ECONOMY

KETER BOOKS

This book is compiled from material originally published in the *Encyclopaedia Judaica*

Copyright © 1973, Keter Publishing House Ltd.
P.O.Box 7145, Jerusalem, Israel

Cat. No. 25070
ISBN 0 7065 1333 9

Printed in Israel

CONTENTS

CONTRIBUTORS

David Horowitz: Former Governor of the Bank of Israel, Jerusalem

David Brodt: Head of Macro Economic Planning Authority, Ministry of Finance, Jerusalem

Zeev Barkai: Jerusalem

Dr. Ben-Ami Zuckerman: Deputy-Director, State Revenue Administration, Ministry of Finance, Jerusalem: Lecturer, School of Business Administration, Tel Aviv University

Dr. Kurt Grunwald: Economist

Michael Adin Talbar: Ministry of Commerce and Industry, Jerusalem

Alexander Ezer: Editor

Simha Blass: Engineer: Former Director General of Tahal, Water Planning for Israel, Tel Aviv

Aaron Wiener: Engineer: Former Director General of Tahal, Water Planning for Israel, Tel Aviv

Joseph Adar: Ramat Gan

Prof. Shmuel Hurwitz: Emeritus Professor of Agronomy, the Hebrew University of Jerusalem

Mendel Nun: Kibbutz Ein Gev

Joseph Weitz (deceased): Writer and Former Head of the Development Authority of the Jewish National Fund, Jerusalem

Abraham Rutenberg: Engineer: Former Director. of the Israel Electric Company, Haifa

Menachem Babitz Ing.: Senior Lecturer, Technion, Haifa

Prof. Israel Dostrovsky: President and Professor of Physical Chemistry, the Weizmann Institute of Science

Uri Shraga Würzburger: Managing Director of the Timna Copper Mines, Israel

Moshe M. Felber: Jewish Agency, Jerusalem

Ram Carmi: Tel Aviv

Felix Bernard Wahle: Chamber of Commerce, Tel Aviv

Yuval Elizur: Journalist

Dr. Jacob Picker: Ministry of Finance, Jerusalem

Rabbi Zvi Herman: Former Member of the Jewish Agency Executive, Former Managing Director of the Zim Israel Navigation Company, Haifa

Colonel (Res.) Moshe Peled: Israel Defense Forces: formerly Ministry of Transport, Jerusalem

Moshe Eliahu Berman: M. Eng., F.I.E.E., Former Director of Engineering, Ministry of Communications, Tel Aviv

Dr. Moshe Hesky: Former Adviser, Philatelic Services, Israel Ministry of Posts

Meir de Shalit: Former Director General, Ministry of Tourism, Tel Aviv

GNP = Gross National Product
IDF = Israel Defense Forces
IL = Israel Pound
LP = Palestine Pound

1 ECONOMIC DEVELOPMENT

ECONOMIC DEVELOPMENT IN THE INITIAL PERIOD. The economic life of the Middle East is determined by the scarcity of natural resources and the aridity of the area: out of 2.6 million square miles, only about 25% had an average rainfall of more than 5 in. (125 mm.). From time immemorial the economy was predominantly agrarian, with a semi-feudal system of land tenure, practically no industry worth mentioning, and a limited use of money. It was a typical subsistence economy, with an underdeveloped society and a low standard of living. The towns were of limited importance, serving mainly as administrative centers, and market places for agricultural produce, with some commercial activity and an artisan class operating small workshops. The few indigenous industries, such as the manufacture of soap and handwoven textiles, were fragmented into many small enterprises.

The Arab Economy. Still in the early 20th century, the primitive Arab economy of Palestine was semi-feudal and semi-self-sufficient, devoting up to 65% of its resources to agriculture. The Arab village was an almost completely self-sufficient unit, not yet emancipated from the century-old feudal usages. The exchange of goods was of minor importance and the use of money was limited. The village community was bound by tradition: its forms of life and work had been preserved unchanged for generations. This type of economy has been described as follows:

> The owners of large landed property—families or groups of families—take little if any interest in the agricultural development of their lands. The fellahin who work these lands live in a state comparable to that of the serfs under the

Carolingian dynasty. Hardly 20% of the gross proceeds of the soil is left to its cultivator. It may almost be said that landlords are engaged not in exploiting the land, but those who cultivate it (M. Delbes, in *Bulletin de l'Union Economique de Syrie,* 1928).

Improved means of communication and transport, however, drew the country into the orbit of the world market. Money became the measure of economic value and was adopted as the sole medium of exchange. The fellah became aware of new needs and a new standard of living, although his income remained barely sufficient to keep body and soul together. The first result of this contact with the modern world was increased exploitation of the peasant by the landlord and the moneylender. As the fellah's need for cash increased, he became dependent upon the usurer, who was often simultaneously the landlord and grain dealer. The large landowners did not hesitate to take advantage of the weak position of the indebted peasant: the smallholder was "bought out" and proletarized, while large properties accumulated in the hands of a few rich landlords. In this way, the economic medium-sized farm unit gave way to large estates on the one hand and dwarf holdings on the other. Nor was this the end of the process: gradually the dwarf holdings also crumbled and passed into the hands of the large landowners. As the fellah could not hold his own or compete with goods produced by modern methods overseas, he sank into debt and dependence on the labor market. The transition from small proprietor to landless laborer was common. As the Government of Palestine stated in its Memorandum to the Palestine Royal Commission in 1936: "It is generally alleged that the Palestinian fellah is born in debt, and dies in debt." The share expected by the owner from the tenant was very high (as much as 30% of the gross returns or 50% of the net income), though the advantages of improved methods and mechanization, the concomitant of large land-holdings in other countries, were lacking. Uncertainty of tenure was a deterrent against the amelioration of the soil. Official reports of the British

Administration in Palestine in the 1920s describe the poverty of the peasantry and the desolation of the country. One such report (Cmd. 1499 (1921), p. 4) stated:

> It is obvious to every passing traveler, and well known to every European resident, that the country was before the War and is now undeveloped and underpopulated. The methods of agriculture are for the most part primitive; the area of land now cultivated could yield a far greater product. There are in addition large cultivable areas that are left untilled. The summits and slopes of the hills are admirably suited to the growth of trees, but there are no forests. Miles of sand dunes that could be redeemed are untouched, a danger by their encroachment to the neighboring tillage. The Jordan and Yarmuk offer an abundance of water power, but it is unused. Some industries—fishing and the culture and manufacture of tobacco are examples—have been killed by Turkish laws; none have been encouraged; the markets of Palestine and the neighboring countries are supplied almost wholly from Europe. The seaborne commerce, such as it is, is loaded and discharged in the open roadsteads of Haifa and Jaffa; there are no harbors. The religious and historical associations that offer most powerful attractions to the whole of the Western and to a large part of the Eastern world, have hitherto brought to Palestine but a fraction of the pilgrims and travelers who, under better conditions, would flock to her sacred shrines and famous sites. The country is underpopulated because of this lack of development.

Beginning of Jewish Settlement. It was against this background that the Jewish resettlement of the land was started in 1878. The development of agriculture was characterized by the penetration of active Western forces into a backward, primitive agricultural economy, and their revolutionizing influences on the fabric of life and economy. The transformation was both economic and technological. Extensive investment of capital, transition to modern agriculture both at home and abroad, and new technical methods that raised the productivity of labor and the fertility of soil, combined to shift the emphasis from primitive self-sufficient farming, based on low productivity 3 and cheap labor, to a highly commercialized, modern agricultural industry. The new ventures upon which Jewish settlers embarked wrought fundamental changes in the character of the country's agriculture. At the outset, they were confronted with several tasks essential for further development: the productivity of labor had to be raised by labor-saving devices; the fertility of the soil had to be increased; and agriculture and industry had to be varied and ramified by the introduction of new products.

The transformation was, inevitably, gradual. By 1914, 47 Jewish villages had been established, with about 12,000 inhabitants and 110,000 acres of land—a modest achievement. This was still a small proportion of the Jewish population, which included a substantial proportion of religious Jews in the towns, who were mainly supported by funds from abroad. The towns had a definite oriental character: artisans, coppersmiths, shoemakers, and potters worked only for the local market, and the general pattern had not changed for many centuries. The rhythm of economic life was slow; there was little division of labor. The Jewish villages encountered formidable difficulties, which they overcame only with the generous support of Baron Edmond de Rothschild [1], who introduced viticulture on a large scale. The paternal system of administration instituted by the Baron left little room for the initiative of the farmers and only at the end of the century, in 1899, was the administration turned over to the Jewish Colonization Association (ICA), which tried to promote self-reliance and diversify agriculture. In the course of time the cultivation of wheat was introduced in some areas and orange groves assumed increasing importance, but the attempt to develop the growing of almonds failed.

THE INTERWAR PERIOD. Within the interwar period the Jewish population of Palestine increased at a pace unexcelled anywhere else. The total increase, aggregating 815,540, i.e., 125.6%, is quite unusual in the 20th century.

[1] Lived in Paris and was patron of Jewish settlement in Erez Israel, (1845–1934)

Table 1. Increase in Permanent Population of Palestine, 1922–39

	Jews		Non-Jews		Total	
	No.	% of 1922	No.	% of 1922	No.	% of 1922
Permanent population 1922	83,700	100.0	565,258	100.0	648,958	100.0
Natural increase	93,505	111.6	366,411	64.8	459,916	70.8
Net immigration	297,305	354.8	48,319	8.5	345,624	53.3
Border adjustment in north			10,000	1.8	10,000	1.5
Total increase	390,810	466.4	424,730	75.1	815,540	125.6
Permanent population 1939	474,510	566.4	989,988	175.1	1,464,498	225.6

Sources: 1) *Jewish Population in Palestine.* A demographic survey by D. Gurewitz and A. Gertz, Jewish Agency Statistical Department, Bulletin No. 21, Jerusalem, Nov. 1940.
2) Quarterly Bulletin of Vital Statistics of Palestine, Office of Statistics of the Government of Palestine, 4th quarter of 1939.
3) Census of Palestine 1931, Vol. 1, Palestine, Part I.—Report by E. Mills, 1933.
4) Statistical Abstract of Palestine, 1941. (Estimates of "unrecorded births" minus deaths, as mentioned by Mills.—sub (3). p. 45; distributed between Jews and non-Jews at the ratio of 1:9.)

5

The growth came from two sources: natural increase and immigration—the Arab population multiplying mainly through natural increase and the Jews chiefly by immigration. The increase in the population of Palestine during the 17 years 1922 to 1939 is reflected in Table 1.

Natural Increase. Natural increase in Palestine was among the highest in the world. In 1936, for example, it reached 28.8 per 1,000 of the population, four times as large as in Europe. Of course, a distinction must be made between the rate of natural increase in the Jewish and Arab population. Although the rate among the Jews was high, it did not exceed the level frequently found in countries absorbing a large immigration at the end of the 19th century. However, it was extraordinarily high for a population of European origin and must be attributed to the age distribution, i.e., the very high proportion of men and women between the ages of 15 and 45. On the other hand, the Muslim population had the highest rate of increase in the world as a result of a very high birth rate (52.8 per 1,000 of the population in 1936) and a relatively low mortality rate (19.9 per 1,000 in the same year). This birth rate, which was similar to that in Egypt (41 to 44 per 1,000) and in some underdeveloped countries, is characteristic of primitive peoples who are not accustomed to birth control. Such high birth rates, however, are usually linked with high mortality rates, so that the rate of natural increase remains relatively low. The Muslim population was an exception to this rule because of the low mortality rate in comparison with other underdeveloped countries, which was a result of the special conditions of Palestine. The high standard of living of the Jewish population, the percolation of Jewish capital into the Arab economy, and the Mandatory government's efforts to raise the level of hygiene and improve the Arab population's health conditions and standard of living, were reflected in the rapid decrease of the mortality rate, particularly among infants. These trends are shown in Table 2.

6   The economic development of Palestine was so rapid that

Table 2. Mortality and Birth Rates of the Muslim Population

	Average 1927–29	Average 1937–39	Decline
Mortality rate	28.6	20.3	−29%
Birth rate	52.6	47.8	− 9%

the sociological and psychological changes in the Arab population did not catch up with it.

Immigration. The economic integration of immigrants in Palestine stood out against the background of limited and declining immigration elsewhere. The number of immigrants absorbed in Palestine between 1933 and 1937 was, relatively, the highest in the world, while production, consumption, and national wealth increased in the interwar period more rapidly than the population. But the expansion of production was not the only criterion of the success of integration. The modernization of the economy of Palestine and its transformation from a semi-agrarian country to a modern industrial one, as well as the progressive division of labor, led to an increase in sources of income other than agriculture—a well-known feature of rapid economic development. Of particular significance is the growth of services, which far exceeded the growth of population and production. Table 3 reflects the occupational distribution of the population according to the census of 1931.

From 1931 to 1939, the proportion of Jews in the total population of Palestine increased from 18% to 29%.

Economic Equilibrium. The problem of economic equilibrium and stability was especially important in Palestine, which was subjected to the impact of new, dynamic forces. The import of capital was particularly important in this pattern of development and was reflected in the import of equipment and means of production. This was, of course, accompanied by the import of consumer goods for the sector of the population engaged in the establishment of the new economy. Thus, the deficit in the

Table 3. Occupational Distribution of the Population of
Palestine, 1931

	Jews		Non-Jews	
	Number	%	Number	%
Administration	3,410	2.2	21,008	2.8
Agriculture	27,017	18.0	492,920	64.9
Building and Industry	50,441	33.5	91,170	12.0
Commerce	28,665	19.1	67,932	8.9
Transport, mining, and quarrying	9,629	6.4	40,991	5.4
Household services	5,264	3.5	11,384	1.6
Professions	17,490	11.6	17,991	2.4
People living on capital gains	8,545	5.7	15,252	2.0
Total	150,461	100.0	758,648	100.0
Unspecified	19,889	—	25,959	—
Unproductive	4,260	—	9,451	—
Total	175,610		794,058	

trade balance, the import of capital for investment, and the increase in bank deposits were interdependent, as reflected in Table 4.

The clear connection between the deficit in the balance of trade, Jewish investment, and the import of Jewish capital reflected the interdependence of these factors. They had to be supplemented by non-Jewish import of goods and capital, as shown in Table 5.

As might be expected, the import of capital in the interwar period exceeded the excess of imports over exports. The volume of imports declined automatically with the decrease in the import of capital. Two facts are salient in this context: the excess of imports over exports closely approached the volume of investment and current consumption was to an increasing degree satisfied by production for the local market or the proceeds of export. In a country marked by rapid development and large-scale immigration, economic progress is linked with large imports and a deficit in the trade balance. As long as immigration is high, production must lag behind the increase in population; and as long as the new branches of production are in their infancy, the population engaged in establishing the new capacity for production is supported by import of capital, which is reflected in the import of goods and services.

Part of the materials required for the new investment in Palestine during this period was produced in the country. Foremost among these were building materials—a fact of particular importance, as the investment in building represented about half the total investment, and the share of wages is exceedingly high in this type of investment. The labor force was absorbed by expanding enterprises and by the investment sector. In the periods of recession, at least part of the labor force set free by the contraction of investment was absorbed in the enterprises established to satisfy consumption in the period of expansion. In the period of expansion and immigration, there was an accumulation of surpluses that were used later in the period of contraction.

Agriculture. Agriculture in Palestine was divided into three separate sections, each characterized by certain distinctive features:

(1) Citriculture, based on modern technical methods and high capital investment, employing hired labor, and producing chiefly for export. The industry was divided almost equally between Jews and Arabs.

(2) Indigenous agriculture, characterized by primitive farming methods, semi-feudal forms of land ownership, and a low standard of living. This form of agriculture, which was almost entirely in Arab hands, was to a high degree self-sufficient. Cereal growing predominated, but milk, eggs, fruits and vegetables were also produced.

(3) Modern mixed farming, based on intensive cultiva-

Table 4. Trade Balance and Jewish Capital Imports (in millions LP)

Year	Import	Export	Trade balance (exc. gold)	Import of Jewish capital	Jewish invest-ments	Increase of bank deposits
1920	5.08	0.85	− 4.23	Individual figures not available		—
1921	5.87	1.50	− 4.37			0.10
1922	5.47	1.26	− 4.21			0.50
1923	4.95	1.41	− 3.54			0.10
1924	5.40	1.38	− 4.02			0.40
1925	7.53	1.47	− 6.06			0.50
1926	6.52	1.49	− 5.03			0.20
1927	5.78	2.15	− 3.63			−0.10
1928	6.53	1.66	− 4.87			0.10
1929	6.87	1.75	− 5.12			0.40
Total (1920−29)	60.00	14.92	−45.08	.04	.02	2.20

Year						
1930	6.64	2.08	− 4.56	3.00	} 7.20	0.30
1931	5.64	1.82	− 3.82	3.00		1.00
1932	7.48	2.62	− 4.86	3.00	3.33	2.00
1933	10.26	2.61	− 7.35	7.00	6.13	5.27
1934	14.36	3.50	−10.86	11.37	9.71	3.73
1935	17.02	4.52	−12.50	14.21	10.67	0.70
1936	12.66	4.27	− 8.39	8.39	7.00	0.29
1937	15.11	6.45	− 8.66	6.00	6.00	−0.70
1938	11.02	5.68	− 5.34	7.97	4.70	1.81
1939	13.88	5.47	− 8.41	8.19	5.00	1.91
Total (1930–39)	114.07	39.32	−74.75	72.13	59.74	16.31

Source: *Census of Palestine,* 1931.

Table 5. Import of Goods and non-Jewish Capital (in millions of LP)

	Direct import % goods by the government	Capital imports (grants and loans)	Capital imports by Iraqi Petroleum Co.
1924–29	.94	5.06	—
1930–39	5.13	5.04	2.77

tion and irrigation, to supply the urban population. Production was concentrated on dairy farming, poultry raising, and fruit and vegetable growing. This type of farming was almost entirely Jewish and provided the farmer with a relatively high standard of living. Most of the land was publicly owned, and the farms were financed mainly by public and semi-public funds, with a view to creating an agricultural basis for Jewish settlement.

Cereal Growing. Grain was grown by both Jews and Arabs, but under vastly differing conditions. As the main branch of indigenous agriculture, it was the typical occupation of the peasant (or fellah) but of minor importance among the Jews. About 52% of the income of Arab farms was derived from cereal growing, as compared with only 11% in Jewish farms and 30% in Palestinian agriculture as a whole. There were also great differences in yields. As a result of scientific methods of cultivation (such as crop rotation and extensive use of fertilizers) and a high degree of mechanization, the Jews succeeded in obtaining about 110 kg. per dunam of wheat and 154 kg. of barley (four dunams=one acre). This contrast in production methods within one small country was the natural consequence of the different conditions prevailing in the two economies. The self-sufficient primitive Arab farm suffered from a lack of capital resources, but enjoyed an abundance of cheap labor. It was natural, therefore, that it should dispense with modern labor-saving devices and concentrate on human labor. The Jewish farms, on the other hand, had ampler capital resources, but the standard of living and wages were higher. They therefore tended to reduce manual labor to a minimum and increase the share of machinery.

The size of the Palestine cereal crop was dependent on weather conditions. The improved methods of farming, with their increased yields, affected too small an area to influence the total output. Fluctuations between good and bad years were wide and were an extremely important factor in the general economic welfare of the country. The fellahin who were about half the population, depended mainly on cereal crops for their livelihood. The urban grain supply also depended largely on the size of the crop; in good years dependence on imported grain and flour was markedly relieved, as shown in Table 6. The chief distinguishing feature of cereal growing was its failure to keep pace with the expansion in output that was so characteristic of all branches of the economy. Crop fluctuations were due entirely to climatic variations, and there were no long-term structural changes.

Table 6. Palestine's Supply of Wheat and Flour: Import and Local Production (metric)

	Local production of wheat		Import of wheat and wheat flour[1]	
	Tons	% of supply	Tons	% of supply
1933	44,000	31.4	96,000	68.6
1934	83,000	50.9	80,000	49.1
1935	104,000	61.9	64,000	38.1
1936	76,000	54.3	64,000	45.7
1937	127,420	63.3	73,987	36.7
1938	44,435	40.9	64,279	59.1
1939	89,190	45.0	108,927	55.0

[1] 1 ton of flour = 1.348 ton of wheat.
Source: *Statistical Abstract of Palestine* (1941) pp. 3, 61.

Mixed Farming. The development of mixed farming in Palestine was due mainly to Jewish settlement: its rapid growth was made possible by two factors: the large sums of capital invested in irrigation and farm intensification; and the expansion of the local urban markets for food. Development along lines of public or semi-public settlement was imperative in a country such as Palestine, where private capital would not be attracted to a form of farming in which initial losses were inevitable and a reasonable profit—even after the passage of some years—was no more than doubtful. In 1937 some 10,000 families, or 34,000 people, were dependent for their subsistence on Jewish mixed farming, which covered an area of 380,000 dunams These were divided between labor and other settlements as shown in Table 7.

The total area of land in these settlements expanded considerably from the commencement of Jewish settlement, but the size of the farming unit decreased, as is seen from the fact that, while the number of workers increased by 410% (1925–36), the number of cattle by 215%, and the number of poultry by 600% (from 1927), the area of land

Table 7. Population and Land Area of Jewish Mixed Farm Settlements, 1937

	Population		Total of cultivated land area (dunams)
	Families	Persons	
Labor settlements	7,000	22,000	280,000
PICA settlements [1]	430	1,600	50,000
Other smallholders' settlements	2,500	10,000	50,000
Total	9,930	33,600	380,000

[1] Settlements established on publicly owned land, dispensing entirely with hired labor. Figures refer to these settlements only, as no other statistics are available. The labor section, however, was predominant.

expanded by only 160%. This development reflected the intensification of mixed farming and the transition from branches of agriculture requiring large areas of land (such as cereal growing) to dairy, poultry, and vegetable farming.

Outstanding Features of Palestinian Agriculture. Three outstanding features emerge from any survey of the individual branches of agriculture in Palestine.

The first is the shift in emphasis from extensive cereal growing to intensive mixed farming.

The second is the relatively high proportion of the demand supplied by imports. As home production rapidly increased, the growth in population and its demand for foodstuffs outstripped the capacity of the local farms. The most important causes of this feature were: (a) The lower prices of the imported products—as a result of more advantageous production conditions in other countries or of export premiums granted by governments to agricultural exporters. These price differences were particularly marked in the case of some forms of dairy produce and of cattle for slaughter. (b) Competition from adjacent countries, based on cheap labor. Syria, in particular, enjoyed an unusually advantageous position vis-à-vis the Palestinian market, as the trade agreement between the two countries provided for the free import of Syrian goods into Palestine. (c) A profitable basis of production had not yet been established for certain types of products that were still being supplied almost entirely from abroad. Examples were cattle for slaughter, butter, onions, garlic, and potatoes out of season. Vegetable growing, milk production, and egg and poultry farming had already developed mature and profitable methods of production, so that they were able to supply a large portion of the home market, but in the other areas local production was still unprofitable.

The third outstanding feature was the unusual method whereby the major section of the country's modern mixed farming was financed. The total investment in Jewish mixed farming amounted to LP7,000,000, which was divided as shown in Table 8. A considerable proportion of this total

Table 8. Total Investments in Jewish Mixed Farming (in LP)

Investments in labor settlements	3,600,000
Investments in PICA settlements	400,000
Investments in other smallholders' settlements	3,000,000
Total	7,000,000

was invested by public Jewish funds without expectation of profit. Losses were incurred in order to clear the path for a new form of farming necessary to the country as a whole. Public capital was utilized both for the fundamental work of settlement, such as irrigation and the introduction of modern machinery and fertilizing methods, and for the experimental and scientific work on which settlement was based. It is no exaggeration to say that the actual process of settlement was financed mainly through Jewish public funds without the expectation of a reasonable return and without the assistance of the Mandatory authorities.

Citriculture. The citrus industry expanded more rapidly in Palestine than in any other country. The area under citrus cultivation increased fivefold within a decade. The growth in the citrus area and the size and value of the export crop are illustrated in Tables 9 and 10.

In 1936–37 Palestine took third place in the list of citrus-exporting countries. Owing to the small size of the

Table 9. Area under Citrus in Palestine (dunams)

Year	Total	Jewish
1927	60,800	24,000
1931	129,000	70,000
1932	164,000	90,000
1933	204,000	120,000
1934	260,000	145,000
1935	278,000	153,000
1936	298,000	155,000
1939	299,500	155,000

Table 10. Export of Palestine Citrus (in thousands)

	Oranges		Grapefruit		Total (incl. lemons)	
	LP	Cases	LP	Cases	LP	Cases
1926/27	846	2,669	—	—	849	2,677
1930/31	728	2,425	16	40	745	2,470
1931/32	1,725	3,585	58	106	1,785	3,698
1932/33	1,961	4,230	129	245	2,097	4,490
1933/34	2,430	5,158	184	353	2,621	5,534
1934/35	2,829	6,510	342	792	3,183	7,331
1935/36	2,215	4,997	305	850	2,548	5,897
1936/37	3,378	9,191	466	1,534	3,873	10,796
1937/38	3,346	9,573	504	1,794	3,880	11,444
1938/39	3,865	13,056	445	2,067	4,356	15,265
1939/40	1,642	6,449	224	988	1,918	7,590

Source: *Statistical Abstract of Palestine* (1941) p. 72.

population, the citrus industry depended almost wholly on export. The local population could not possibly consume more than the culls, which accounted for only 10% of the crop. This problem was particularly urgent, as the non-exportable fruit constituted a very high proportion of the crop owing to the large area of new groves. Palestine was in an exceptionally difficult position for the expansion of its export outlets. Because of its international legal status under the Mandate, it was compelled to maintain, without discrimination, an open door to the products of all member-states of the League of Nations and was thus precluded from negotiating trade treaties with other countries. Furthermore, the entire citrus crop had to be marketed in less than four months, as compared with a seven- to eight-month shipping season in Spain and nearly the whole year for the United States. This meant that prices were reduced by the glut of fruit arriving on the market at approximately the same time.

Transport conditions were particularly bad. It was not until 1937 that the Jaffa-Haifa highway was completed, and single railroad track to Haifa was quite incapable of coping properly with the peak traffic during the shipping season. The situation was very greatly improved by the building of the trunk road to Haifa, but the crop was growing so rapidly that constant road improvements were needed to keep pace with the increasing transport demands. The fact that there was no deep-water harbor in the orange-growing district round Jaffa where fruit could be loaded safely in all weathers was also a grave drawback. To ship all the fruit from Haifa was physically impossible, and the attempt added greatly to transport costs. Palestinian citriculture also suffered from the fact that the growers were divided into two communities—Jews and Arabs.

While the organization of the Jewish section of the industry, though far from perfect, was much better developed than that of the Arabs, political differences kept the two communities apart, so that the Arabs, who were not successful in organizing their own cooperatives, remained outside the Jewish cooperatives. In addition to these special difficulties, the growers had to contend with a more general problem, which was inherent in the expansion of the crop and was bound, sooner or later, to alter the very nature of the Jaffa citrus trade. The Jaffa *(Shamouti)* orange had been a luxury item, so that marketing meant disposing of a small quantity at as high a price as possible among the richer strata, who were not greatly affected by small price variations. But with the doubling and trebling of the Palestine crop, the special scarcity of the *Shamouti* had disappeared. A survey of Palestine's citrus markets from 1934 to 1940 is given in Table 11.

Industry. The rapid process of industrialization taking place in Palestine was limited mainly to the Jewish sector of the population. Arab industry consisted mostly of small handicrafts, which accounted for less than 20% of total industrial output. The one exception was the Nablus soap industry (see below). In the early 1930s a larger Arab metal works, a match factory and a rice mill were established, but they had not yet commenced production. The growth of

Table 11. Palestine's Citrus Markets

Country	1934/35		1935/36		1936/37		1937/38		1938/39		1939/40	
	Cases	% of total	Cases	% of total	Cases	% of total	Cases	% of total	Cases	% of total	Cases	% of total
Belgium	124,002	1.7	84,392	1.4	243,892	2.2	517,931	4.6	1,132,462	7.4	972,072	7.3
Czechoslovakia	62,069	0.9	77,872	1.3	177,790	1.7	280,683	2.5	111,821	0.7	101,994	0.8
Finland	35,659	0.5	44,028	0.7	74,901	0.7	107,286	0.9	149,398	1.0	124,273	0.9
France	170,586	2.3	114,170	1.9	289,254	2.7	217,541	1.9	596,192	3.9	582,158	4.3
Germany	509,494	6.9	222,644	3.8	318,273	3.0	210,710	1.8	115,227	0.8	111,205	0.8
Holland	367,895	5.0	344,679	5.9	612,486	5.7	1,093,198	9.6	1,612,706	10.5	1,448,264	10.8
Norway	105,791	1.4	107,533	1.8	158,298	1.5	280,324	2.5	393,541	2.6	261,443	2.0
Poland	163,086	2.2	273,205	4.6	307,791	2.8	383,592	3.4	493,701	3.2	388,132	2.9
Rumania	170,027	2.3	137,622	2.3	219,699	2.0	246,670	2.2	311,942	2.0	268,036	2.0
Sweden	108,325	1.5	162,220	2.8	312,794	2.9	483,353	4.2	857,458	5.6	767,620	5.7
U.K.	5,244,337	71.5	4,009,503	68.0	7,714,608	71.6	7,046,601	61.8	8,988,028	58.7	7,855,961	58.7
Other	269,575	3.8	319,433	5.5	344,573	3.2	525,601	4.6	547,960	3.6	504,534	3.8
Total	7,330,846	100.0	5,897,301	100.0	10,774,359	100.0	11,393,490	100.0	15,310,436	100.0	13,385,692	100.0

19

Jewish industry between 1921 and 1937 is shown in Table 12.

Special Conditions Favoring Industrialization. Industrialization in Palestine was closely connected with the process of immigration. Capital was imported directly by the immigrants themselves, which explains the availability of a large volume of capital in a new country at a time when there was a severe decline in the normal migration of capital. These imports of capital faced a limited field of investment, so that any possiblity of industrial expansion was eagerly taken up. The volume of industrial investment and its percentage of total Jewish investment are shown in Table 13.

Industrial investment in Palestine had the great advantage of the availability of both experts and skilled labor. Many of the capitalist immigrants had been engaged in industry abroad, and it was only natural that they should return to the occupation for which they were best trained. Industrial experts without capital found little difficulty in inducing investors with idle capital to finance their ventures. The immigration of skilled laborers facilitated the process.

Perhaps the most important factor in the movement toward industrialization was the expansion of the home market. While manufacturers in other countries had become accustomed to contracting markets and limited purchasing power, in Palestine they were confronted with a market that was expanding in consonance with the inflow of new immigrants and new capital. The opening of new factories depended directly on this growth in demand. There was a certain technical minimum of output below which production was not profitable, and it was not until the market was large enough to absorb this minimum that many of the new factories could start work.

An additional stimulus was given to industrialization by the system of capital "transfer" from Germany. The capital of Jewish refugees could not be exported from Germany in cash, and the range of goods that could be exported instead was very limited. Industrial machinery was one of the most

Table 12. Development of Jewish Industry, 1921–37

	1921/22	1929	1933	1937
Number of enterprises	1,850	2,475	3,388	6,307
Personnel	4,750	10,968	19,595	27,260
Capital invested (LP)	600,000	2,234,000	5,371,000	12,700,000
Value of annual production (LP)	500,000	2,510,000	5,352,000	9,060,000
Consumption of electricity (kwh.)	—	2,214,000	6,576,000	30,478,000

Table 13. Relationship of Jewish Investment in Industry to Total Jewish Investment

	1932	1933	1934	1935	1936	1937
Total Jewish investment (LP)	3,000,000	6,000,000	9,000,000	10,000,000	6,500,000	5,300,000
Investment in industry (LP)	500,000	500,000	1,500,000	1,800,000	1,200,000	1,000,000
Percentage	17.0	8.0	17.0	18.0	18.0	19.0

prevalent media of transfer. It was transferred to Palestine, either directly by private Jewish entrepreneurs—who saw in this medium the one chance of saving their capital—or directly through industrial shares issued in Germany, the share-capital thus raised being transferred by the new company in the form of machinery. The most important industrial enterprises that were established in Palestine were partly financed on such a basis.

According to the 1937 census of Jewish industry taken by the Jewish Agency, industrial personnel, investment, and production were distributed as shown in Table 14.

(1) In Palestine, as in all young industrial countries, industry was concentrated mainly on the production of consumer goods, which, it is estimated, occupied 75% of

Table 14. Jewish Industry, 1937

	Personnel	Investment (LP)	Production (LP)
Foodstuffs	3,480	1,850,000	2,300,000
Textiles	1,300	430,000	380,000
Clothing	3,460	290,000	540,000
Metal	2,760	740,000	790,000
Machinery	1,150	250,000	300,000
Wood	2,980	500,000	810,000
Leather	1,790	200,000	410,000
Printing and paper	2,390	600,000	580,000
Chemicals	730	1,050,000	720,000
Stone and Cement	2,480	1,820,000	1,060,000
Electricity	540	120,000	140,000
Miscellaneous	1,770	300,000	280,000
Total	24,830	8,150,000	8,310,000
Concessions:			
Palestine Potash	920	4,530,000	750,000
Palestine Electric	1,510		
Total	27,260	12,680,000	9,060,000

manufacturing capacity, only 25% being engaged in making capital goods.

(2) Palestine's industry was overwhelmingly dependent on the home market. Ninety to ninety-five percent of the output was consumed locally.

(3) Inadequate industrial protection and Palestine's legal inability to impose discriminatory tariffs meant that about half of the country's industry was contending with keen foreign competition.

(4) Only about 40–45% of the industries used local raw materials, the remainder being dependent on supplies from abroad.

(5) About one-third of Palestine's industry centered on the building market, and about 10% on supplies for citriculture.

(6) The relative weight of industry within the economy was on the increase. In the years 1936–37, the gross value of production (Jewish and Arab) approached LP10,000,000.

(7) The capital influx, which had been so pronounced a feature in Palestine until 1936, provided a stronger incentive for investment in industry than existed in most other countries.

Building. Building played an extremely important role in the country's economic growth. Housing—one of the very few commodities that cannot be imported—was inadequate for the rapidly growing population, and building naturally served as the point of departure for new workers until they could be absorbed in the expanding apparatus of general production. In the initial period of each wave of immigration and expansion, the construction of houses was the main economic activity. In 1925–27 not only was the absolute number of construction workers high, but their share in the total labor force reached as much as 43%. In the period of consolidation that followed, the proportion and number decreased, and the workers were slowly absorbed into the other branches of production, which had been expanding steadily due to the market created by the building trades. The building trade, therefore, provided a   **23**

Table 15. Share of Building in Palestine's Economy

	Jewish building workers	% of all Jewish workers	Jewish investment in building (LP)	% of total Jewish investment
1925	7,800	43.0	—	—
1932	4,000	13.5	1,094,000	39
1933	7,000	16.7	2,884,000	51
1934	11,500	19.2	4,554,000	50
1935	16,500	19.4	5,730,000	56
1936	13–14,000	15.8	3,700,000	57
1937	11,000	10.6	2,800,000	52

remunerative field of employment and investment during the initial phases of each spurt in economic development. The high proportion of investment and the large share of the labor force that the construction industry absorbed may be seen from Table 15.

The building industry offered certain advantages, particularly in a young and small country. In the first place, the high percentage of wages in total investment was invaluable in increasing purchasing power. The need for consumer goods was stimulated, and thus the reabsorption of labor set free by a temporary saturation of the building market was facilitated. The whole of Palestine's economic life fluctuated in correspondence with the building movement, which became as sensitive a barometer of business conditions as iron and steel output in some other countries. The extent of these fluctuations was seen by the wave-like graph of building activity since 1924 and the correlation between building and other characteristic indications, such as imports and government revenue. The dominant influence of building in Palestine provides a partial explanation of the violent fluctuations in the country's economic life. Whereas the supply of ordinary consumer goods is easily adjusted to demand, many years must elapse before the supply of houses can be increased or decreased in accordance with market variations. Thus it is not difficult to understand why trade fluctuations in Palestine, where so much economic activity centered on the building industry, were particularly severe. On the other hand, the actual length of the fluctuations was shorter than in other countries.

Foreign Trade. Four unusual features characterized Palestine's foreign trade: (1) the exceptional size of trade per capita, in relation to the relatively backward stage of the country's development; (2) the large adverse trade balance, which, reckoned per capita, was the highest in the world; (3) the lárge proportion of capital goods imported; and (4) the concentration of exports mainly on one product and one market. Up to 80% of Palestine's export trade consisted of citrus fruits, and over 70% of these were concentrated on the British market. Of the country's total exports, about 60% were sold to Britain. These phenomena were, in reality, four aspects of one and the same circumstance. In such a young, rapidly developing country of immigration and settlement, high imports and an adverse trade balance were inevitable accompaniments to progress. As long as an intensive stream of immigration was being absorbed and new farms and factories were daily being established, home production inevitably lagged behind the needs of the growing population, both in consumer goods and productive apparatus. Until the young local industries were set in motion, the new population employed in producing the industrial equipment had to be fed, clothed, and housed with imported goods. Imports, therefore, had to be looked upon in the main as a form of capital investment; hence the high proportion of investment goods imported.

It is not surprising that under these conditions the export trade remained relatively undeveloped. In the years of rapid development, manufacturers were barely able to satisfy the demand of the local market, let alone develop export outlets. In addition, the products of new industries needed time to be perfected. The one product of high quality that Palestine could produce, and for which the home market

Table 16. The Balance of Payments of Palestine, 1922—47 (in

Current account
   Merchandise trade
   Transactions with armed forces in Palestine
Total

Unilateral transfers (net)
   Immigrant transfers
   Transfers by Jewish public institutions
   Transfers by non-Jewish public institutions
   Transfers by government
Total

Capital account (net)
   Private investments
   Government investments
   Balance abroad and investments of banking system
   Balance abroad and investments of Palestine Currency Board
Total

Total

Errors and omissions

Source: Michael Michaely, *Foreign Trade and Capital Imports in Israel* (Tel Aviv, Am

offered insufficient scope, was the orange, and the volume of citrus exports grew with speed and success. In all other fields, Palestinian production was still too young and untried to have had much time for, or success in, the expansion of an export trade. Exports did pay for a certain portion of the imports, and a further portion was offset by invisible exports, such as the tourist traffic, remittances to charitable and religious organizations, remittances arriving through the Jewish public funds, interest on government millions LP)

	1922–39		1940–47		1922–47	
	Credit	Debit	Credit	Debit	Credit	Debit
	52	171	129	313	181	484
	8	—	180	—	188	—
	60	171	309	313	369	484
	75	—	35	—	110	—
	25	—	40	—	65	—
	6	—	4	—	10	—
	3	—	7	—	10	—
	109	—	86	—	195	—
	26	—	—	10	16	—
	—	2	—	9	—	11
	—	6	—	48	—	54
	—	9	—	35	—	4
	26	17	—	102	16	109
	195	188	395	415	580	593
	—	7	20	—	13	—

Oved, 1963; Hebrew), p. 2, Table 1.

investment abroad, etc. This situation is reflected in Table 16 (prepared by Dr. L. Gruenbaum (Gaathon) for the Jewish Agency Economic Research Institute).

Communications. The stage of internal development which characterized the country at this time necessitated an unusually high level of foreign trade per capita. There was continual immigration on a large scale; a modern economy was being created; new farms and factories were being established, and building activity called for the import of 27

Table 16a. Population and shipping, 1935 and 1936

Year	Population (end of year)	Tonnage entering	Tonnage per head
1935	1,144,000	5,564,000	4.9
1936	1,242,000	5,006,000	4.0

raw materials and equipment. All this stimulated shipping activity, which, per capita, appeared to be the highest in the world (see Table 16a).

There was a tourist traffic of 50,000–100,000 a year, and immigration reached 60,000 in 1935. Palestine was also important as the starting point for one of the two trans-desert motor roads to Baghdad—through Haifa and Amman.

Internal Transport. In comparison with the well-advanced shipping activity, internal transport was backward and undeveloped. The road network was still very small: in 1936, only about 800 miles (1,200–1,300 km.) of all-weather roads, which meant 8 miles of road per 100 sq. miles of territory. The road and rail systems had not been planned primarily to suit the country's commercial needs. The chief railroad line, for example, was built to facilitate the advance of the British army from Egypt during World War I and had never been adapted to everyday requirements. What should have been the main trunk road from Tel Aviv to Haifa was not completed until as late as 1937 for fear of competition with the less convenient, but state-owned, railroad. The existence of the railroad was, in fact, a determining influence on road-building policy. Roads were built as feeders to the railroad and not as alternatives. Some were constructed only when their strategic necessity became evident. The road to Metullah, which was built at lightning pace at the time of the Druze rebellion in Syria, is an early example. For the most part, however, strategic and commercial interests coincided in the actual layout of road or rail.

The backwardness of internal communications was due not only to the general policy of the government, but also to the peculiar twofold structure of the country's economic life. The Arab producer, on the one hand, had barely emerged from his primitive, self-contained economy; he was tied to the soil and made next to no demand for transport facilities for himself or his products. On the other hand, the Jews were actively developing a modern economy, closely bound with the world at large, and dependent on overseas sources for equipment, raw materials, and even, at the beginning, foodstuffs.

Public Finance. The Palestine treasury favored orthodox ideas of finance and the principle of minimum state interference in the affairs of the community. Faced, until 1936, with a revenue mounting at an extraordinary pace—as the result of increased immigration and rising prosperity—the treasury aimed at preventing expenditure from increasing in sympathy and so piling up a respectable surplus as a reserve for times of need. The result was a yearly excess of revenue over expenditure and a steadily rising surplus, which reached the extraordinary size of LP 6,270,000 in 1926—more than the total annual budget. The policy of accumulating large surpluses was open to controversy in view of the fact that Palestine was an underdeveloped and in many respects primitive country: its education and health services were sadly lacking, an agricultural development scheme to lift the peasant out of the rut of poverty and indebtedness was called for by more than one visiting expert, and the road and rail network could bear considerable improvement.

Growth in Expenditure Since 1929. Although government expenditure did not increase as rapidly as revenue, there was an advance in per capita expenditure from LP 2.54 in 1929/30 to an estimated LP 5.54 in 1937/38, as Table 17 shows. In spite of this advance, expenditure per capita in Palestine, though very much higher than in the surrounding countries, was still extremely small compared with progressive countries and established economies in Europe. The **29**

Table 17. Government Expenditure in Palestine

Year	Expenditure (LP)	Settled population (mean)	Expenditure per capita (LP)
1929/30	2,245,989	882,511	2.54
1933/34	2,704,856	1,038,331	2.60
1934/35	3,230,010	1,104,605	2.92
1935/36	4,236,202	1,194,529	3.55
1936/37	6,073,502	1,269,965	4.78
1937/38	7,297,688	1,318,077	5.54
1938/39	5,692,672	1,351,639	4.21
1939/40	6,004,738	1,404,759	4.27

Sources: *Statistical Handbook of Jewish Palestine* (1947), 380; *Statistical Abstract of Palestine* (1941), 21.

development of budgetary expenditure over the years 1931–32 to 1937–38 is summarized in Table 18.

According to these figures, the expenditures of the government more than doubled from 1931 to 1937. The increase was noticeable in all fields—the greatest being in "public works—extraordinary." Social expenditure on health education, agriculture, and "public works—recurrent" increased in proportion to the expansion of the total budget and also showed a per capita increase. The increase in expenditure on agriculture was particularly noticeable. There were two outstanding features in the composition of the budget: the very small debt charges and the low expenditure on social services. The favorable debt situation could be attributed to the prosperity of the country and the large import of capital by private individuals, which facilitated development without recourse to large foreign loans.

Capital Imports, Credit, and the Banking Structure. The financial conditions were determined in the main by the import of capital, which was estimated in 1935 at LP10–12 million, while the total volume of production—including agriculture, industry, and building—barely exceeded LP20

Table 18. Government Expenditure in Palestine (in LP)

	1931/32	1937/38 (Budget proposal)	Percentage increase
Debt charges	124,396	158,900	28
Defense, police and prisons, Transjordan Frontier Force	724,130	1,356,608	87
Administration and miscellaneous	764,551	1,551,064	103
Health and education	255,157	524,739	106
Agriculture and forests	83,762	226,825	170
Public works—recurrent	236,513	437,917	85
Public works—extraordinary	101,038	639,653	533
Special non-recurrent expenditure	88,078	181,461	106
Total	2,377,625	5,077,167	113

million. The impact of such large amounts of capital on a relatively small economy was bound to have a profound influence on economic development. The influx of capital had an inflationary effect: on the one hand springing directly from the injection of new capital—like currency inflation in other countries —and, on the other hand, owing to the expansion of credit based on the import of new capital. This credit expansion was small in proportion to the capital imports that formed its basis, indicating a restrictive, rather than an inflationary, credit policy, but it was so large in relation to the size of the economy that its stimulating effect resembled those of inflation in other countries. The credit inflation, however, had the exceptional advantage of being linked with an immigration that brought with it a demand for goods and services. The new capital, therefore, did not remain idle, but percolated throughout the entire economy.

The inflationnary tendency which lasted throughout the prosperity period lacked one feature that was characteristic of inflation in other countries: there was no tendency toward a general rise in the price of commodities. The reason for this is clear. A disproportionately large percentage of commodity supplies was covered by imports and not by home production, and the price of imports was, of course, independent of local conditions, particularly as the local customs tariff was low. At the same time, the prices of commodities of local origin—such as houses, perishables, land, services, labor, and bulky building materials—showed unmistakable signs of inflation during the boom years. This does not mean that there were no radical shifts within the price structure, but rather that general price fluctuations were relatively small. Other parts of the world have been developed by immigrants of the laboring classes, the capital being provided by groups of capitalists remaining abroad. This system requires the developing country to provide regular interest payments abroad on its capital supply, which often constitute a severe drain on its still unconsoli-

dated finances. In Palestine, the settlers imported their own capital requirements, with the result that the country had an extraordinarily small foreign debt. It was this influx of "refugee" capital that determined the expansionist character of Palestine's economy. The mechanism by which capital influx was transformed into credit inflation may be described as follows: the new capital caused an increase in bank deposits disproportionate to the normal turnover in the country, which weighed on the financial structure of the banks and forced them into an expansionist credit policy, for which the large amount of deposits (some LP17 million during 1936 and 1937) provided a safety valve.

Labor. The Jewish working class was unique in nature and origin. It was neither an organic stratum in a strictly defined economic body nor the product of the usual urbanization of the rural community. It was built up through immigration and the occupational and class redistribution inherent in the construction of a new economy. Table 19, which indicates the numerical growth of the working class in comparison with the growth of the Jewish community, provides sufficient proof of the movement of Jews into the working class. This transition was interwoven with a second process, usually defined in Palestine as "productivization": a movement away from the occupations on the fringes of the economy toward the more basic occupations and trades.

Table 19. Growth of the Jewish Working Class

Labor census	Earners		Jewish population (mean)	
	No.	Index	No.	Index
1926	25,187	100	149,500	100
1937	105,000	417	388,970	260
1938	107,000	425	402,244	269
1939	112,000	445	429,605	287

Sources: Statistical and Information Department of the Histadrut, *Bulletin*, n. 9, 11; *Statistical Abstract of Palestine* (1941), 21.

Most of the Jews abroad were engaged in small trade or in the liberal professions and their transformation into a working class was, economically, technically, and psychologically, one of the most fundamental processes in the creation of the Jewish community.

Changes in the class and the occupational distribution of Jewish labor were combined with a movement from town to village—in direct contradiction to the usual drift away from the countryside. This shift was necessitated by the peculiar occupational distribution of Diaspora Jewry, already noted, the Jewish immigrant having to convert himself into a manual worker, very often into an agricultural laborer, as well as by the basic aim of creating a many-sided, well-balanced economic structure. The Arab working class, on the other hand, was created as a direct result of the impact of capitalism on the country's primitive rural economy. Palestine and the other countries of the Middle East were now coming under the influence of world forces and shaken out of the self-sufficient village system that had prevailed for centuries. Wages in the Arab sector were extremely low, however, and the standard of living bordered on the primitive.

Composition of the Jewish Working Class. The composition of the Jewish working class was profoundly influenced by one further deviation from the normal pattern of labor development. The new labor economy was financed by the funds of the Jewish national institutions and by direct support from Jewish labor abroad. In this way, certain key positions in Palestine's economic life, which either exerted no attraction for private capital (such as mixed farming) or were occupied by labor from the outset (such as transport) became an integral part of the independent labor economy. Some positions, such as the almost monopolistic control of the building market that labor possessed in the early days, were lost in the course of time, as private capital gradually penetrated into the field, but in the main labor continued to hold its own, side by side—sometimes in competition and sometimes in cooperation—with private enterprise.

The result of this dual sociological structure was that the Jewish working class was not composed entirely of hired wage-labor. A considerable proportion of the workers was engaged directly within the labor economy. The workers employed in mixed farming were for the most part neither peasants, in the usual sense of the word, nor ordinary hired laborers. They lived and worked in collective or cooperative farms or in joint enterprises based on varying degrees of cooperation. These farms varied in form from the moshav, or smallholders' settlement, with joint sale and purchase, joint use of machinery, a prohibition of hired labor, and national ownership of land, to the kibbutz, the completely collective commune, with joint production and consumption. The members of the transport and producers' cooperatives in the towns were the urban counterpart of the independent agricultural worker. These did not differ in form from the usual producers' cooperatives in Western countries, but, numerically and economically, they were of much greater importance in Palestine than elsewhere. Finally, a number of economic institutions were established directly by the comprehensive General Federation of Jewish Labour—the Histadrut.

Working Class Organization. The Histadrut was organized on the basis of one big union subdivided into trade sections. Its numerical strength may be gauged from Table 20, which shows the extraordinarily high percentage of the population it represented. The organization of Arab labor was still in its initial stages. A number of separate Arab trade unions had been formed, but few of them actually functioned. Some Arab workers were organized by the Histadrut into Arab sections of Jewish unions, but though some success attended this policy in the years preceding 1936, the strained relations of 1936 and 1937 brought this movement to an end. The few mixed Arab-Jewish unions—notably that of the railroad, post, and telegraph employees—almost ceased to exist after 1936.

The Labor Economy. It is difficult to estimate the relative influence of the independent labor economy within the

Table 20. Growth in Histadrut Membership

	Members of Histadrut		Total Jewish population		% Histadrut members in total Jewish population
	No.	Index	No.	Index	
1920	4,433	100	83,790 (1922)	100	5
1925	10,085	228	121,725	145	8
1931	30,060	678	172,028	205	17
1933	47,819	1,079	209,207	249	23
1936	98,636	2,225	370,483	442	27
1937	100,000	2,256	388,970	464	26
1938	108,000	2,436	402,244	480	27
1939	117,000	2,639	429,605	513	27

Sources: Statistics and Information Department of the Histadrut, *Bulletin* No. 9, p. 11. *Statistical Abstract of Palestine* (1941), p. 21.

economic life of the country, but there is no doubt that this sector formed one of the most powerful "concerns" in Palestine. Some of its economic activities were run through centralized institutions or companies, others by the method of autonomous cooperative enterprise. The Histadrut had its own financial institution—the Workers' Bank; it centralized the activities of the agricultural settlements through the Agricultural Audit Union; it organized supplies to a fair part of the community through the wholesale purchasing organization, Hamashbir Hamerkazi; it organized the sale of agricultural produce through its marketing cooperative, Tenuvah; it influenced a considerable section of the building market through its contracting organization, Solel Boneh; it carried out citrus planting through its citrus contracting institution, Yakhin; it planned and constructed workers' housing through its housing company, Shikun; it ran its own insurance company, Hassneh; it participated in the financing of public works through the Bizur Company; it centralized the transport and industrial producers' cooperatives through its

Cooperative Center. Inevitably, such ramified and comprehensive activities profoundly affected the economic development of the country, especially as they were coordinated and centralized within one institution, Hevrat ha-Ovdim, which had the right to control the various subsidiary institutions by law, as well as by custom and the system of labor organization.

The Arab Economy. The primitive Arab economy, as we have seen, was in many respects in a separate category. The usual economic problems of capitalism—trade fluctuations, finance, inflation and deflation, balance of payments—were almost completely absent from the Arab economic organization, which was centered—to the extent of 60–65%—on more or less self-sufficient agriculture, with specific problems of its own.

The Transformation of the Arab Village. The Palestinian village was an almost completely self-supporting unit, not yet emancipated from the century-old usages of the feudal system. Exchange of goods was of minor importance, and the use of money was limited. The village community was bound by tradition, and the forms of life and work had been preserved unchanged from past generations. The effect of the impact of capitalist forces on the economy, which was similar in all countries of the Near East, was by no means wholly unfavorable. The consequences of the break-up of smallholdings were neutralized by the new opportunities opened up to the rural population by the development of the country. The beneficial aspect of economic modernization was accentuated by the special influence of Jewish settlement: the towns grew as wages rose and employment facilities increased, and the Muslim urban population grew more rapidly than the population in the countryside, as Table 21 shows.

In addition, the increased revenue enabled the government to execute large public works projects, which employed a considerable proportion of the surplus rural population and provided those still engaged in cultivation with an additional source of out-of-season income. The 37

Table 21. Muslim Population in Palestine

	Urban		Rural	
	No.	Index	No.	Index
Census 1922	139,074	100	451,816	100
Census 1931	188,075	136	571,637	126
Estimate 1936	229,000	165	619,000	137

increased employment opportunities offered an outlet for the surplus rural population, which in other Near Eastern countries weighed heavily on the whole structure of the economy.

Another, even more important, opportunity for the Arab farmer was provided by the expansion of the urban market for foodstuffs. From 1922 to 1936 the urban population of Palestine expanded from 264,000 to 582,000, mainly as a result of Jewish immigration. The townsfolk consumed large quantities of foodstuffs and absorbed a fair proportion of the total output of the Arab farms. The development of markets for the products of intensified farming was of decisive importance for the progress of the Arab rural economy. The increase in Arab-owned poultry by 127% since 1930 was a characteristic symptom of this process.

Agricultural machinery was purchased by the Arab villages in larger quantities. Intensive methods of cultivation were adopted, and more remunerative crops sown. The farmer also received direct assistance from the government, which, backed up by a prosperous treasury, was able to adopt a fairly progressive and generous policy. Rural taxes were reformed and a rural property tax imposed, replacing the heavy burden of tithe and "werko." In difficult years, taxes were remitted: from 1930 to 1936 the government remitted LP600,000 of rural taxes and granted agricultural loans amounting to LP 169,000. Farming was also directly improved by the selection of seeds, provision of saplings and stocks, and, in general, by the work of the government experimental stations. Finally, the grain cultivator was protected from foreign competition by a system of duties on wheat and barley based on a sliding scale, which guaranteed a minimum profit for the farmer. The development of Arab citriculture, involving the investment of large capital sums, bears witness to the influx of capital into the Arab economy. The area of citrus groves owned by Arabs expanded from 22,000 dunams in 1922 to 147,000 in 1936. The semi-feudal, closed structure of the Arab rural economy was tottering under the impact of the new forces that had penetrated into the Near East since World War I, but in Palestine the impact was softened by the vast new possibilities opened up by Jewish settlement. The development of the Arab economy was the result of these two divergent forces.

Growth of the Arab Town. In the Arab town, the changes were scarcely less pronounced than in the village. The process of industrialization, though less marked than among the Jews, had not left the Arab world untouched. In the period between the end of World War I and the Government Industrial Census of 1928, 1,373 new Arab enterprises were established, representing an investment of LP613,000. From 1931 to 1937 another 529 Arab enterprises (companies, cooperatives, and partnerships) were registered. The increase in the Arab urban population was also reflected in the growth of the municipal budgets—particularly in the mixed towns. An Arab middle class was gradually developing. Merchants, industrialists, clerks, and the free professions gained ground at the expense of the rural community. The number of Arab officials in government services increased. The growth of this new stratum was accelerated by the sale of land to Jews at very high prices. Within the five years 1932–36, 209,000 dunams of land were sold to Jews at a price of LP 4,510,000. Such an influx of capital must have had a profound influence on the formation of the new Arab middle class. At the same time, there was a growth in the Arab wage-earning class. The new employment opportunities in the towns and in the expanding citrus area attracted landless peasants from the countryside and stimulated an immigration of Arabs from the neighboring countries. The fact that this new wage-earning class was still unorganized and the fellahin community from which it derived was weak and poverty-stricken meant that wages remained low and conditions of work primitive. The result was a more strongly pronounced class distinction within the Arab population than among the Jews. To sum up: a semi-feudal, almost self-sufficient, rural economy was being transformed under the impact of new forces working in two contrary directions. On the one hand, the impingement of modern conditions converted the self-sufficient, closed village into an exchange economy, increasing the cash requirements of the peasant and aggravating his indebtedness. The fair-sized land holding gradually disappeared, giving way to dwarf holdings and large landed properties. On the other hand, the wealth created by Jewish settlement and industrialization counteracted some of the adverse effects of this process: a market was created for agricultural produce, and the fellah was enabled to go over to more intensive farming; the government expanded its agricultural, health, and education services; new employment opportunities were created in the towns; and public works were established, offering the farmer an extra out-of-season income. In the towns, land sales at high prices, industrialization, and the expansion of commerce created a middle class with a concomitant accumulation of capital. The town assumed a more important place in the Arab economy and, with it, there emerged an Arab wage-earning class, employed in the cities and in the expanding citrus plantations.

THE PALESTINE ECONOMY DURING AND IMMEDIATELY AFTER WORLD WAR II. *Inflation and Full Employment.* The war economy in Palestine reflected such characteristic phenomena as the transition from a deflationary to an inflationary condition, increased liquidity on the money market, the expansion of production and decline of imports, autarkic tendencies, and an increasing influence of governmental and military establishments on economic conditions. The excess of receipts over expenditures in the balance of payments had a considerable influence on the economy. The circulation of currency, the scope of bank credit, and the liquidity of the money market were all rising rapidly. The profitability of various branches of the economy, both in industry and mixed farming, was improved. On the whole, the developments were favorable, despite a depression in citrus and the contraction of building activity. The developments in industry, mixed farming, and services generated a prosperity based on a war economy and facilitated the absorption of goods and labor. This improvement in economic conditions was generated by non-economic and external forces, which stimulated economic activity in much the same way as during the period of prosperity in 1933–35, which also had its origin in non-economic factors. In the 1930s it was immigration, the influx of capital, building activity, and investment that were instrumental in creating conditions of prosperity. In the 1940s the war economy and the expenditure of the British army produced similar conditions. The scope of building activity and of investment, which was extraordinarily broad in the Palestinian economy, contracted after the outbreak of the war.

Finance. Economic conditions called imperatively for an expansion of credit to facilitate large-scale investment in the expansion of agricultural and industrial production, and to meet the increased demand for working capital created by a general rise in prices. Owing to inflationary tendencies, deposits increased from LP47 million in September 1943 to LP82.5 million in the last month of the war, while the rise in the circulation of currency was even more pronounced: from LP6.3 million in 1939 to LP47 million in 1945. The war effort in Palestine was financed neither by the local government nor from the country's internal resources, but by the Imperial British Government, which paid for its purchases from Palestine with money provided from Britain. In this way the war economy was based on a kind **41**

Table 22. Jewish Capital Imports

Year	LP
1940	5,180,000
1941	4,350,000
1942	5,500,000
1943	8,340,000
1944	10,010,000
1945	11,780,000
Total	45,160,000

of invisible export and expansion, which created a considerable surplus in the balance of payments. While in the 1930s the surplus in the overall balance of payments was the result of the import of Jewish capital, another, no less important factor—the British indebtedness to Palestine citizens and banks—was now operative, and was reflected in Palestine balances in British banks and British securities. The import of Jewish capital during the war years is shown in the Table 22.

The influx of capital, mainly public, played a smaller role, however, in creating a surplus in the balance of payments. The expenditure of the British army was of a

Table 23. Increase in Assets Abroad as an Indicator of Visible Surplus in Balance of Payments (round figures)

Period	LP
October 1939–December 1940	4,300,000
1941	8,300,000
1942	21,200,000
1943	28,300,000
1944	20,200,000
January–September 1945	10,200,000
Total	92,500,000

Table 24. Expenditure of Allied Troops in Palestine

Period	LP
September–December 1939	2,841,000
1940	8,637,000
1941	14,433,000
1942	28,639,000
1943	33,866,000
1944	25,229,000
Total	113,645,000

much larger scope and influence. The growth of Palestine balances abroad, shown in Table 23, indicates the effectiveness and scope of these factors. The expenditure of the British and allied troops in the country, as estimated by the Palestine government statistician, is shown in Table 24.

The import of Jewish capital, aggregating LP45 million, and the expenditure of the British army, totaling over LP113 million, resulted in the accumulation of capital, particularly as consumption was limited by import restriction. Thus the capital surplus was reflected in the foreign balances of Palestine citizens, companies, and banks. This process generated inflationary pressures in the Palestine economy. The currency in circulation increased from July 1939 until September 1945 by 748% and bank deposits by 412%. Under these monetary conditions, inflation was inevitable, particularly as the supply of goods and services was limited by administrative controls and by the diversion of means of production to the war effort. Difficulties in communications, the shortage of shipping space, and the occupation of some Far Eastern countries by the Japanese and of European countries by Germany, while local production was partly diverted to military needs, led to a considerable increase in prices: the official price index rose by 254 points in comparison with 1939.

Expansion of Agricultural Production. The war economy in Palestine also led to the reinforcement of self-sufficiency, **43** based primarily on the expansion of agricultural and industrial production. The total increase in the Arab agricultural sector was estimated at 15–20% and the output of Jewish agriculture doubled. On the other hand, citriculture was seriously affected by its virtual exclusion from foreign markets: output declined from 18 million cases in 1938–39 to 5 million at the end of the war. Moreover, since some of the plantations were neglected during the war, the contraction of citriculture had an adverse effect on the balance of payments even after the war.

Expansion of Industry and Contraction of Building. Industry was greatly stimulated by the war. The elimination of external competition, restriction of imports, military purchases, and the opening of neighboring markets to Palestine's industrial exports stimulated industrial expansion. The increase in the scope of work and employment is reflected in Table 25.

The index of Jewish industrial production reached its apex in May 1943: 236 points, with September-October 1939 as the base. On the other hand, construction contracted as a result of (a) the diversion of labor to industry, military employment, and mixed farming, and (b) a shortage of building materials, leading to a shortage of housing and a rise in rents.

Foreign Trade. A serious contraction took place in the foreign trade of Palestine during the war. Nominally, imports increased from LP14 million in 1939 to LP28 million in 1944. However, the physical volume of these imports declined and is estimated at only LP8.5 million at 1938 prices. The decline in exports was even more pronounced, as the export of citrus represented two-thirds of Palestine's total exports before the war.

Employment and Wages. The inflationary pressures were most pronounced in the labor market. Unemployment, which was prevalent before the war, disappeared, as reflected in Table 26. Thousands of new workers were drawn into the process of production and thousands more 44 joined the British army. During the war, some 55,000 Jews

Table 25. Indices of Industrial Development

Month	No. of workers		Work days		Total wage bill	
	Jewish Agency figures	Government figures	Jewish Agency figures	Government figures	Jewish Agency figures	Government figures
October 1938	100	100.0	100	100.0	100	100.0
September 1939	103	86.9	105	97.0	108	95.7
September 1940	112	104.1	115	116.2	120	113.4
September 1941	146	117.8	157	138.3	179	144.9
September 1942	177	137.4	197	164.6	327	264.9
September 1943	202		231		677	
September 1944	202		228		744	
September 1945	185		212		819	

Calculated on the basis of Jewish Agency and government figures.

Table 26. Unemployment Among Jews

December 1938	3,123
December 1939	13,947
August 1940	12,819
August 1941	3,986
August 1942	1,304
August 1943	380
August 1944	356
August 1945	357

reached the country and were absorbed in its economic activity: in industry, mixed farming, and work for the war effort, as well as in the British army—in addition to the absorption of labor previously unemployed in building, citriculture, etc. A serious shortage of labor developed, and a substantial number of women joined the labor force, particularly in branches engaged in the war effort. Until 1943 the index of wages lagged behind the rise in the cost-of-living index. However, the shortage of labor later accelerated the rise in wages, so that both nominal and real wages increased.

The Arab Economy During the War. Profound changes took place in the pattern of the Arab economy during the war. The accumulation of capital led to modernization in this sector and reinforced tendencies apparent before the war due to the percolation of Jewish capital into the Arab economy. This is borne out particularly by the spectacular increase in deposits in the two Arab banks between the years 1940–45; from LP246,000 to LP7.1 million—i.e., about thirtyfold. The income from cereal growing, which represented 85% of the total income of the Arab economy, increased 7.5 times, while the cost of production increased to a much smaller extent. Practically all agricultural produce—milk, eggs, vegetables, olives, fruit—increased in price, with the one exception of citrus, which was seriously affected by the war. The livestock in the Arab economy increased continuously: from 152,000 head of cattle in 1937

46

to 215,000 in 1943. The fellah's farm income increased thanks to a fivefold rise in the prices of agricultural produce. The increase in the quantity of produce brought to market by the Arab agricultural sector was estimated at 28%. There was also some development in Arab industry, which benefited from the general prosperity, particularly in textiles, flour mills, etc. In 1942, according to the government census, Arab industrial production aggregated some LP 5,650,000 in value and investment LP 2,131,000. Some 50,000 Arab workers were employed by the army and the number employed by the government increased simultaneously, while wages in the Arab economy rose considerably.

Postwar Trends. The Palestine economy had undergone far-reaching changes during the war. Owing to import restriction and increased self-sufficiency, some parts of the economy were contracted and others inflated: some branches of industry had expanded considerably, far beyond the capacity of the local market to absorb their output. The favorable balance of payments led to the accumulation of capital in the form of balances held in Britain. The artificial prosperity seriously affected competitive capacity, as the cost of production rose excessively, making it more difficult to reconvert to peace conditions. During the war the development of the economy was determined by full employment of labor and of productive capacity; inflationary tendencies, reinforced by rising national income, expanding purchasing power, rising prices, and a surplus in the balance of payments; autarkic tendencies caused by the separation of the country from its source of supply, contraction of shipping space, rise in freight charges, etc.; increasing government intervention and increasing weight of the military and governmental sectors. The operation of these factors changed and in some respects distorted the economic structure of the country. The tremendous demand created by the army and the increased purchasing power insulated the country from normal economic conditions. The economy was thus determined by physical and not by economic factors.

It was under these conditions that the country entered into the period of transition from a war to a peace economy. For two years after the end of the war, industrial capacity was fully employed, notwithstanding the contraction of governmental and military orders, owing to the pent-up demand which could not be satisfied during the war because of physical shortages. The accumulated purchasing power reinforced this demand, stimulated production, and was conducive to full employment. However, with the increasing contact with world markets, price discrepancies became evident and imports increased considerably: up to 117% of the 1939 volume. Sterling balances were accumulated thanks to the transfer of dollars from the United States and to British army expenditures for the purchase of goods and services. These balances, including British securities, amounted to LP55 million, but one part of it belonged to the Arab sector and another was spent to cover the deficit in the balance of trade immediately after the war.

IN THE STATE OF ISRAEL—1948–72. The increase in Jewish population is the most distinctive and decisive feature in the State of Israel's economic affairs. During the period 1948–72 almost 1,200,000 immigrants were absorbed, while natural increase added over 850,000 souls. Today, the bulk of Israel's population consists not of those who established the State, but of those who settled or were born there after its establishment. An increment of this magnitude is bound to have a sweeping effect on the entire economic fabric, as well as on current economic processes, as new arrivals become consumers before they can be economically integrated and play an active part in the process of production. The occupational distribution of the Jewish population in the Diaspora reflects a predominance of commercial, clerical, and free professions. The difference on the occupational distribution of Israel's labor is reflected in Table 27.

The bulk of the immigrant population had to undergo occupational reorganization, but this process and the

Table 27. Occupational Distribution of Israel's Labor Force (percentages)

	1958	1962	1967	1969	1971	1972
Agriculture	17.6	15.5	12.6	9.7	8.5	8.0
Commerce, finance, insurance	12.3	12.3	13.5	18.4	18.4	19.3
Construction and public works	9.8	9.7	7.6	8.1	8.9	9.5
Electricity, water, sanitation	2.2	2.1	2.2	1.1	1.1	0.8
Industry	22.4	25.0	24.6	24.0	24.1	23.7
Personal services	7.6	7.6	8.1	8.1	7.3	7.3
Public services	21.9	21.7	24.1	22.7	24.3	24.1
Transportation, communication, storage	6.2	6.1	7.3	7.9	7.4	7.3
Total	100.0	100.0	100.0	100.0	100.0	100.0
Total in thousands	655	777.1	835.0	945.0	997.0	1,045

resultant economic growth were facilitated by the availability of a nucleus of highly skilled labor—technicians, experts, scientists, manufacturers with experience gained abroad, designers, engineers, agronomists, diamond cutters and polishers, horticulturists, irrigation engineers, and the like—which established the essential preconditions for rising productivity. The knowledge of industrial and agricultural techniques also accelerated economic growth, while the establishment and rapid growth of schools of higher learning, laboratories, libraries, etc., sponsored by the government and various groups from abroad, and the spread of scientific knowledge combined to increase Israel's potentialities. The immigrant population thus contained a sufficient proportion of skilled and trained manpower to provide the qualitative background for the process of transplantation, and the enterprising qualities of the 49 population also seem to have been adequate to the task. Rapid economic growth was thus facilitated by the process of co-migration, i.e., immigration with a concurrent increase in the labor force combined with the necessary investment of capital and rise in productivity.

Major Trends. The goal of Israel's economic policy may be said to be threefold: rapid economic growth, reinforcement of competitive capacity, and close integration into the world economy (the latter being the point of departure for Israel's efforts to build a bridge to the European Common Market). The functional link between economic growth and import of capital and investment is very perceptible in Israel, and thanks, inter alia, to the sustained import of capital, remarkably rapid economic growth has been achieved under extremely difficult conditions.

First, the demographic growth far exceeded the rate in underdeveloped countries; in the period 1948–72 the population was almost quadrupled. Second, the geopolitical and military background hardly favored development; boycott and blockade were a serious handicap, and the geopolitical situation entailed heavy expenditure on arms. Third, the country was faced with a lack of water and a scarcity of natural resources—no coal, iron, or substantial oil wells. Fourth, part of the new population was accustomed to European standards of living, which had to be maintained within a poor and still infant economy. Fifth, the occupational structure and cultural background of a section of the population were not adapted to local needs, and an occupational realignment of most of the population could not be deferred. Sixth, people coming from eighty countries, with nearly as many languages, and sometimes centuries apart in cultural sophistication, had to be welded into ethnic and national unity. Seventh, the restricted scope of the home market excluded the economics of scale in industrial production. In such circumstances it was essential to enlarge productive capacity, as the economy also had to provide a livelihood for an unusually large increment in population. The work had to be done under great strain and inflationary hazards: the trebling of the population, the crippling burden of defense, and massive expenditure on development, which in itself created inflationary pressures. Although conditions were difficult, a steady growth was maintained, as shown by an average annual rise in the gross national product by some 10% in real terms during 1949–72 and a rise of nearly twentyfold in exports during 1950–72: from $45.7 million to $918.4 million. In 1949 only 16% of imports were covered by income from exports: in 1972 the proportion exceeded 67%. In 1949, a population of 1.1 million was supplied with up to 50% of its foodstuffs from local production: in 1972 a population of more than 3.1 million derived about 90% of its foodstuffs from local sources and at a much superior nutritional level. The area under irrigation increased more than sixfold: 40 times more electricity was produced. At the same time, net reserves in gold and foreign currency rose from nearly nil to $1,070 million. These are but a few indications of the achievement.

Very large amounts of capital were brought in during the first 25 years of Israel's statehood in the form of money involving no financial obligation on the part of the state now or hereafter: gifts from world Jewry, West German reparations, and grants-in-aid from the United States government. This capital was supplemented by loans, such as Israel's own Independence and Development Loans, the long-term loan of the Export-Import Bank, World Bank loans and commercial credits, and equity for investment. This capital made investments of some IL53 billion (or IL51 billion at 1964 prices) possible in the years 1950–72. The loans matured quickly and furthered a reduction in the per capita import surplus from $230 in 1949 to $128 in 1972 and a greater rise in per capita exports: from $27 in 1949 to $725, notwithstanding a concurrent rise in the standard of living.

Another of Israel's distinctive characteristics is its socio-economic structure: there are pronounced differences between its parts, governmental, private, and cooperative

sectors coexisting within the economy. The investment of
large amounts of public capital makes for the emergence of
a tripartite mixed economy of this kind. The labor-coopera-
tive sector, controlled by the Histadrut, represents a very
substantial and independent economic element and part-
nership between groups belonging to the private and
cooperative sectors, or between both together and the
governmental sector, are frequent. The relationship between the sectors is sometimes one of cooperation,
sometimes of conflict, and always of competition. The
dimensions of the three sectors, which are of great interest,
are shown in Table 28.

Annual economic growth in real terms, which in few
other countries exceeded 5%, averaged 10% in Israel during
the decade 1950–60. The rate of growth was fairly even,
moreover, with the exception of the years 1966–67, when it
slowed down as a result of the economic policy of
consolidation.

Agriculture. There was a very pronounced growth in
agriculture, which may be divided into two sections, each
with its own distinctive features: citriculture, based on
modern technical methods and high capital investment,
employing hired labor, and producing mostly for export;
and modern mixed farming, based on intensive cultivation

Table 28. Net Domestic Product by Sector, 1953–60 (percentages).

	NDP (1)	Public sector (2)	Histadrut sector (3)	Private sector (1)−(2 + 3)
1953	100.0	19.4	20.3	60.3
1955	100.0	19.4	18.0	62.6
1957	100.0	20.9	20.6	58.5
1958	100.0	20.0	20.0	60.0
1959	100.0	21.6	20.3	58.1
1960	100.0	21.1	20.4	58.5

and irrigation, producing food for the urban population, and concentrating on dairy farming, poultry breeding, and fruit and vegetable growing, with some admixture of mechanized cereal growing. Higher agricultural output, which is among the most valuable components of economic growth, gave the rapidly expanding population an ample supply of foodstuffs. The objectives of agricultural policy—adequate stocks of home-grown food and more agricultural exports—could only be achieved by higher productivity and a shift from less to more remunerative crops. Simultaneously, there was an expansion in agricultural exports from $6.5 million (after a decline during World War II) in 1949 to $160 million in 1972, consisting mainly of oranges, grapefruit, and other varieties of citrus. The economic significance of the extension of citrus groves lies in the high capital investment per wage earner and a tendency to substitute capital for space; this is of great significance for a small country with a high population density.

The rise in agricultural exports other than citrus was smaller, but from 1965–72 it accelerated from $45–53 million. Most of this is out-of-season vegetables and fruit; climatic and soil differences between Israel and Europe, which is almost the sole market for these products, are turned to good account. The rapid expansion of mixed farming may be attributed to the large sums of capital invested in irrigation and more intensive cultivation, and to the enlargement of local urban demand. The shift to more expensive foodstuffs, such as fruit, vegetables, eggs, and dairy produce, increased the value of farm produce.

Available data indicate not only a rising per capita consumption, but an even larger expansion due to the rise in population. In arid Israel, this structural change could be achieved only by extending the area under irrigation, as Table 29 shows. Since the establishment of the State, some 450 new farm villages have been founded and the production of older ones has been greatly enlarged. Some IL4,700 million (at 1964 prices) were invested in such

Table 29. Irrigated Area, 1948/49–1971/72 (selected years, thousand dunams)

	1948/49	1954/55	1960/61	1966/67	1971/72
Field crops	65	265	467	525	642
Fish ponds	15	37	53	59	56
Orchards	150	285	522	679	694
Vegetables potatoes ground nuts	54	237	235	259	300
Miscellaneous (auxilliary farms, nurseries, etc.)	16	66	83	94	98
Total	300	890	1360	1616	1790

villages and in the development of water resources, over the years 1950–72.

In the years 1948–72 the value of agricultural production (at constant prices) rose by more than tenfold and production per capita was more than doubled. The irrigated area was increased fivefold, herds of milch cows were quadrupled, the number of tractors was multiplied by nineteen, and the area under citriculture was tripled. New crops and new methods of cultivation were introduced, with notable advances in yields. The make-up of agricultural production is shown in Tables 30 and 31.

The rapid growth of agricultural production resulted in almost complete self-sufficiency in most foodstuffs, and even surpluses of eggs, vegetables, potatoes, and dairy produce. Prices accordingly declined after 1959 and a system of farm subsidies was adopted. A portion of the subsidies, which totaled IL200 million in 1972, was meant to stabilize the scope of production and the prices of farm

produce, so as to prevent price increases, which, owing to

Table 30. Total Agricultural Output by Branch (percentages)

	1965/66	1967/68	1968/69	1969/70	1970/71	1971/72
Poultry farming	21.4	19.6	19.4	20.0	20.4	20.7
Cattle farming	15.8	15.0	14.6	15.0	13.4	13.5
Other livestock	7.4	8.3	7.7	7.9	8.0	6.7
Total livestock	44.6	42.9	41.7	42.9	41.8	40.9
Citrus	18.1	21.6	20.3	19.2	22.5	23.3
Other orchards	11.8	9.7	11.2	10.3	9.7	10.6
Vegetables and potatoes	9.8	10.8	10.9	11.8	10.3	11.2
Field crops and miscellaneous	15.7	15.0	15.9	15.8	15.7	14.0
Total crops	55.4	57.1	58.3	57.1	58.2	59.1
Total	100.0	100.0	100.0	100.0	100.0	100.0

Table 31. Growth in Agricultural Production (indices based on 1948–49 prices)

	1948/49	1952/53	1960/61	1965/66	1969/70	1970/71	1971/72
Field crops	100	250	638	784	825	933	1,088
Vegetables and potatoes	100	245	348	470	620	670	700
Citrus fruits	100	137	213	355	509	571	571
Other fruit	100	165	608	1,077	1,100	1,240	1,470
Milk	100	177	374	479	579	589	614
Eggs	100	152	558	543	605	650	637
Honey	100	136	174	424	340	400	420
Meat (live weight)	100	135	838	1,175	1,800	1,800	1,935
Fish	100	217	430	689	607	713	713
Total	100	183	491	656	838	931	993

the escalator clause in practically all wage agreements, would have led to rises in costs of production in industry, building, transport, and services. But the purpose of a large proportion of them, as well as of tariff protection against competing imports, was to raise the level of farming incomes. As in most developed countries, the average farming income in Israel is less than the average in the economy as a whole, but the gap is not excessive. Citrus growers and well-established farmers in the vicinity of dense conurbations are most favorably situated, though in recent years even farmers in new villages in development areas have begun to show a marked improvement in income, despite their lack of experience, skill, and full equipment.

Industrialization. Israel has been undergoing an accelerated process of industrialization, as shown by Table 32. A set of circumstances peculiar to Israel must be sought to explain this process. The motives for industrialization that were once usual in colonial territories are not present in Israel. In a territory that was for many years a source of raw

Table 32. Development of Industry, 1959—71

Year	Number of enterprises	Personnel (thousands)	Capital investment (IL million)	Consumption of electricity (million kwh.)
1959	4,662	142	160	630
1962	5,494	179	281	994
1963	5,835	193	359	1,037
1964	5,998	204	402	1,106
1965	6,615	206	383	1,225
1966	6,600	209	291	1,285
1967	5,986	187	229	1,285
1968	5,994	218	470	1,534
1969	5,773	226	671	1,654
1970	5,926	233	813	1,840
1971		240	1,056	2,071

materials and a market for the industrial goods of more developed countries, the advantages of establishing local industries are realized sooner or later. Cheap labor, proximity to raw materials, and a market on the spot eventually attract capital from the metropolis, and new industries spring up. But such stimuli to industrialization are lacking in Israel: there is no cheap labor and there are few raw materials. Industrialization in Israel, accordingly, is different: it is closely bound up with immigration. The capital is imported directly by the immigrants themselves or as public capital through the Development Budget, which explains the availability of so much capital in a new country. Perhaps the key factor has been the expansion of the home market and the opening of new factories to meet the rising demand. According to surveys of Jewish industry taken by the government in 1962, 1965, and 1969, industrial personnel and production were divided among various branches as shown in Table 33.

The following points are worth noting: (1) In Israel, as in all young industrial countries, industry concentrated on the production of consumer goods—it was estimated that 65% of it is engaged in that field and only 35% in turning out capital goods. (2) It was overwhelmingly dependent on the home market—77% of total output was consumed locally. (3) The bulk of Israel's industries used imported raw materials. (4) The relative weight of industry within the economy was rising (in 1971–72 the gross value of its production amounted to IL14,185 million). (5) Capital influx served as a powerful stimulus to industrial investment. (6) The rate of industrialization was rapid, and depended on an economy of growing population and demand. The absorption of immigrants would have been all but impossible without it. Agriculture could not assimilate a large increment of population in a short time, and besides, agricultural development itself depends on the expansion of urban markets. Demographic growth also promotes diversification of industrial production by creating the technical and economic minima of production required for the

Table 33. Israel's Industry, 1962–71/72

	Employed persons (thousands)				Production (thousand IL)			
	1962/3	1965/6	1969/70	1971/72	1962/3	1965/6	1969/70	1971/72
Foodstuffs	24	28	31	32	730	1,318	1,966	2,705
Textiles	22	25	20	22	391	675	779	1,308
Clothing	7	9	20	22	98	171	477	751
Metal products	13	16	22	25	186	368	814	1,348
Machinery	8	10	10	11	162	276	430	560
Wood, wood products, and furniture	13	13	10	11	203	320	329	447
Leather, and products	5	4	4	4	59	80	104	132
Chemicals and petroleum	8	8	9	10	302	352	591	1316
Paper and products	3	3	4	4	41	56	103	171
Printing and publishing	3	3	4	4	90	125	211	322
Rubber and plastics	8	8	8	9	99	166	246	302
Mining and quarrying	5	6	8	9	127	205	408	612
Non-metallic mineral products	3	4	4	4	84	170	222	339
Diamonds	11	11	8	9	256	368	395	550
Basic metal industries	7	7	10	9	187	293	563	1,175
Electrical machinery and equipment	4	4	5	5	129	178	339	392
Transport equipment	7	8	14	17	121	228	625	916
Miscellaneous	17	21	15	18	234	417	441	839
Total	168	188	206	225	3,599	5,706	9,043	14,185

Table 34. Share of Industry[1] (in millions IL at current prices)

	Investment			National Income		
	Investment in industry	Gross fixed domestic investment	Share of industry (%)	Income originating from industry	National income	Share of industry (%)
1952[2]	67	327	20.5	184	827	22.2
1955	75	637	11.8	399	1,695	23.5
1958	160	941	17.0	623	2,717	22.9
1960	198	1,122	17.6	845	3,418	24.7
1962	340	1,942	17.5	1,276	4,783	26.6
1964	469	2,758	17.0	1,809	6,951	26.0
1967	237	1,929	12.3	2,111	9,485	22.2
1970	823	4,815	17.1	3,925	15,477	25.4
1971	1,056	6,575	16.1	4,769	19,082	25.0
1972	1,400	8,442	16.6	5,830	23,795	24.5

[1] Including manufacturing, construction, mining, and quarrying. [2] Including electricity.

Table 35. Industrial Exports, 1950—72

	Percentage increase in industrial exports	Industrial exports as percentage of total commodity exports
1950	——	58.1
1952	− 7.4	60.9
1954	49.0	54.9
1956	15.0	56.0
1958	− 2.0	58.2
1960	25.5	69.1
1962	18.9	74.8
1964	13.4	80.4
1966	19.0	78.9
1967	3.0	78.0
1968	25.1	80.3
1969	13.4	81.0
1970	6.8	81.1
1971	25.2	81.4
1972	23.0	82.9

establishment of industries. The importance of industry in Israel's economic life is mirrored in Table 34. The rising relative momentum of industrial exports, which have an important bearing on Israel's crucial economic problem, the balance of payments, is shown in Table 35.

It would appear that industry developed mainly in three directions: production on the basis of locally available raw materials (citrus, Dead Sea minerals, and cotton); production based on skill, where the value of raw materials is a fraction of that of the end-product (chemicals and pharmaceuticals, certain kinds of machinery, instruments, fashion goods, and electronics); the use of small, light raw materials, so that transport costs are negligible in relation to value and manufacture is entirely independent of the geographical origin of the raw materials (furs and diamonds). The pattern of development is shown in Table 36.

Building. One of the effects of immigration is a vast investment in construction, which totaled IL15 billion in

Table 36   Israel's Industrial Economy, 1958/72

	1958	1960	1962	1964	1966	1968	1969	1970	1971	1972
Industrial output (in million IL)*	2,012	2,595	3,400	4,426	4,929	6,156	7,135	7,867	8,850	9,820
Index	100	129	169	220	245	306	354	391	440	408
Industrial exports (in millions U.S. $)	81	145	201	281	375	480	558	597	748	920
Polished diamonds	(34)	(56)	(84)	(118)	(165)	(194)	(216)	(202)	(265)	(385)
Index of industrial exports	100	179	248	347	463	586	685	737	923	1,136
Number of persons employed in industry: index	100	115	143	163	162	176	195	207	216	226
Output per person employed: index	100	112	118	135	151	173	182	189	204	216
Net investments in industry: index	100	107	141	162	118	173	234	265	308	357

* Based on 1958 prices.

the period 1950–72 at 1964 prices. Immigrants generate an incessant demand for housing, which is partly financed by the capital inflow. Import of capital alone could not stimulate economic activity so rapidly. The capital had to be diffused through all strata of the population, and the building trades have been very much to the fore in effecting the diffusion. An exceptionally high proportion of the investment in building is paid out in wages, thus creating a market for agricultural and industrial products. In this way new capital invested in building has an instant and meaningful impact on all branches of the economy and on its growth. Throughout most of Israel's history, there was not enough housing for the swiftly increasing population, and building naturally became the workers' point of entry into the economy until they could be absorbed in the expanding network of agricultural and industrial production. At the onset of each tide of immigration and expansion, the construction of housing was the principal task; the proportion of building workers in the total labor force came to as much as 9.5% in 1972.

Services. Variation in the occupational pattern of society enlarged the share of "tertiary" stages of production. The percentage of industrial products and of services in the family budget rises with standards of living. Thus, the percentage of personal expenditure devoted to the purchase of food declined, while spending on services rose as shown in Table 37. When there are large sectors of governmental and public enterprise, this tendency is strengthened by the expansion of administrative staff. This process is particularly true of a welfare state like Israel, with expanding health, social, and educational services, scientific institutions, and so forth.

Income and Consumption. Personal incomes rose rapidly and continuously, owing to capital import, rising wages, the increase in the gross national product in real terms, and restitution payments from West Germany. Demand rose parallel with the rise in incomes, which again raised the level of consumption and investment. As both private and 63

Table 37. Composition of Personal Expenditure, 1960 – 72

	Average 1960–65	1967	1969	1971	1972
Food, drink, and tobacco	33	31	28	27	25
Durable goods	9	7	12	9	10
Other goods	17	16	18	17	16
Services	41	46	42	47	49

public consumption expanded more than the population did, per capita consumption rose as well.

Although the average real income of the population rose steadily after 1948, the increase was not divided equally among the various sectors of the population, and the inequality in incomes steadily widened, as shown in Table 38. Although the income differential widened, however, it is still among the narrowest in the world. A relatively more even distribution of income raises total consumption, as it mainly benefits the sections of the population with a high propensity to consume. The highest rate of rise was registered until 1965 in the purchase of durable consumer goods. Table 39 gives the real rate in the decade 1959–1972 (the drop in the years 1966 and 1967 was due to the economic recession).

The rise in the purchase of goods that are characteristic of a high standard of living, such as electric refrigerators, washing machines, record players, mixers, and vacuum cleaners, is very noticeable. Travel abroad also increased considerably. Simultaneously, more food of higher quality was consumed. The trend toward a relative decline in the proportion spent on food is a further sign of a rising standard of living.

Public consumption was very heavy and the cumulative amount of money injected by the government into the economy during most of the period of statehood was

Table 38. Distribution of Urban Family Incomes, 1954—68/69*

Deciles	1954	1957/58	1963/64	1968/69
Lowest tenth	2.5	1.8	1.5	1.5
Second tenth	4.5	3.5	3.6	3.3
Third tenth	6.3	5.4	5.2	5.0
Fourth tenth	7.6	6.9	6.6	6.4
Fifth tenth	8.7	8.3	7.9	7.9
Sixth tenth	9.5	9.4	9.1	9.3
Seventh tenth	10.4	10.6	10.7	11.0
Eighth tenth	12.5	12.6	12.8	13.2
Ninth tenth	15.3	15.9	15.9	16.6
Upper tenth	22.7	25.6	26.7	25.8
Lorenz index of inequality	293	350	364	368
Average nominal income, in IL	2,618	3,196	6,931	10,853
Index of real income	100	101	158	206

* Percentage of total incomes received by each decile (tenth of the total number of families in ascendancy order of incomes).

Table 39. Purchases of Durable Goods (at constant 1961—72 prices)

	Percentage increase over preceding year
1961	16
1963	20
1964	24
1965	5
1966	-8
1967	- 19
1968	70
1969	38
1970	- 16
1971	2
1972	18

Table 40. Share of Government Consumption Expenditure in National Product, 1950–72

Year	Percentage
1950	20.1
1953	18.7
1956	26.6
1959	19.1
1963	20.5
1966	22.8
1967	30.1
1968	29.6
1969	30.7
1970	35.8
1971	34.0
1972	31.6

considerable. This development must, however, be viewed in the context of defense needs and vast investment for absorption of immigration, economic development, and the creation of sources of livelihood for newcomers. The share of the State Budget and of total public consumption within the total national income was therefore substantial (see Table 40).

Balance of Trade and the National Product. The salient feature of Israel's balance of payments is a substantial excess of imports over exports on current account, while the overall balance of payments almost invariably showed a surplus, due to a surplus on the capital account, until 1968. These facts are brought out in Table 41. Like most small countries, Israel must assign a substantial proportion of its resources to export. This fact once again brings the question of competitive capacity into sharp relief. It is likely that any further rise in exports will be mainly to developed countries, which today absorb about 87% of them. Israel's agricultural produce, grown in a subtropical climate, is plainly not marketable in countries of similar climatic and natural conditions, but sells satisfactorily in the temperate zones.

European countries buy its fruit, especially citrus, and out-of-season vegetables. Production on a small scale for a population of three million cannot be economical. Artificial growth under a protective tariff would entail divergence from world economic trends and distort the pattern of production. Israel's economy, after rapid expansion, must now take its decisive steps toward maturity and integration in world markets. Hence the efforts to build a bridge to the Common Market, which now buys nearly one-third of the country's exports.

Total exports rose from $46 million in 1950 to $2,275 million in 1972, but imports increased concurrently. The problem here is one of competitive capacity. While rapid physical expansion proceeded, the attainment and maintenance of competitive capacity were somewhat neglected, and inflation, of course, undermined it. Exports rose much more quickly than imports; but as even in 1967 exports were only two-thirds of imports, they did not catch up. However, the growing percentage of exports covered by imports confirms the view that remarkable progress was made. The gap was bridged by a very substantial import of capital, which also found expression in the import of capital goods, so important from this point of view. Table 42 gives a list of the main categories of goods imported.

Investment and Import of Capital. Net capital imports in the years 1950–72 totaled IL13 billion (gross 17 billion dollars) and made possible investment of IL51 billion (at current prices): about 15% of which went to industry, mining, and electricity; 9% to agriculture and irrigation; 17% to transport and communications; 34% to housing and building; and the remainder to trade and services. The money came from a variety of sources, but the overwhelming bulk of it was from public and semi-public funds. Import of capital made it practicable to dispense with a rapid increase in domestic saving and to avoid any drastic reduction of living standards, which must have ensued if resources had been diverted from consumption to investment. Moreover, there were no capital charges on account   67

Table 41. Balance of Payments (in millions U.S. $)

	1960	1962
Goods and Services		
Exports, f.o.b.	210	271
Imports, f.o.b.	− 442	− 556
Trade deficit	− 232	− 285
Net invisibles (except investment income)	− 71	− 128
Investment income	− 43	− 48
Total invisibles	− 114	− 176
Deficit on goods and services	− 346	− 461
Unilateral transfers		
Private donations[1]	123	137
Restitution	101	138
Reparations	73	43
Government transfers	14	8
Total unilateral transfers	311	326
Residual deficit[2]	− 35	− 135
Capital (net)		
Private foreign investment	44	82
Independence and development bonds	28	33
Other medium and long-term capital	35	105
Short-term and errors and omissions	30	56
Total capital	137	276
Change in foreign exchange reserves[3] (a minus indicates an increase)	− 102	− 141

[1] Includes immigrants' transfers in cash and kind. [2] Deficit on goods and services minus total unilateral transfers.
[3] Includes net foreign exchange position of commercial banks.

1964	1966	1968	1970	1971	1972
349	475	649	802	977	1,202
− 733	− 736	− 997	− 1,286	− 1,622	− 1,798
− 384	− 261	− 348	− 484	− 645	− 596
− 126	− 126	− 237	− 632	− 420	− 389
− 54	− 59	− 71	− 118	− 107	− 91
− 180	− 185	− 308	− 750	− 527	− 480
− 564	− 446	− 656	− 1,234	− 1,172	− 1,076
168	176	299	463	529	702
134	110	143	204	231	292
17	−2				
8	3	−7	−17	8	56
327	287	435	650	768	1,050
− 237	− 159	− 221	− 584	− 404	−26
143	71	9	10	47	123
36	8	78	136	184	188
128	102	103	512	512	401
− 36	− 55	− 21	44	39	− 192
271	126	169	702	782	520
− 34	33	52	− 118	− 378	− 494

Table 42. Commodity Imports, 1962—71(in millions U.S. $)

	1962	1964	1966	1968	1970	1971
Food and beverages	83.1	109.6	132.0	125.9	167	185
Oilseeds	23.4	28.7	33.7	30.3	29	54
Wood	26.7	29.7	23.7	30.3	35	42
Textiles	22.9	30.9	26.8	35.3	50	59
Chemicals	34.6	42.6	48.6	73.0	100	116
Metals	58.3	70.4	63.4	103.0	158	146
Raw diamonds, net	67.2	102.3	124.9	162.1	154	224
Fuel	40.1	46.6	58.3	62.7	70	90
Other raw materials	60.0	74.9	86.0	105.2	150	170
Machinery, electrical and communication equipment	117.5	123.5	122.7	180.7	286	327
Automotive vehicles	32.4	52.2	33.7	48.5	77	81
Ships and aircraft	29.5	67.2	26.3	43.7	74	200
Furniture and household appliances	2.1	6.1	6.1	5.9	8	9
Miscellaneous	31.5	37.8	34.8	55.8	74	84
Total	629.3	822.5	821.0	1.062.4	1.432	1.787
Less: import returned and adjustment	15.5	19.1	25.7	27.0	6	1
Total commodity imports, net	613.8	803.4	795.3	1.035.4	1.426	1.786

of principal or interest for a good part of the capital, such as reparations and restitution funds from West Germany, gift funds collected by Jewish communities all over the world, and United States government aid, though interest had still to be paid on loans and private investors abroad received dividends.

The rapid rise in gross national product and economic growth was due to an extraordinary increase in population as a result of immigration, the skill and know-how brought into the economy in the wake of it, the import of capital invested in the economy, and higher productivity. The rise in capital stock per head was estimated at 7.5% per annum in 1950–60 and some 6.5% a year between then and the end of 1967, and 7.5% per annum between the years 1968 and 1972. These considerable increases confirm the assumption that increment of the capital stock not only matched but even outstripped the growth of population. Tariff protection was an extra incentive to industrial investment in a sheltered market.

The Problem of Savings. The formation of capital in Israel requires careful scrutiny in the light of the facts recorded in Table 43. The high rate of disinvestment in the public sector was a consequence of expenditure on defense, absorption of immigration, and social welfare. This negative saving was made possible by unrequited receipts from abroad. An investigation held in 1957–58 showed that household saving in Israel had risen to a level similar to that of Western countries, that is an average of some 5% of income after deduction of taxes. The most usual form of saving was in housing, although investment in financial assets (encouraged, apparently, by linkage of securities to the cost-of-living index) and in saving schemes had latterly risen as well. In Israel, as elsewhere, the self-employed are the best savers and are prone to invest in their own enterprises. White-collar workers are the most reluctant savers and finance their investment mainly by loans.

Personal restitution payments from Germany increased   71

Table 43. National Saving as Percentage of Net National Product, 1950–72 (current prices)

	1950	1954	1956	1958	1960	1962
IL million	17	− 9	−133	105	233	90
Percentages	4.1	−0.5	−5.7	3.6	5.1	1.4

	1964	1966	1968	1970	1971	1972
IL million	449	240	− 719	− 1,426	−634	− 171
Percentages	5.4	2.2	− 5.6	− 8.3	−3.0	− 0.7

consumption spending in the private sector. When the incremental consumption is deducted from the domestic income of the private sector, the saving out of such income is low. This is true for the public sector and nonprofit institutions as well, and is especially significant in respect to the latter in view of the large weight of foreign transfer receipts in their total income.

A different picture emerges from a comparison of national saving in Israel with that in the other countries. The rate for Israel during the years 1957–60 came to 3.7%, which was exceeded by all other countries except Panama and Peru. The reason for the low level of national saving in Israel was the heavy weight of unilateral transfers. Whereas national saving in other countries is actually the amount saved out of the total resources at the disposal of the economy, the situation was entirely different in Israel, where unrequited transfers during the period discussed amounted to 13% of national income. An important new channel for saving that developed in the early 1960s is the stock exchange. In the years 1961–63, security quotations in the market showed a steady and rapid rise, but there was a marked decline from October 1963 onward, as Table 44 shows.

The principal cause of these developments was the fact that the excessive rise in 1961–63 went beyond the inherent

Table 44. Index of Ordinary Share Prices, 1961—72

1960	100.0
1962	131.0
1963	191.6
1965	155.6
1967	114.3
1968	126.6
1969	134.8
1970	122.1
1971	132.0
1972	207.8

Table 45. Share of Investment in Total Economic Resources (1955 prices) 1950—72

	Total economic resources (million IL)	Total investment (million IL)	Investment as percentage of resources
1950	3355	1118	33.3
1952	4080	1134	27.8
1954	4735	1059	22.4
1958	6770	1551	22.5
1960	8163	1780	21.8
1962	10397	2341	22.5
1964	12628	2930	23.2
1966	13582	2469	18.1
1967	14182	1916	13.5
1969	19164	3501	18.3
1970	21232	3895	18.3
1971	23113	4597	19.9
1972	25150	5061	20.1

value of the shares and was not warranted by the yield. The downward trend was reinforced by the general decline in the liquidity of the economy due to the large excess of imports over exports and, to a lesser extent, by the government's disinflationary policy. Table 45 shows the share of investment in the total resources of the economy.

There was much change in the sources of investment over the years. The development after devaluation in 1962 betrays certain long-term trends. The overall national saving in 1962 (disregarding unrequited transfers from abroad) was at a rate of 2% of the national income—positive but relatively small. Import of capital provided the financial resources for 93% of the total net investment. In the early stages of development, investment in the infrastructure of the economy was of prime importance. Generation of electricity, extension of irrigated areas, housing for immigrants were, of course, financed by government and other public sources.

Finances. Financial development in Israel from the establishment of the State until 1965 was marked by continuous monetary expansion. The rise in the two components of means of payment—deposits on call and currency in circulation—was continuous. Until 1965, the most striking feature of the economy was the complete absence of the usual business cycle: at no time could it be classified as one of recession. The traffic was all one-way: dynamic growth and inflationary pressure were never lacking. Only in 1965–67 did Israel's first and only economic recession take place. Table 46 shows the rise in money supply up to 1972 (these are nominal) especially after the recession.

The ratio of deposits on call to currency in circulation was about 2:1, with frequent fluctuations, however.

If it be assumed that the rise in money supply indicates a rise in effective demand, an assumption which seems well warranted in the case of Israel, a disparity will develop between monetary expansion and the growth of real resources at constant prices. This disparity led to a rise in prices that was the product of a larger effective demand as an autonomous factor, on the one hand, and of a rise in costs, on the other. The interrelation between gross national product in real terms, excess of imports over exports, rising prices, and rise in money supply is indicated in Table 47.

The rapid rise in the money supply was due to three

Table 46. Money Supply, 1948—72 (in million IL)

End of year	A Cash held by public	B Demand deposits	C = Total money supply	Demand deposits as a percentage of total money supply (%)
1948	30.6	70.2	100.8	69.6
1950	64.8	125.0	189.8	65.9
1952	106.0	151.2	257.2	58.8
1954	146.6	201.9	348.5	57.9
1955	172.6	247.2	419.8	58.9
1956	228.3	289.0	517.3	55.9
1957	230.9	345.8	570.2	60.0
1958	251.4	408.5	659.9	61.9
1959	259.9	466.0	725.9	64.2
1960	299.5	580.7	880.2	66.0
1961	344.0	625.1	969.1	64.5
1962	409.3	847.3	1256.6	67.4
1963	525.0	1084.3	1609.3	67.4
1964	590.3	1117.1	1707.4	65.4
1965	657.4	1241.5	1898.9	65.4
1966	751.1	1256.7	2007.8	62.6
1967	965.8	1572.7	2538.5	62.0
1968	1091.2	1807.3	2898.5	62.4
1969	1128.9	1841.0	2970.1	62.0
1970	1280.7	2103.9	3384.6	62.2
1971	1584.4	2756.9	4341.3	63.5
1972	1974.2	3613.1	5587.3	64.7

factors, operating in varying degrees at different times: credit extended to the government—that is, deficit financing of the state budget; expansion of credit to the public; and monetization of surplus balances of foreign currency. Until 1952, the main cause was deficits in the state budgets; in 1953–56 it was the expansion of credit to the public; after 1959 it was the accumulation of foreign currency surpluses.

State Finances. The deficit financing of state budgets was due to demographic growth, the geopolitical and military

Table 47. Interdependence of Real GNP Import Surplus, Money Supply, 1950–72

	Real GNP[1]	Import surplus	Money supply		Bank credit	Prices[2]
1950	100	100	100		100	100
1952	138	130	136		159	171
1954	162	108		184	229	242
1956	202	92		273	292	287
1957	219	82		304	354	310
1958	236	101		348	420	330
1959	266	126		383	520	340
1960	284	117		464	657	352
1961	312	121		511	815	385
1962	345	112		662	1055	418
1963	385	121		848	1075	456
1964	425	155		899	1244	478
1965	459	162		1000	1399	522
1966	461	154		1058	1830	560
1967	472	198		1119	2320	570
1968	543	184		1277	2821	581
1969	607	156		1308	3355	597
1970	655	188	442	1490	4097	651
1971	709	230	428	1911	3006	743
1972	776	305	372	2460	6162	849

[1] Based on 1955 prices.
[2] GNP prices, calculated from current and constant price series.

situation, and the scarcity of natural resources. As a result of these factors, state budgets rose more rapidly than the population and the gross national product (with the exception of the years 1950–52, when the GNP climbed suddenly from a very low level). The share of government expenditure in the gross national product is given in Table 40. The ordinary state budget was financed chiefly by internal revenue and the development budget by external sources, such as the Independence and Development loans, grants-in-aid, reparations, and the counterpart funds of food surpluses from the United States. Figures are given in

Table 48. Sources of State Budgets (percentages of total receipts)

	Taxes	Other domestic collections	Grant from abroad and reparations	Foreign loans	Loans from the Bank of Israel[1]	Other internal loans[2]	Total[3]
1949/50	42.3	0.6	5.9	24.2	19.1	7.8	100
1952/53	61.4	4.4	16.5	14.6	–	3.1	100
1956/57	53.7	10.0	11.8	13.2	7.0	4.2	100
1960/61	63.8	13.2	8.2	8.1	1.5	5.3	100
1964/65	64.4	10.2	3.8	14.9	–	6.7	100
1966/67	63.6	11.2	0.9	12.9	2.8	8.6	100
1967/68	49.2	12.6	0.1	16.2	4.8	17.1	100
1968/69	54.6	12.5	0.1	13.4	9.0	10.4	100
1969/70	47.5	9.0		12.2	21.0	10.3	100
1970/71	48.8	8.9		20.1	5.9	16.3	100
1971/72	57.2	11.3		16.7	4.3	10.5	100
1972/73	58.0	12.4		13.2	3.5	12.9	100

[1] Until 1951–52, from banking system.

[2] Including absorption loans.

[3] Discrepancies are due to rounding.

77

Table 49. Development Budgets* (in million IL). 1949/50–1972/73

1949/50	35
1951/52	73
1953/54	154
1955/56	257
1956/57	237
1957/58	343
1958/59	364
1959/60	374
1960/61	375
1961/62	502
1962/63	504
1963/64	677
1964/65	779
1965/66	884
1966/67	790
1967/68	943
1968/69	1,163
1969/70	1,573
1970/71	1,460
1971/72	2,274
1972/73	2,252

* Excluding debt repayment and working capital.

Table 48. The growing impact of the development budget is clear from Table 49.

In internal revenue, the distribution between direct and indirect taxation was subject to some alterations over the years. Until 1956–57 there was a steady rise in the share of direct taxation, which may be ascribed to the establishment of tax collection machinery and remarkable advances in its efficiency. Since 1957–58 the share of indirect taxation has gone up, which reflects surcharges on import as expressing a gradual change in the effective rate of exchange of the Israel pound. Table 50 shows the distribution of government expenditure by main items.

Expansion of Credit. Monetary expansion, so prominent in fashioning the design of Israel's economy, originated not

Table 50. Distribution of Government Expenditures (percentages)

	Defense, police, and special budgets	Development expenditure[1]	Debt repayment[2]	Other services	Total
1949/50	29.5	39.8	2.3	28.4	100
1950/51	23.2	47.2	4.2	25.4	100
1952/53	29.6	37.4	5.2	27.8	100
1954/55	23.7	33.7	14.5	28.1	100
1956/57	39.5	23.8	9.3	27.4	100
1958/59	24.8	30.2	10.2	34.8	100
1962/63	25.2	21.9	19.9	33.0	100
1964/65	28.7	22.7	17.3	31.3	100
1966/67	23.0	19.6	15.3	42.1	100
1967/68	27.1	16.9	13.5	42.5	100
1968/69	28.4	15.2	18.0	38.4	100
1970/71	45.3	13.3	15.4	26.0	100
1971/72	40.0	15.7	16.0	28.3	100
1972/73	31.8	12.8	21.6	33.8	100

[1] Excluding debt repayment and working capital.

[2] Capital and interest.

only in government finances but also in expansion of credit to the public. Credit has been fairly fast, expanding ever since the establishment of the State. Evaluation of the effects of this phenomenon will depend a great deal on a comparison between the rise in the volume of production and the rise in money supply. Table 47 shows the ratio of growth of the money supply, credits, and gross national product. The expansion of credit far exceeded the rise in the volume of production.

Monetary policy, applied in the form of quantitative credit controls, restrained credit expansion within certain limits, however. The restraint was achieved by the credit control mechanism of the central bank—the Bank of Israel (see Banking, page 257). The principal device employed is the requirement that commercial banks maintain a pre-scribed ratio between liabilities and liquid assets, which are narrowly defined as deposits with the central bank. The nominal liquidity ratio was 65% at the end of 1967, but the actual ratio was diminished by exemption of 25% of liabilities, so that the minimum, in the form of deposits with the central bank, was 40% (and in 1972,48%). The unsterilized 25% was used for qualitative control of credit. Restrictions of this severity on monetary policy became imperative in the light of rising prices and the deterioration in the balance of payments. The source of inflationary pressures since 1959 was mainly different from those that existed in the first years of statehood. In the post-1959 period, the chief cause of monetary expansion was the influx of capital, mainly by unilateral transfers such as reparations and restitution payments from West Germany, gift funds, loans, and direct investment. The consequent rapid rise in foreign currency reserves led to an imported inflation. The rise in reserves was monetized, which produced inflationary pressures from demand and cost at one and the same time. Effective demand grew, and wages and incomes rose quickly. The pressures thus led to the expansion of the money supply, a rapid rise in prices, and excess of imports over exports, as shown in Table 47. The correlation between the three aspects of the monetary situation is clear. A very large import of capital must make for inflationary pressures if the influx of new capital exceeds the deficit in the current account of the balance of payments. Reserves of foreign currency consequently rise. This process of accumulation and the creation of surpluses was intensified in 1962 by a new devaluation, which was rendered unavoidable by antecedent developments, which had made the existing rate of exchange unrealistic.

New Economic Policy, 1962. The main feature of the new economic policy in 1962 was the devaluation of the currency, which averted a serious economic crisis and produced a strong momentum in reconstruction and development. In 1962, because of a deterioration in the balance of trade and some weakening of internal stability, the government was again confronted with the urgent necessity for a new departure in economic policy. To this was added the ever-present need for integration in the world economy, accentuated by the emergence and consolidation of the Common Market.

The 1962 reform was unique in economic history because it involved a phase of constant and rapid rise in foreign currency reserves. The sources of the rise in reserves and the accumulation of foreign currency were unilateral transfers of capital, which involved a grave risk of monetary expansion and a rise in purchasing power that could ultimately have affected the achievements of the new economic policy. The new rate of exchange, three Israeli pounds to one U.S. dollar, wiped out the artificial preference for imports and established an objective criterion for determining the economic justification and soundness of enterprises and economic operations. This reform in itself contributed to the integration of Israel's economy in the world market. The removal of distortions in the price pattern was tantamount to the removal of distortions in the design of production. Even more significantly, it made for selectivity of future investments.

The reform was, of course, reflected in physical **81**

development as well. Economic growth went on at an average rate of more than 10%. The volume of investment expanded by IL547 million in 1962 over 1961 and by IL226 million in 1963 over 1962. The annual growth rate of investment in real terms was 13.6% in 1962, 3.5% in 1963, and 21.9% in 1964. The number of gainfully employed persons rose by 5.5%, mainly in the building trades and in industry. The drop in unemployment synchronized with a new wave of immigration that started in 1959-60 and continued until 1964-65. In 1964 the population rose by 4%; at the same time unemployment declined and full employment was reached. The rise in the gross national product was due not only to the growth in manpower, but also to a 5% rise in worker productivity. The large influx of capital led to monetary expansion on a very large scale in 1962 and 1963—some IL640 million or 66%. Only a small part of this was due to expansion of credit. The government framed a surplus budget, reduced its debt to the Bank of Israel, and was a disinflationary agent. The main cause of the expansion was conversion of foreign currency surpluses.

The main purpose of the 1962 new economic policy, and particularly of devaluation, was to improve the balance of trade. After a few months there was indeed a certain improvement, but it was of brief duration. The new rate of exchange attracted more capital in 1962, with the result of a surplus in the balance of payments and, ipso facto, a corresponding rise in reserves by $110 million; in 1963 there was again a surplus and a rise of $88 million in reserves. This tremendous expansion in the liquidity of the economy, a rise in the means of payment by 66% and IL640 million, again had unfavorable consequences for the balance of trade, which deteriorated in 1964, with a rise of $134 million in the excess of imports over exports. In 1964, the effects of the devaluation petered out to some extent, owing to the rise in prices and incomes, and a new policy was initiated, aimed at slowing down economic activity, which had again become overheated.

Economic policy during the years 1965-67 was aimed,

first and foremost, at two targets: improvement of the balance of payments, and the stabilization of prices, including the cost of money. In addition, it was intended to bring about a long-run structural change, and although this was not been fully attained, first signs in this direction could be discerned. As to the first two points, definite results were obtained: in 1967 the trade deficit declined by about $120 million as compared with the previous year, after a decrease of $70 million in 1966 and $64 million in 1965. The narrowing of the trade gap was of great significance when viewed in the light of the steady deterioration—at the rate of 7% per annum—during the years 1961 to 1964, reaching a peak in 1964, when the deficit grew by $134 million, or 31%, within a single year. Exports grew considerably: they were 46% higher in 1967 than in 1964. Prices were stabilized to a degree unprecedented in Israel's economic history: from May 1966 to October 1967 they did not rise at all, whereas they had gone up by 7.1% in 1965 and 7.8% in 1966. The cost of money declined considerably. From June 1966 to October 1967 net interest (i.e., after deduction of 25% income tax) on various series of the Government's Short-term Loan, ranging from 3 to 12 months, was reduced by 12–27%. The interest rate on bill brokerage in the three largest banks declined from 17% to $13\frac{1}{2}$%—a change of 21%. Furthermore, these figures applied only to a decline in the rate of interest on bank credit. The share of bill brokerage in total credit simultaneously fell from 40% to 27%; in other words, bank credit increased and bill brokerage credit decreased much more. This change in the composition of credit led to a further reduction over and above the 21% already mentioned.

The growth of the real product in 1967 was 2.2%, but the composition of the increase was also important. While there was a 21% decrease in construction, agriculture showed an impressive advance of 21%. In industry there was a slight decline, approximately 5%, but the trend in the last months of 1967 was upward. These achievements were made, of course, at a certain price: the growth of unemployment, the **83** deceleration of economic growth, an excessive rise in prices and production costs, and a decline in investment, which had undesirable implications for the future of the economy. Some distress was also caused to part of the population. On the other hand, as we have seen, there were important positive features: the improved balance of payments; the normalization of certain economic processes; the slower expansion of private consumption; and the hope and prospect of further economic consolidation and of a steady movement toward economic independence. At the end of 1966, the Government and the Bank of Israel adopted reflationary monetary and fiscal policies: steps were taken to increase employment; tax collections were slowed down; concessions to private investors were extended, and commercial bank reserve requirements reduced.

AFTER THE SIX-DAY WAR—1967–72. The year 1967 marked a turning point in Israel's economic development. The first half of the year saw a continuation of the standstill in the growth of the national product discernible since the end of 1965. The reflationary measures adopted by the government and the Bank of Israel in the latter part of 1966 did not have much of an impact in the first half of 1967—though in certain spheres the trend may have begun to change—since the influences slowing down the growth of aggregate demand during the period of economic restraint continued to operate at full force. During the period of prewar tension and hostilities, ordinary economic activity was largely curtailed, but a turning point was reached around the middle of the year. The expansionary monetary policy, particularly the increase in government expenditure (mainly on defense), the deficit financing of the war, and the increased liquidity all augmented local demand. In the middle of 1967, the gross national product began to expand at the rapid annual rate of some 10.5%. The recovery embraced most sectors of the economy, and was especially striking in the public sector and industry. In construction, which had suffered more than any other sector from the recession, the decline in activity was checked in the second half of the year and signs of an upswing became apparent. This expansion, which led to a decline in unemployment and an increase in employment and real economic growth, carried over into the years 1968–72, as may be seen from Table 51.

The main characteristic of the Israel economy during the period 1967–70 was its susceptibility to strong pressures. The causes of these pressures upon the limited available resources and factors of production (including labor) are well known: defense requirements absorbed more than a quarter of the national product and the volume of investment was unprecedentedly large, yet necessary to enable the state to shoulder the burden of this security expenditure. In other words, the expansion of investment was essential to assure that the mounting defense outlays did not increase the relative weight of defense within total expenditures; otherwise, little would have remained for other uses. Immigrant absorption, though not on the tremendous scale of the first years of statehood, now entailed an enormously greater expenditure per family and person, owing to its different composition. The cultural and economic background of those hailing from the affluent countries, along with the high living standards in Israel, contrasted sharply with the situation during the years of mass immigration.

These pressures on the limited productive factors made themselves felt through overemployment. The shortage of labor drove up wages and salaries, thereby detrimentally affecting the price level and the competitiveness of the economy, and led to a deterioration in labor relations. Consequently, purchasing power increased and consumption expanded, as shown by Table 52.

Excessive monetary expansion and a rise in the turnover velocity of money also affected the price level and the balance of payments, the central problem of Israel's economy. After a rapid increase in 1966 and 1967, due to the reflationary policy and the Six-Day War, the growth of the money supply slowed down in 1968 and 1969, but

Table 51. Main Economic Indicators, 1970—72 Percent Increase

	Average 1961—65
Resources and uses (constant prices)	
Total domestic uses	10.5
GNP	10.3
GNP per capita	6.2
Private consumption	10.3
Private consumption per capita	6,1
Public consumption	10.6
Gross investment	11.3
Balance of Payments ($)	
Imports[1]	12.0
Exports[1]	15.6
Import surplus[1]	8.8
Capital imports, long and short term	5.8
Foreign currency balances[2]	25,6
Population and Employment	
Average population	3.9
Number of employed	4.8
Rate of unemployed from total manpower	3.8[3]
Prices and Nominal Income	
Average monthly wage per employee	13.6
Wage per hour of work	13.3
GNP prices	8.0
Consumer price index (annual average)	7.4
National income	18.8
National income per capita	14.3
Finance	
Money supply (annual average)	17.6
Bank credit to the public (annual average)[4]	19.6

[1] Goods and services; imports c.i.f., exports f.o.b. [2] Foreign currency balances at Bank of Israel at end of year. [3] 1963—65 only. [4] In 1961—63, bank credit only.

or Decrease (−) Compared with Previous Year

Average 1966–69	1970	1971	1972	Average 1970–72
	11.3	6.1	6.1	7.8
7.4	8.0	8.2	9.5	8.6
4.3	5.0	5.0	6.0	5.3
6.9	3.4	4.4	8.4	5.4
3.8	0.6	1.4	4.9	2.3
18.0	27.8	0.5	−1.6	8.1
2.7	11.5	17.6	10.1	13.0
14.6	22.2	14.1	5.8	13.8
14.0	8.6	30.2	18.8	18.9
− 15.4	41.5	−3.3	− 13.1	5.9
− 13.8	84.7	21.8	10.3	35.5
4.0	6.5	60.0	85.7	46.1
3.0	2.8	3.0	3.3	3.1
1.8	1.8	3.5	5.0	3.4
6.7	3.8	3.5	2.8	3.5
7.7	16.6	15.4	16.1	16.1
7.3	17.5	15.6	14.9	16.0
3.7	9.1	14.1	14.2	12.5
3.5	6.1	12.0	12.7	10.2
11.5	16.9	23.1	24.7	21.5
8.3	13.7	19.5	20.7	17.8
13.3	5.0	22.4	30.0	18.6
17.9	18.7	23.4	20.2	20.8

Table 52. Growth of Real Total and Per Capita Consumption, 1967—72 (percentages)

	Total	Per capita
1967	1.4	− 1.7
1968	12.0	8.3
1969	10.8	8.0
1970	3.4	0.6
1971	4.4	1.4
1972	8.4	4.9

accelerated again from 1970, as can be seen in Table 53.

The deceleration of monetary expansion in 1968 and 1969 was the result of the depletion of foreign currency reserves in those two years by $330 million, which reduced the liquidity of banking institutions and thus restrained the growth of money supply. Since 1970 this factor no longer operated. The problem of the money supply and monetary expansion is of decisive importance for the balance of payments, since—to use a metaphorical expression—"pounds eat dollars." The larger the domestic purchasing power in terms of local currency, the more goods and services can be imported directly from abroad, and the more the populace will consume the national product, which, in a country poor in natural resources, has a relatively high import component. Monetary expansion also affects exports, since the local market absorbs goods which otherwise might be sold overseas. Moreover, it drives up domestic production costs, thus reducing the competitiveness of export goods. Another aspect of the same problem is the trend toward inflation, as reflected in Table 54.

The three years following the Six-Day War were characterized by vigorous efforts to counter these pressures by expanding the economy and increasing the national output. These efforts were largely successful. The gross national product grew by some 65% between the middle of 1967 and the end of 1972, while the volume of investment during the period reached some IL33,000 million at

Table 53. The Money Supply, 1967–72

	Balance at end of year (IL million)	Percent increase in end-year balance	Average annual balance (IL million)	Percent increase in average annual balance
1967	2,539	26.4	2,366	20.3
1968	2,899	14.2	2,815	19.0
1969	2,970	2.5	3,015	7.1
1970	2,385	14.1	3,166	5.4
1971	4,341	28.3	3,876	22.4
1972	5,587	28.7	5,035	30.0

Table 54. Price Indexes, 1967–72

	Consumer price index (annual average, 1969 = 100)	Percent annual increase	Wholesale price index of industrial production (annual average, 1968 = 100)	Percent annual increase
1967	95.6	1.7	97.7	1.1
1968	97.6	2.1	100.0	2.4
1069	100.0	2.5	101.9	1.9
1970	106.1	6.1	108.8	6.8
1971	118.1	11.3	118.8	9.2
1972	133.3	12.9	132.6	11.6

constant prices. During the five years 1967 to 1972, approximately 210,000 immigrants came to Israel, and this helped to alleviate the shortage of manpower. Other factors contributing to accelerated economic growth were the existence in 1967 of unutilized reserves of productive factors and an increment of some 30,000 workers from the administered areas and East Jerusalem. There were also huge capital imports during that period and a decline in foreign exchange reserves, while large-scale imports provided the economy with additional resources.

To sum up, it may be said that the activation of productive factors idle during the recession period, the incremental manpower supplied by immigration, the employment of workers from the administrated areas, and capital imports on a large scale made possible a high level of economic activity and a rapid rate of growth, simultaneously with a greater and successful defense effort—thus meeting a challenge unprecedented in Israel's history. However, all this involved a huge increase in the import surplus, which was financed by the growth of the external debt and a decline in foreign currency reserves. The central problem facing the country's economy was thus the strain on the balance of payments.

The heavy depletion of foreign currency balances in 1969 was a red warning light, since these balances to all intents and purposes set the limits for the country's economic and military activities. Until 1968 the overall balance of payments showed a surplus, although there was a considerable deficit on current account, but in 1968 and 1969 there were, for the first time, large deficits in the overall balance as well. Foreign currency reserves, which had increased so long as the overall balance was in surplus—i.e., when capital imports of all types exceeded the deficit on current account—declined by a total of $330 million when capital imports became insufficient to cover the current deficits. Table 55 shows the development of the balance of payments in the years 1967–72.

The decline in foreign currency reserves was arrested in

Table 55. Imports, Exports, and Current Deficit[1], 1967–72

	Imports	Exports	Current deficit
1967	1,480	949	531
1968	1,846	1,199	647
1969	2,183	1,317	866
1970	2,703	1,469	1,234
1971	3,115	1,912	1,203
1972	3,350	2,775	1,075

[1] Including trade with the administered areas.

1970, the level stabilizing at some $400–420 million. This was not due to an improvement in the current balance (which in fact worsened considerably in 1970, the current deficit increasingly by $370 million during the year), but to an increase in capital imports. The latter development was in turn a result of larger receipts from the emergency fund-raising campaigns conducted abroad and the sale of State of Israel Bonds, as well as the incurring of other, less convenient, foreign debts. The external debt at the end of 1970 reached $2,600 million, and, was $3,400 million by the end of 1971 and $4,000 million by the end of 1972—a very high figure not only in relation to the population of the country but also in comparison with its gross national product. An external debt of this size imposes a heavy burden upon the national product of future years.

Thus Israel moved further away from economic independence during these years—an inevitable development in a war period. The most important and decisive criterion for measuring the country's approach to economic independence is the weight of the balance of payments deficit within total available resources (GNP plus the import surplus). Whereas in 1966 the deficit was equal to 10% of total available resources, the figure rose to some 18% in 1969 and was estimated to have reached 20% in 1970, and was reduced to 17.5% in 1972.

Export growth slowed down appreciably, from 16% in 1968 to 11% in 1970, and came up to 30% in 1971 and 19% in

1972. The main reason for the deceleration in 1970 was the conditions prevailing in the international market, which severely hit two of the main export branches—citrus and diamonds. Agricultural exports other than citrus and industrial exports other than diamonds expanded during the first ten months of 1970 by 52 and 12% respectively as compared with the corresponding period of the previous year. Hence the picture was more encouraging outside citriculture and the diamond industry, though there was some deceleration in the growth of industrial exports in 1970. Another difficulty with which the economy had to contend was the rise of prices abroad. Since Israel's imports were larger then her exports, every increase in the general price level abroad cost the economy precious dollars.

Another indicator of change in trends is the breakdown of incremental resources and uses. Though the weight of imports within incremental resources moved up sharply in the first ten months of 1970 by 62 and 12% respectively as 1970, from 35% the year before to 50%, there was a marked improvement in incremental uses: in 1970 the increase was IL4,610 million, of which private consumption absorbed some 13%, public consumption over 52%, gross investment 19%, and exports approximately 16%. This compares with a total increase of IL3,664 million in 1969, which was distributed as follows: private consumption 40%, public consumption 27%, gross investment 21%, and exports about 12%. Except for the fact that the proportion of resources channeled to exports was still too small, these were desirable developments, indicating the diversion of productive factors from private consumption to the defense effort, while investment remained at an optimal level. That some progress was made was also confirmed by preliminary consumption estimates for 1970, which showed that the total increase probably amounted to only 3.4% (in sharp contrast to 1969), while per capita it came to a mere 0.6%, compared with about 8% in 1969.

The trends widening the balance of payments deficit gained momentum in 1970, and the year was characterized by an attempt to mitigate them. A policy of economic restraint was followed by the government and the Bank of Israel in order to check the growth of the current deficit and the contraction of foreign currency reserves.

Certain long-term trends in Israel's economy emerged or were reinforced during the 1967–70 period. These may be summarized as follows:

(1) A change in the structure of the economy, involving the occupational reshuffle of the population.

(2) An increase in labor productivity, through a shift to branches with a high value added and also as a result of mechanization and the application of scientific methods.

(3) The agricultural revolution, which was paving the way for overcoming the limitations of space, water, and narrow markets.

(4) Industrialization, which is not hampered by any limitations of space and is based on large-scale investment, know-how, and skill.

(5) A shift from staple to sophisticated industries, based mainly on science and with a high value added.

(6) The allocation of an increasing share of output to export, thereby basing the economy to a greater extent on the exchange of goods through international trade and making it more export oriented—a precondition for the successful economic development of any small country.

ECONOMIC DEVELOPMENTS. The year 1972 was one of continuation and intensification of trends which became evident during the previous year: overheated economic activity, rapid economic growth, substantial increase of population, a high level of immigration, unequalled since 1964, high level of investment, over-employment, over-liquidity, large excess of imports over exports, increased inflow of capital, large share of defense expenditure in the Government budget, high level of public expenditure, excessive monetary expansion, rapid rise of prices and inflationary pressures which became more pronounced in the course of time.

While the average population during the year was 3.3%

higher than in 1971, the average number employed grew by 5.0%. The Gross National Product was up by 9.5% over the previous year, gross investment by 10.1%, and the means of payment by 30.0%, the same as in 1970. Although exports of goods and services were 19% higher, there was a balancing rise of 16% in the volume of imports, so that the adverse balance fell by 11%. The defense estimates for the fiscal year 1972/73 accounted for 32% of the state budget.

These super-boom conditions were alleviated to some extent by an extensive import of capital of 22% in 1971/72 and more than 10% in 1972.

The economic policy of the Government made serious endeavors to create countervailing forces. In monetary policy, this was done by imposing credit restrictions and high reserve requirements on the banks. In its fiscal policy the government reduced expenditure, particularly in the development budget, and postponed the implementation of some projects, such as public building. The last step in this direction during the year and the most far-reaching was the devaluation of the Israel pound by 20% in August 1971 after the promulgation of the Nixon plan. As far as the currencies not linked to the dollar were concerned, an additional devaluation was effected by the change in the rate of exchange of the dollar with these currencies in December 1971 after the Washington agreement.

The results of the years 1970 and 1971 are summarized in the following tables of the main indicators of economic developments:

The inflationary pressures created by the conditions reflected in the above indicators had their effect on both the excess of imports over exports, which increased substantially, and on the price level. Prices reflected in the cost-of-living index increased by 11.3% in 1971 and by 13.5% in 1972, while average nominal wages per month increased in 1971 by 15.4% to IL878 and in 1972 by 14.2% reaching IL890.

94   The particular conditions of Israel have been greatly

Table 56. Population and Employment (in thousands)

	1970	1971	1972	Changes (%) 1970 to 1971	Changes (%) 1971 to 1972
Average population	2,958	3,046	3,147	3.0	3.3
Average number of employed	963	997	1,047	3.5	3.0
Percentage of unemployed in the labor force	3.8	3.5	2.8		

Table 57. Resources and Use of Resources (in Millions of Israel Pounds at 1971 Prices)

	1970	1971	1972	1970 to 1971 (%)	1971 to 1972 (%)
Resources					
Gross National Product	21,528	23,293	25,505	8.2	9.5
Import surplus	5,551	5,455	4,990	-1.7	-9.7
Total resources	27,080	28,748	30,495	6.2	6.1
Use of resources					
Private consumption	13,302	13,892	15,065	4.4	8.4
Public consumption	7,884	7,923	7,795	0.5	-1.6
Thereof: Defense expenditure	(5,476)	(5,400)	(5,060)	(-1.6)	(-6.1)
Other public consumption	(2,408)	(2,523)	(2,735)	(5.3)	(7.9)
Gross investment	5,894	6,933	7,635	17.6	10.1
Exports	6,241	7,741	8,825	24.0	14.0

Table 58. Balance of Payments[1]

| | 1970 | 1971 | 1972 | Increases | |
				1970 to 1971	1971 to 1972
	(millions of $)			(per cent)	
Imports	2,703	3,115	3,350	15.2	7.5
Exports	1,469	1,912	2,275	30.2	19.0
Excess of imports over exports	1,234	1,203	1,075	−2.5	10.6
Net import of capital (excluding administered areas)	1,243	1,511	1,670	21.8	10.3
Foreign currency balances in Bank of Israel	361	576	1,070	59.5	85.8

[1] Including administered areas

Table 59. Other Indicators

	1970	1971	1972	1970 to 1971	1971 to 1972
				(per cent)	
Product per employed person (IL 1971 prices)	22,357	23,363	24,367	4.5	4.3
National income per capita:					
a. In IL at current prices	5,230	6,255	7,550	19.6	20.7
b. in dollars at the official rate of exchange	1,495	1,662	1,798	11.2	8.2
c. in dollars at the effective rate of exchange	1,230	1,295	1,360	5.2	5.0
Private consumption per capita (IL at 1971 prices)	4,500	4,560	4,780	1.4	4.9
Means of payment, annual average (IL millions)	3,166	3,876	5,035	22.4	30.0

influenced by external non-economic factors, such as the demographic expansion caused by the high level of immigration, in which the inflow from the U.S.S.R. became substantial, the impact of the population of the administered areas both on employment, alleviating the shortage of labor, and on marketing, and the spectacular rise of standards of life in the administered areas. The rhythm and directions of Israel's economy in the period 1967–70 were determined and dominated by political and military events. Idle factors and underutilized production capacity were galvanized once more by effective demand. The demand generated by the war effect absorbed as much as one-quarter of the Gross National Product.

In those years, the economy was chiefly characterized by, on the one hand, a susceptibility to strong pressures upon limited resources, capacity of production, and manpower, and, on the other hand, by large import of capital and rapid economic growth.

Economic developments in 1972 have been marked by a continuation of trends prevailing in 1971, such as inflationary pressures, over-full employment, and intensive economic activity. On the one hand, these tendencies stimulate economic growth, as reflected in the increase of the Gross National Product, but, on the other hand, they affect the stability and balance of the economy. They are reflected in Table 60.

SUMMARY. The central feature of the development of Israel is that whole communities have been transplanted to, and established in, the country, with the necessary capital, manpower, and skill, as well as purchasing power for the creation of an internal market. The various elements of economic growth and the dynamic reaction of the economic structure to the process of migration released new economic forces. The settlement of Israel was therefore the transplantation of a population: the transfer in sudden, large, wavelike motions of an immigrant population possessing the prerequisites of skill and capital and automatically providing its own internal market. This rapid mass **99**

Table 60. Selected Economic Indicators, 1971 and 1972
(preliminary estimates)

	1971	1972
Rise in means of payment	22.4%	30.0%
Rise in prices of goods and services for private consumption	11.3%	13.5%
Real rise in average wages	3.5%	0.6%
Rise in private consumption per capita (in real terms)	1.4%	5.0%
Rise in output of manufactures	11.2%	11.0%
Rise in agricultural output	11.1%	7.6%
Rise in construction	7.0%	12.8%
Exports of goods and services	$ 1,912 m	$ 2,275 m
Imports of goods and services	$ 3,115 m	$ 3,350 m
Excess of imports over exports	$ 1,203 m	$ 1,075 m
Exports as percentage of imports	60%	67%

movement within a short period of time constituted a
non-economic driving power. Israel's economy has been
subject to many dynamic, powerful, and contradictory
trends and tendencies. Its problems are formidable, sometimes overwhelming. The attempt to achieve balanced
growth, maintain dynamic development, and confine it
within a framework of stability and equilibrium necessitates
unpopular policies. The excessive rise in consumption per
capita and standards of living must be restrained if a
balance in the external payments account is to be achieved,
and the low rate of internal saving must be increased if
investment is to become gradually independent of unilateral
transfers of capital. These measures have become all the
more urgent since 1967, in view of the continuing
deterioration in the balance of payments. To achieve these
aims, a surplus budget, a wages and incomes policy aimed
at restraint, and severe limitation of credits are indispens-
able. The Israel government's income and fiscal and
monetary policies have all these objectives in view, within

the limitations imposed by the demands of defense, immigration, and debt repayments.

The large import of capital into the country is derived mainly from public and semi-public sources and passes through the channels of the government or public organizations like the Jewish Agency. These circumstances are responsible for the creation of a very large sector of public and semi-public economic enterprises in agriculture, industry, transport, building, and almost every branch of the economy. Investment by the State through the Development Budget and public institutions is practically impossible without planning and priorities established by these public investors. At the same time, the government's policy and the exigencies of the situation, as well as the need to build a bridge to world markets, converge to reinforce a general tendency toward liberalization of the economy. This policy of a liberalized economy, based on a larger sector of public and semi-public enterprises and therefore committed to planning and priorities, is fraught with difficulties and contradictions.

Finally, the socioeconomic structure of the economy is unusually diversified. The governmental, private, and cooperative labor sectors coexist, in a kind of symbiosis, in an economy subordinated to the overriding broad political objectives of the State. The very fact of the investment of immense amounts of public capital provides the precondition for the development of a kind of mixed economy. It is too early to pronounce final judgement on this experiment. On the face of it, the philosophy behind this maze of crosscurrents is a pragmatic one, arising out of the conditions of the economy and society. Its core is acquiescence in coexistence between a diversity of socioeconomic entities and flexibility in their mutual adaptation. It is noteworthy, too, that this experiment in rapid economic growth and control of inflation, development in the framework of stability, economic expansion under democracy, control and liberalization, and pluralism in socioeconomic forms is being implemented in a small country and within a relatively short period of time.

2 ECONOMIC PLANNING

Functions of Economic Planning. The function of the Economic Planning Authority in the Ministry of Finance is to work out medium- and long-range economic plans, to coordinate the plans of the various ministries, to propose long-term plans for social policy, and to prepare comprehensive plans for balanced regional development.

Economic planning, as carried out in Israel, is basically a systematic, coordinated presentation of policies the implementation of which is calculated to lead the economy to its goals. It is not a vague forecast of future expansion, but a systematic quantitative presentation of economic and social objectives and of the economic policies required to attain them.

It thus involves establishing an order of priorities among social targets as part of the formation of long-range economic policy. As the basis of planning, clear alternatives must be presented, so that definite choices may be made between them.

Economic planning in Israel, therefore, provides a general framework for economic policy and facilitates control over economic activity. Its aim is to create in the economy the overall conditions required for the functioning of the various economic sectors and units.

The aims of economic planning and the means employed are based on a set of given external assumptions. The national economy of Israel, more than that of other nations, depends on factors which are difficult to predict in advance, e.g. immigration, defense expenditure, and capital imports. This uncertainty hampers accurate planning, but, on the other hand, these factors emphasize its vital importance.

Economic planning presents a comprehensive and consistent framework for the future expansion of the economy, based on an assessment of the interdependence of external assumptions, economic and social aims, means of implementing policy, and developments in individual fields. Economic planning founded on these principles can be a basis for analyzing and examining the possible consequences of changes which occur from time to time in these assumptions and the development of one sector or another.

PLANNING METHODS. The first step in the planning process is the determination of overall targets for the expansion of the economy and the charting of policy guidelines which follow from them. At this stage, detailed programs for the development of the various branches of the economy are drawn up by the government departments concerned.

The dovetailing of the departmental programs into a single comprehensive forecast and an examination of the economic consequences involved are an essential part of the work. At this stage, an effort is made to pinpoint the central problems and bottlenecks which confront the economy. As a general rule, the integration of the separate programs makes it necessary to modify them in order to adapt them to the aims of the national economy while preserving their internal consistency. The sectional programs are adapted, with the guidance of the Economic Planning Authority, by the ministries concerned, and the amended, coordinated program of ends and means constitutes a master-plan for the economic policy of the Government and a framework for the activity of its departments for a number of years.

The Economic Planning Authority, established in 1962, has submitted to the Government a number of programs for the development of the national economy. The first was submitted to the Government in 1964, its target-year being 1969. This plan, after much discussion, was not published. The second program covered the development of the national economy for the years 1968–71. This plan, drawn up in 1966–67, which was the first to include a comprehensive survey of economic problems, was published in March 1968. The central task confronting the economy in 1968 was defined as: "How to increase the national product at the same rate as in 1955–64 while making efforts to preserve the balance of foreign trade and, at the same time, to reduce the dependence on capital imports." The third program was the development plan for the years 1971–75, worked out in 1969–70. It aimed at grappling with the central economic problem which had left its imprint on the expansion of the economy, i.e. the high level of defense expenditure.

Post-facto evaluation is an integral part of the work of the E.P.A. While preparing plans for the development of the economy, the Authority keeps a close watch on their implementation and on the implementation of individual development projects, and submits reports to the Government and the Knesset on its principal findings. Economic Plan for 1972–76. The plan for 1971–75 has been brought up to date for the years 1972–76. It focuses on two central problems: the high level of defense expenditure (both in local and foreign currency), and the need to absorb some 250,000 immigrants during the five-year period. The plan is designed to facilitate the handling of these problems by creating conditions that will, in the long run, reduce the economy's dependence on capital imports, while maintaining full conditions of employment.

The Gross National Product is expected to increase during the period at an annual rate of 7.3% to a total of IL33,150 million in 1976 (calculated on the basis of 1971 prices). The number of employed persons will grow by about 170,000 to 1,177,000 at the end of the period. The largest increase, about 60,000, will be in industry, while employment in agriculture will remain stable. There will also be increases in other branches of the economy, especially in educational and other services. Domestic Product per worker should rise during the period by an annual average of $4\frac{1}{2}$%. A 10% increase in capital stocks is foreseen, so that the ratio of capital output will be relatively high towards the end of the period.

Capital stocks will grow approximately $14\frac{1}{2}\%$ a year, primarily in industry, where some IL7,800 million will be invested. As a result, capital stock per employee in industry will increase to about IL48,000 as compared with IL35,000 in 1971 (at 1971 prices).

A considerable increase in capital stock per employee is also expected in transport and communications, a branch in which IL7,700 million is to be invested, and capital stock in 1976 will be about 70% higher than in 1971. The growth of capital assets in commercial and social services will be somewhat less than that in industry and transport: IL7,150 million will be invested in commerce and services, IL1,100 million in education, IL700 million in health services, and about IL900 million in facilities for tourism.

Industry is scheduled to make the greatest contribution to the growth of the National Product, its output increasing at a rate of 11% annually. The source of this growth is expected to be the demand for industrial products by the armed forces and increased exports and production geared toward import substitution. Considerable efforts will have to be made to attain these rates of growth, especially regarding the accelerated growth of industrial exports excluding diamonds. These are expected to increase by 20% annually and to total $1,180 million in 1976, as compared with $470 million in 1971.

Agriculture will experience continued expansion, but at a slower rate than the average for the economy. This is the consequence of limitations on production factors— water and soil—and also on the prospective demand for agricultural produce. According to the plan, agricultural production will rise at the rate of about 5% annually and an effort will be made to stimulate exports.

Transport and communications are mainly concerned with the infrastructure of the economy and this branch's expansion depends on development in other branches. For example, the growth of imports and exports will determine the modifications needed in the merchant fleet and the development of ports, while the expansion of tourism will call for more aircraft and motor vehicles as well as the extension of the road network and the communications system. The output of this branch should rise by an average of 8% annually.

Building output should increase by about 7% annually. The principal aims of this industry will be to provide adequate housing for the 250,000 immigrants expected over the period, to eradicate slums, and to house young couples. A total investment of IL12,500 million is earmarked for these purposes.

A slower rate of growth is expected in the services, with about 30,000 more employed in education and 13,000 in health services.

One of the principal limitations on the continued developments of the economy is the shortage of foreign exchange. In order to reduce the adverse balance of payments—about $1,200 million in 1971—further measures will be taken to curtail the increase in imports and to expand exports. Steps will be taken to replace imports by economical local manufactures, while exposing to competitive imports local products which at present enjoy high protective tariffs. The main efforts will be to increase exports by a consistent and unflagging line of policy. The Government will maintain the profitability of exports in relation to production for the home market, while the availability of production resources will be assured by restricting the increase in private consumption to a rate not exceeding $2\frac{1}{2}$% annually.

According to the Development Plan, exports should increase by 14.2% annually, amounting to $3,500 million in 1976 as compared with $1,800 million in 1971. Imports for 1976 should be about $4,500 million in 1976, representing an annual increase of about 8.2%. Total imports over the five-year period will amount to about $19,150 million, of which some 22%—$4,200 million—will be direct or indirect defense imports. Therefore according to the forecast imports will exceed exports, by $950 million in 1976, and the total accumulated deficit over the entire period will amount to about $5,400 million. Assuming that all the requisite foreign capital can be obtained, the total foreign debt at the end of 1976 will be $5,400 million.

Public consumption in 1976 will be IL9,280 million, as compared with IL7,380 million in 1971, representing an average annual increase of about 3.3%. According to the forecasts on which the plan is based, defense consumption will rise by about 10% annually until 1976 and the proportion of defense expenditure in the GNP will be reduced (in comparison with 1970 when it stood at about 30%). It is assumed that negative savings in the public sector will disappear during the period as the result of an increase in tax revenue.

The increased absorption of resources by the public sector is designed to ensure that the increase in private consumption keeps in step with what the economy can bear. To balance the increased burden on the general public, the Government will ensure that the standard of living of the lower-income groups will rise by more than the 2.5% average for the population at-large.

3 TAXATION

IN THE OTTOMAN PERIOD. Under Ottoman rule there was a wide variety of unrelated taxes, most of them levied on property or on the produce of the land. Assessments were often arbitrary, and a large proportion of the revenue was absorbed by tax farmers and other go-betweens. Though the rates were not high, taxation weighed heavily on the population, particularly the fellahin and other productive elements. Property tax *(werko)* varied from 0.4 to 1% of the value of the property and the tax on livestock from 0.8 to 4%. The tithe, said to have been adopted by Islam from biblical sources *(ma'aser)*, amounted at first to one-tenth and later to one-eight of the produce and was collected from the cultivator. Customs duties were collected both on imports (at rates rising eventually to 11%) and on exports, though at a trifling rate, as well as on certain goods transported within the empire. There was an excise duty on liquor and tobacco was a state monopoly. Various fees were charged, mainly on transactions registered in the *tabu* (land registry), and there were local authority taxes and fees on the sale and slaughter of cattle.

BRITISH MANDATE (1917–48). This period saw a shift from taxes on property toward taxes on consumption and, finally, income. By 1922 customs and excise duties accounted for more than half of the total tax revenue; the proportion rose to nearly 60% in 1933, falling to 40% in 1938 and remaining at the same level until the end of the Mandate. Property taxes, on the other hand, provided less than one-third of the revenue in 1922, 10% in 1933, 6% in 1938, and 8–9% from 1942, while fees and stamp duties provided a steady 18–21%. A progressive income tax, based on the British model, was introduced in 1941 and, by 1945, accounted for nearly 20% of the revenue. The Jewish population ultimately carried about twice as large a share per capita of the total tax burden as the Arabs, owing to their higher average incomes. Tithe and *werko* were gradually replaced by urban and rural property taxes. Vacant urban land was taxed on its capital value, while taxes on all other property were assessed on net annual value. Customs duties were levied at specific or *ad valorem* rates, and excise on tobacco and liquor became a substantial source of revenue. Protective duties, particularly against foreign dumping, were imposed at the request of the nascent Jewish industry and agriculture, although Article 18 of the Mandate prohibited differential rates against member states of the League of Nations. The Arab population was successful in resisting proposals for estate and land value increment taxes.

IN THE STATE OF ISRAEL. Israel, which is handicapped by a heavy security burden (about 25% of its national product went to meet security needs in 1970), also has had to spend large sums on the integration of immigrants and the development of the economy. In all these activities, the government plays a central role, and the principal taxation problem in the 1970s was the need to increase revenue despite the already high rates of taxation. Tax revenue in the fiscal year (April 1–March 31) 1968/69 was 28% and 38% in 1972 of the national product, in comparison with around 40% in countries like France and Sweden (see Table 61), but the burden on part of the economy was heavy. The rapid growth of government expenditure in recent years was not accompanied by a proportionate increase in tax revenue. As a result, there was a decrease in the role played in the budget by direct and indirect taxes, which financed about half of government expenditure, compared with about three-quarters in the past. About half of the tax revenue was derived from direct taxes and half from indirect taxes (see Table 62). The position in comparison with that in some other countries may be judged from Table 63. **109**

Table 61. Percentage of Revenues from Taxes and Compulsory
Payments in the National Product for the Year 1968

Sweden	42
France	37
Austria	36
Norway	38
Holland	38
Western Germany	35
Denmark, Gt. Britain, Finland, Belgium	35; 34; 33
Chile	30
Italy	30
Israel	28
Uruguay, Ireland	26; 28
Tunisia, New Zealand	26; 26

Table 62. Composition of Tax Revenues, 1964, 1969 and 1972

	1964	1969	1972
Income taxes	37.6	44.5	44.3
Property taxes	5.1	4.0	3.8
Expenditure taxes	49.1	47.3	49.5
Other local revenues	8.2	4.2	2.4
Total	100.0	100.0	100.0
Value (in million IL)	2,170	4,268	10,715

Table 63. Proportion between Direct and Indirect Taxes in
Various Countries (generally in 1968)

	Indirect Taxes	Direct Taxes	
United States	30.4	69.6	100.0
West Germany	39.4	60.6	100.0
United Kingdom	47.2	52.8	100.0
Japan	39.6	60.4	100.0
Canada	48.4	51.6	100.0
Israel	51.3	48.7	100.0
Spain	43.5	56.5	100.0
Greece	62.8	37.2	100.0
Denmark	47.4	52.6	100.0
Chile	47.7	52.3	100.0
Tunisia	63.4	36.6	100.0

Direct Taxes. These include income tax and various property taxes. Income tax was deducted by employers at source when paying wages or salaries and then transferred to the authorities. The income-tax laws were modified every few years in order to adapt them to changing condition, particularly increased prices and incomes. Exemptions and allowances for individuals in the fiscal year 1972/73 were as follows: The first IL3,540 of annual income was exempt. In addition, married men received exemptions in respect of IL1,260 for a wife, IL1,200 for each of the first two children and, since 1968/69, IL1,320 for every additional child. Cost-of-living payments were exempt, and there were allowances for parents, other relatives, costs of study, unmarried persons over 30, men over 60, and women over 55. Tax credits were given in respect of payments for medical treatment, retirement pensions, and life insurance. Residents in border and new villages and in the Negev got special concessions. New immigrants were exempt from income tax on IL1,200 monthly for their first 18 months in the country, IL700 for the next 12 months, and IL200 for the 12 months after. They also received certain exemptions from death duties, property taxes, and customs.

Tax rates were progressive, the marginal rate ranging from 18% for the lowest taxable incomes to 63% for taxable incomes of IL42,000 and over (Table 64). Rates were high in the middle brackets, in comparison with those prevailing in other countries, as shown in Table 65. The highest rate of taxation in the United States is about 90%, in comparison with about 60% in Israel, but the income required in the United States to reach this rate is higher than in Israel.

The table exaggerates the income tax rates in Israel as a result of the use of the official exchange rate, which did not reflect the true purchasing power of the currency. In addition, the defense levy, 15% of income tax paid, which was imposed after the Six-Day War was reduced to 10% in the fiscal year 1971/72 and abolished in 1973. Between 1964 and 1969 there was an increase in the proportion of 111

STATE BUDGETS, 1971/72–1973/74

REVENUE IN IL

	Actual	Estimates	Forecast
	1971/72	1972/73	1973/74
TOTAL REVENUE	**14,481,393,190**	**17,815,550,000**	**19,800,000,000**
1. Ordinary Revenue	9,301,588,628	12,892,550,000	15,130,000,000
2. Revenue from Loans and Capital Payments	5,179,804,562	4,929,000,000	4,670,000,000
1. ORDINARY REVENUE	9,301,588,628	12,892,550,000	15,130,000,000
TAXES AND COMPULSORY PAYMENTS	*8,557,352,451*	*10,715,550,000*	*12,900,000,000*
Taxes on income and property	*3,111,563,722*	*3,925,700,000*	*4,581,200,000*
Income tax and defense levy	2,877,157,171	3,600,000,000	4,174,000,000
Land betterment tax ($^2/_3$)	36,142,117	74,700,000	88,200,000
Property tax	198,264,434	251,000,000	319,000,000
Taxes on expenditure	*4,155,264,275*	*5,457,550,000*	*6,682,880,000*
Customs and import levies	1,965,821,764	2,645,550,000	3,125,000,000

Purchase tax (95%)	921,271,356	1,258,600,000	1,696,700,000
Excise tax	262,099,165	310,000,000	362,000,000
Fuel tax	417,614,463	500,000,000	580,000,000
Foreign travel tax	69,005,346	86,000,000	110,000,000
Stamp tax	165,296,817	227,000,000	305,000,000
Entertainment tax	2,281,500	3,000,000	4,000,000
Defense stamp tax	147,706,406	191,000,000	240,000,000
Surtax and exchange differentials	33,535,401	12,000,000	4,000,000
Vehicles fees (58%)	50,937,375	57,400,000	70,180,000
Other fess and licenses	119,694,682	167,000,000	186,000
Compulsory loans and war damage compensation	*1,201,291,581*	*1,210,000,000*	*1,469,000,000*
Saving loan	632,944,165	580,000,000	710,000,000
Defense loan	497,000,000	565,000,000	689,000,000
War damage compensation fund	71,347,416	65,000,000	70,000,000
Allocation for Property Tax	*(−)171,700,000*	*(−)243,000,000*	*(−)350,000,000*
Transferred Revenue to Local Authorities	260,932,873	365,300,000	516,920,000
Direct	197,864,231	278,100,000	402,210,000
Property tax (4.8%)	(171,700,000)	(243,000,000)	(350,000,000)

REVENUE IN IL

	Actual	Estimates	Forecast
	1972	1972	1972
Vehicles tax (21%)	(14,580,676)	(20,800,000)	(25,410,000)
Land betterment tax ($^1/_3$)	(11,583,555)	(14,300,000)	(26,800,000)
Through Ministry of Interior	63,068,642	87,200,000	114,710,000
Purchase tax (5%)	(48,487,966)	(66,400,000)	(89,300,000)
Vehicle Tax (21 %)	(14,580,676)	(20,800,000)	(25,410,000)
2. REVENUE FROM LOANS AND CAPITAL PAYMENTS	5,179,804,562	4,923,000,000	4,670,000,000
REPAYMENTS OF GOVERNMENT INVESTMENTS			
AND LOANS	207,227,218	375,000,000	256,000,000
Depreciation for economic units	3,377,662	5,157,000	5,446,000
Depreciation for business enterprises	57,944,153	58,779,000	72,654,000
Depreciation for State authorities	1,700,000	1,700,000	1,700,000
Depreciation for Government companies	9,532,196	7,200,000	7,200,000

On a/c of investments in communications	85,574,282	48,850,000	92,000,000
From Ports Authority	—	9,000,000	—
From Land Authority	45,258,434	22,964,000	29,500,000
Allocations for Pensions and Compensation	*55,849,336*	*61,700,000*	*77,500,000*
From economic units	16,780,575	17,249,000	20,670,000
From business enterprises	39,068,761	44,451,000	56,830,000
Domestic Loans	*1,574,517,245*	*2,378,000,000*	*2,230,000,000*
From National Insurance Institute	647,910,552	820,000,000	830,000,000
Bank and public loans	926,606,693	1,558,000,000	1,400,000,000
Foreign Loans and Grants	*2,488,824,036*	*2,406,000,000*	*3,276,000,000*
Foreign surpluses	213,000,000	210,000,000	210,000,000
Foreign loans	2,275,824,036	2,196,000,000	3,066,000,000
Advances from Bank of Israel	*650,000,000*	*650,000,000*	—
Non—Recurrent Items	—	*252,000,000*	—
Transfers to Part 1	—	*(−)1,353,350,000*	*(−)1,378,000,000*

REVENUE IN IL

	Actual 1971	Estimates 1972	Forecast 1973
I INTEREST AND PROFITS	*535,992,863*	*572,000,000*	*623,400,000*
General	341,721,552	325,000,000	360,000,000
From economic units	1,307,140	3,662,000	6,019,000
From business enterprises	70,115,501	139,738,000	163,781,000
From government companies	20,200,000	22,000,000	22,000,000
Interest from state authorities	1,600,000	1,600,000	1,600,000
Profits of Bank of Israel	101,048,670	80,000,000	70,000,000
ROYALTIES	*86,439,066*	*92,650,000*	*131,100,000*
From business enterprises	86,439,066	92,650,000	123,500,000
From natural resources	—	—	7,600,000
MISCELLANEOUS REVENUES	*121,804,248*	*159,000,000*	*97,500,000*
Payments on a/c previous budgets	25,126,550	15,000,000	27,500,000
From miscellaneous services	96,677,698	144,000,000	70,000,000
TRANSFER FROM PART 2	—	*1,353,350,000*	*1,378,000,000*

Table 64. Income Tax Payments

Monthly income	Monthly tax payments (IL)		Average rate %		Marginal rate %	
IL	Single	Married +2	Single	Married +2	Single	Married +2
400	15	—	3.8	—	18	—
500	33	—	6.7	—	18	—
600	52	—	8.7	—	19	—
700	72	12	10.3	1.7	20	18
800	94	29	13.4	4.1	22	18
900	117	48	13.8	5.3	23	19
1,000	142	67	14.2	6.7	25	19
1,100	172	90	15.6	8.2	30	23
1,200	203	115	16.9	9.6	31	25
1,300	238	141	18.3	10.8	35	26
1,400	275	170	19.6	12.1	37	29
1,500	315	201	21.0	13.4	40	31
1,750	431	293	24.6	16.7	46	37
2,000	556	403	27.8	20.1	50	44
2,500	835	659	33.4	26.4	56	51
3,000	1,128	931	37.6	31.0	59	54
4,000	1,769	1,513	44.2	37.8	63	58
5,000	2,399	2,139	48.0	42.8	63	63
7,500	3,974	3,714	53.0	49.5	63	63

Table 65. Income Tax as Percentage of Income
Married +2 children

Annual Income[1]	Israel[2]	U.S.A.	Belgium	Gt.Britain	Germany
12,000	6.7	—	7.1	2.0	6.1
18,000	13.4	—	10.8	11.4	10.4
42,000	34.6	6.2	20.9	22.1	17.3
100,000	50.9	15.1	35.3	34.1	29.9

income tax paid by wage earners, and a decrease in 1972, owing to the employees saving loan (Table 66). These high rates excluded any reasonable possibility of raising income 117

STATE BUDGETS, 1971/72–1973/74

	Expenditure in IL		
	Actual	Budget	Budget
	1971/72	1972/73	1973/74
TOTAL EXPENDITURE	**14,338,764,118**	**17,815,550,000**	**19,800,000,000**
1. Ordinary Expenditure	10,904,155,814	12,892,550,000	15,130,000,000
2. Expenditure for Development and Debt Repayments	3,434,608,304	4,923,000,000	4,670,000,000
1. ORDINARY EXPENDITURE	10,904,155,814	12,892,550,000	15,130,000,000
GOVERNMENT AND ADMINISTRATION	*629,558,529*	*774,529,000*	*954,190,000*
Presidency	1,121,712	1,100,000	1,300,000
Knesset	8,856,729	9,889,000	14,070,000
Cabinet Ministers	701,935	900,000	1,100,000
Prime Minister's Office	23,896,369	39,720,000	34,500,000
Ministry of Finance	114,899,723	132,366,000	166,000,000
Ministry of Interior	20,269,893	26,973,000	39,000,000
Ministry of Police	183,193,489	205,786,000	264,000,000
Ministry of Justice	35,519,862	46,720,000	62,850,000

Ministry of Foreign Affairs	105,219,522	115,135,000	142,000,000
State Comptroller's Office	9,367,551	12,740,000	16,370,000
Pensions and compensation	108,244,851	118,200,000	154,000,000
Miscellaneous	17,996,902	65,000,000	25,000,000
Reserve for cost of elections	—	—	34,000,000
MINISTRY OF DEFENSE	*5,546,582,957*	*5,458,950,000*	*6,065,400,000*
LOCAL AUTHORITIES	*428,056,103*	*520,300,000*	*671,920,000*
Transferred Expenditures	260,932,873	365,920,000	516,300,000
Grants to Local Authorities	167,123,230	155,000,000	155,000,000
SOCIAL SERVICES	*2,043,642,522*	*2,223,813,000*	*3,175,400,000*
Ministry of Education and Culture	816,724,309	995,815,000	1,433,300,000
Subvention to Broadcasting Authority	15,357,953	2,500,000	3,000,000
Ministry of Religious Affairs	33,307,368	30,970,000	38,450,000
Ministry of Labor	64,150,506	74,300,000	90,200,000
Ministry of Health	295,619,808	270,850,000	443,000,000
Compensation for invalids (war and Nazi Persecution)	61,201,552	66,000,000	96,000,000
Ministry of Social Welfare	100,403,922	107,000,000	163,500,000

	Expenditure in IL		
	Actual	Budget	Budget
	1971/72	1972/73	1973/74
National Insurance Institute	171,938,235	190,000,000	220,000,000
Ministry of Housing	12,040,370	24,975,000	52,950,000
Ministry of Immigrant Absorption	21,043,475	24,403,000	35,000,000
Price Subsidies	451,855,024	437,000,000	600,000,000
ECONOMIC AFFAIRS	*1,102,774,808*	*1,281,125,000*	*1,448,400,000*
Ministry of Agriculture	63,956,172	64,935,000	82,300,000
Ministry of Development	12,645,612	9,990,000	33,000,000
Atomic Energy Commission	51,600,000	56,250,000	59,600,000
Ministry of Commerce and Industry	59,335,365	97,900,000	135,000,000
Ministry of Tourism	17,973,530	31,070,000	37,000,000
Export Incentives	797,538,347	910,000,000	950,000,000
Ministry of Transportation	27,325,205	42,020,000	49,000,000
Contribution to railways budget	23,399,172	19,000,000	24,900,000

Grants and rebates for transportation	13,304,245	11,000,000	24,000,000
Public works and survey	35,697,160	38,960,000	53,600,000
INTEREST PAYMENTS	*1,151,640,895*	*1,740,000,000*	*2,000,109,000*
RESERVES	*1,900,000*	*893,833,000*	*814,581,000*
Special budgets	1,400,000	803,333,000	700,000,000
General reserve	500,000	90,500,000	114,581,000
2. EXPENDITURE FOR DEVELOPMENT AND DEBT REPAYMENTS	3,434,608,304	4,923,000,000	4,670,000,000
DEVELOPMENT	*2,275,228,490*	*2,251,977,000*	*2,501,650,000*
Government	*12,490,618*	*21,636,000*	*39,000,000*
Government buildings	6,621,703	9,990,000	15,000,000
Police and prisons	4,848,544	8,000,000	21,500,000
Courts	1,020,371	3,646,000	2,500,000
Local Authorities	*37,577,583*	*52,445,000*	*74,500,000*

	Expenditure in IL		
	Actual	Budget	Budget
	1971/72	1972/73	1973/74
Social Services	*1,319,960,077*	*1,188,533,000*	*1,269,300,000*
Education	54,101,144	77,000,000	70,000,000
Higher education	69,983,000	70,000,000	100,000,000
Religious services	3,279,863	2,500,000	4,550,000
Employment and vocational training	6,738,313	13,500,000	19,000,000
Health	39,216,528	44,600,000	110,000,000
Social welfare	4,068,684	11,833,000	31,000,000
Housing	1,142,572,545	969,100,000	934,750,000
Economic Services	*905,200,212*	*989,363,000*	*1,118,850,000*
Agriculture	122,399,375	76,955,000	79,200,000
Water projects	53,000,620	52,450,000	60,000,000

Mines, minerals and electricity	39,381,170	23,976,000	25,250,000
Oil prospecting and pipelines	11,703,756	5,000,000	10,000,000
Industry and crafts	209,488,998	277,800,000	285,000,000
Tourism	22,478,389	30,070,000	40,000,000
Transportation	108,439,699	117,344,000	151,400,000
Roads	65,928,565	81,918,000	103,000,000
Communications	240,249,973	304,850,000	330,000,000
Other enterprises	32,129,667	19,000,000	35,000,000
DEBT REPAYMENT	*1,138,159,814*	*2,125,000,000*	*2,028,210,000*
BUDGETARY REVOLVING FUND	*21,220,000*	*200,000,000*	*40,000,000*
RESERVE FOR DEVELOPMENT EXPENDITURE	*—*	*94,023,000*	*100,140,000*
NON-RECURRENT ITEMS	*—*	*252,000,000*	*—*

ORDER OF ITEMS AS IN OFFICAL HEBREW TEXT.

tax, and the Finance Ministry was even studying eventual reforms to alleviate the position of those with middle-bracket incomes of IL500–2,500 per month. Corporation tax at present is 38% on taxable profits plus a defense levy of 3%. On the remaining 62% profits on income tax of 25% is paid, and a 7% defense loan on the total taxable profits. Table 67 shows the taxes paid by the two categories of corporations. Agreements for preventing double taxation, partially or completely, with Canada, Denmark, Finland, France, Greece, Italy, Norway, South Africa, Sweden, Switzerland, Great Britain, the U.S., West Germany, Belgium and Singapore.

Table 66. Composition of Income Tax Receipts, 1964–1972

	1964	1969	1972
	100.0	100.0	100.0
Wage earners	42.3	47.5	41.3
Self-employed	30.0	28.7	21.0
Corporations	23.4	19.1	20.8
Interest	4.3	4.7	4.6
Employees savings loan			11.7

Source: Bank of Israel reports.

Table 67. Corporation Tax per IL 100 of Profits

	Approved corporation	Ordinary corporation
Corporation Tax	33.0	38.0
Taxable profits	67.0	62.0
Income tax	–	15.5
Defense loan	7.0	7.0
Net profit (if undistributed)[1]	58.0	39.5

[1] Dividend of approved corporation is exempted of tax.

Source: State Tax Administration.

Property tax was paid annually on the assessed value of real estate, vehicles, and stock, reassessments being carried out from time to time in accordance with increases in prices and property values. Property tax was not levied on financial holdings or movable property, with the exception of vehicles.

Indirect Taxes. These mainly affected manufactured goods, but also—though to a lesser extent— services. The major source of revenue was custom duties. For many years the import of many classes of manufactured goods was prevented by administrative orders, but administrative protection was almost completely replaced by high custom duties in order to expose local manufactures to the competition of imported goods. Since 1966, as a further stage in the same process, the custom duties were gradually reduced. Heavy duties were generally imposed on luxuries, while essential commodities, raw materials, and investment goods were taxed at lower rates or exempted. Certain products were even subsidized, so that they were sold in Israel at a lower price than abroad. The duty charged was generally a percentage of the value of the goods when in port (C.I.F.), but sometimes it was a fixed sum or a combination of both methods: a percentage of the value, provided the duty did not fall below a given sum, or a basic figure plus a percentage of any additional value. During the fiscal year 1971/72, for example, out of imports totaling $760 million, about $189 million worth were exempt from duty as materials for export industries, $295 million of other imports were exempt, and $50 million benefited from conditional exemption. Duty was thus charged on $225 million—about 30% of the total. The average duty paid on chargeable imports was IL1.42 per dollar, which represented a rate of about 36%, but variations in rates were considerable (Table 68). In August 1970, a defense levy of 20% was imposed on all imports, with the exception of a small number of essential goods.

Purchase tax was imposed by value on about 35% of all products. Due to the restricted scope of this tax, on the one

Table 68. Taxable Imports and Customs Revenues According to the 1971/72 Rates (in IL 1,000)

Rate of duty —percent	Value of taxable Imports	Revenue from duty	Proportion of imports	Proportion of revenue from duty
Exempt	2,436	331	53.1	20.1
1—5	110	25	2.4	1.5
6—10	220	61	4.8	3.7
11—15	56	13	1.2	0.8
16—20	186	68	4.1	4.2
21—30	193	89	4.2	5.4
31—40	275	134	6.0	8.1
41—50	206	123	4.5	7.5
51—60	294	172	6.4	10.4
61—70	101	75	2.2	4.6
71—80	76	59	1.6	3.6
81—90	143	128	3.1	7.8
91—100	128	123	2.8	7.4
100+	164	214	3.6	13.0
Non-classified	—	31	—	1.9
Total	4,588	1,646	100.0	100.0

Source: 18th Report for 1971/72, Ministry of Finance, State Revenue Administration. A general tax of 20 % is imposed on imports — the income of which is included in the revenue column.

hand, and the need for large revenues, on the other, high rates were levied, especially on luxuries, while essential commodities were taxed at a lower rate or not at all. The stage of manufacture at which the tax was levied generally depended on convenience in collection. Table 9 contains a number of examples of purchase tax charged on selected products. In 1970/71 the tax was imposed on goods to the value of IL3,600,000,000, out of a total personal consumption of IL14,000,000,000. The revenue from purchase tax during the year was IL713,000,000 representing an average rate of 15%. Rates varied widely: the commonest was 11–15%, but on some goods it rose above 100%. Purchase tax was also charged on certain services, such as the hire of halls, entrance fees to night clubs, and driving tuition. Revenue from services in 1970/71 totaled IL13,000,000— about 2% of the total.

Excise duty was charged mainly on fuel, tobacco, and cement. The tax on the first two was a high percentage of the final price paid by the consumer. A higher rate was levied on petrol used by private vehicles than on heavier fuels, such as solar oil and crude oil, used for manufacture, electricity generation, and the like.

Stamp duty was imposed on all invoices above a given sum, as a percentage of the value quoted in the invoice. Entertainment tax stamps were affixed to every admission ticket to cinemas and other places of entertainment. There was also a defense stamp, levied mainly on telephone, electricity, water, and similar bills as a percentage of the amount.

Fees and licenses of various categories were charged on various services offered by the government, e.g., vehicle, radio and television, construction licenses, and passport fees. Revenue was also obtained from foreign-travel tax and court fines.

Compulsory Loans. In addition to taxes, the Israel government also raised compulsory loans from time to time, mainly to cover defense and immigrant absorption and to combat inflation. In 1969, two compulsory loans were imposed: a defense loan, paid by wage earners at the rate of 4% of wages, by employers at 4% of their wage bills (in addition to the other loans paid by them), and by self-employed persons at 7% of their incomes. The defense loan was to be redeemable from 1985 and the savings loan from 1973/74. The total revenue from the two loans in 1971/72 was IL1,130,000,000.

4 TAX REFORM

The need for the reform of Israel's taxation system became urgent at the beginning of the 1970s for two main reasons. First, the burden of taxation (including National Insurance dues) had reached about 50% of the national income—almost a world record. It appeared, moreover, according to the development plan for the decade drawn up by the Economic Planning Authority, that the burden would not be lightened in the foreseeable future. Secondly, as a result of rises in the price level, the growth of the economy, and increases in the rates of income tax and compulsory loans in 1967–1970, a considerable number of taxpayers had become liable for high marginal tax rates. There were signs that this had a negative influence on the will to work and invest, and was leading to growing pressures for the exclusion of various types of income from the basis for the tax. At the same time, the tax threshold (the minimum income liable to tax) had become very low in relation to average wage and even to the minimum wage.

The last systematic examination of the tax system had been undertaken in 1964 by the Zadok Committee and it was, therefore, found necessary to re-examine the system in the light of the capacity of the public to bear the burden and the possibility of undesirable social and economic effects, in order to adapt it to the changes in the economy. Accordingly, Finance Minister Pinḥas Sapir appointed a public committee, headed by District Court Judge Shelomoh Asher and consisting of representatives of the various sectors in the economy and academic experts, to examine the system and propose reforms.

The State Revenue Committee submitted to the committee proposals for substantial reforms in the existing tax system:

1. Comprehensive changes in the system of allowances and the rates of income tax and compulsory loans, which would bring about a reduction of some 20% in the total burden of direct taxation.

2. A change in the basis of assessment of property tax and a general reduction in the burden of the tax.

3. Imposition of a new tax, the Value Added Tax (VAT).

4. A reduction of some 50% in the revenue from existing indirect taxes.

5. Changes in the system of supplementary payments to low-income families, in order to adapt them to the above tax reforms.

Up to April 1973, the Asher Committee had submitted to the minister of finance five interim reports: three dealing with income tax (tax on individuals, business expenses, taxation connected with social insurance and the administration of the income tax), one on property tax, and one on VAT.

The Committee proposed a new system of allowances and rates of income tax for individuals, as shown in Tables 69 and 70, reducing to 65% the maximum rate on tax-liable incomes of over IL54,000 (about $13,000) per annum. Personal and other deductions would be considerably increased, but existing cost-of-living allowances would no longer be exempt from tax (without affecting the exemption of future increases in the c-o-l allowance). The Committee also proposed the abolition of the existing Defense Levy and Compulsory Loan.

The main effect of these recommendations would be a lightening of the total tax burden, with a significant reduction of marginal tax rates, especially in the middle-income range, and a considerable raising of the tax threshold (see Table 71).Their adoption as a whole would cost the Treasury some IL700 million per annum in revenue.

The Committee also recommended greater strictness

in the recognition of business expenses for tax purposes. On the other hand, it proposed a significant increase in the ceiling of exemption from tax for social insurance payments by self-employed persons, while recommending that one-time payments from provident funds and the like, which are now exempt from tax, should become liable in the future.

By the end of 1972 the Committee had not yet completed its deliberations on such subjects as the expansion of the basis for income tax and the taxation of companies.

On the subject of property tax, the Committee proposed a change in the system of assessment for buildings, a reduction in the rate of tax, and a considerable rise in the ceiling for exemption of residential property from the tax.

Particular importance attaches to the Committee's recommendations on the introduction of VAT, which was meant to balance the loss of revenue due to its other proposals. The Committee suggested imposing VAT, as part of a general reform of the tax system, on all goods and services at a uniform rate of 10%, with exemptions for a limited number of vital foodstuffs. For small businesses, the Committee recommended the imposition of a turnover tax at a low rate in place of VAT. The principles of the tax were, generally, in keeping with those followed in most European countries.

In general, the Committee's proposals were founded on the assumption that the price increases resulting from the imposition of VAT would be balanced by the income-tax reductions, so that the total burden would remain unchanged. In order to compensate low-income families which would suffer from price increases but would not benefit from reductions in direct taxation, the Committee approved the Treasury's proposals to increase children's allowances and old-age pensions paid by the National Insurance Institute, as well as social-welfare allowances.

The Government adopted a considerable part of the Committee's recommendations. An amendment to the law

on property tax enacted in 1972 covered all its proposals

on that subject. In April 1972, the Income Tax Ordinance was amended to implement part of the recommendations on income tax for individuals. The Savings Loan was abolished and the Defense Levy was reduced from 15% to 10% of income. The amendment also carried out the proposals on business expenses.

At the beginning of April 1973, a second stage of the tax reform came into effect: the Defense Levy was abolished and tax rates were reduced and allowances increased so as to reduce the burden on individual taxpayers by about 15%, or, together with the concessions of the previous year, by some 25%. The Minister of Finance stated that it was planned to introduce Value Added Tax in April 1974, ushering in a further stage of reform, bearing mainly on indirect taxation.

Table 69. Marginal Rates of Income Tax, According to Asher Committee's Recommendations

Income liable to tax (in IL)	Marginal tax rates (%)
1 — 1,000	25
1,000 — 2,000	27.5
2,000 — 4,000	30
4,000 — 6,000	32.5
6,000 — 8,000	35
8,000 — 10,000	40 (42.5)
10,000 — 12,000	45 (47.5)
12,000 — 14,000	50 (52.5)
14,000 — 16,000	52.5 (55)
16,000 — 18,000	55 (57.5)
18,000 — 22,000	57.5 (60)
22,000 — 36,000	60 (65)
36,000 — 51,000	62.5 (65)
Over 54,000	65

NOTE: Figures in parentheses apply to bachelors.

Table 70. Main Tax Allowances According to Existing Law and

Nature of exemptions

A. Personal and familial
    Resident of Israel
    For wife
    For 1st and 2nd children
    For 3rd and subsequent children
    For child on army service
    For bachelor over 30
    For widow(er) or divorce(e) with children

B. For working women
    For working mother (separate assessment)

    For wife (joint assessment)
    For working mother (joint assessment)

    For wife helping in husband's business
    For 1st child of above
    For 2nd child of above

Miscellaneous
    For old age (men over 60 and women over 55)
    For old age (men over 65 and women over 60)
    For 25—45% disability
    For 50% disability and over
    For paralysed, etc. wife or child
    For above in an institution
    For support of incapacitated relatives

Notes: 1. With one child. 2. With two children. 3. With three

	Sum exempt (in IL per annum)	
Existing		**Proposed**
1972	1973	
1,700	3,420	2,820
800	1,260	1,200
500	1,260	1,020
1,000	1,320	1,200
200		264
400	720	800
1,000		1,500
650	900	720[1]
		840[2]
		960[3]
		1,080[4]
650	900	650
250[5]	600	720[1]
		840[2]
		960[3]
		1,880[4]
325	480	420
		300
		120
325	480	480
650	1,020	960
550	780	780
900	1,320	1,320
650	1,200	900
850	1,800	1,140
300	456	360

children. 4. With four children. 5. For first child only.

Table 71. Tax Threshold, According to Existing Law and Asher Committee's Recommendations (in IL per Month)

Family status	According to existing law		According to Asher Committee's proposals		Increase (%)
	1972	1973	Without children's allowances	With children's allowances	
Bachelor up to 30	222	300	247	247	11.3
Bachelor over 30	264	363	300	300	13.6
Married, wife not working					
No children	314	411	353	353	12.4
One child	375	521	442	474	26.4
Two children	438	631	532	596	36.1
Three "	561	747	637	730	30.1
Four "	686	863	742	850	23.9
Five "	794	979	847	964	21.4
Six "	903	1,089	953	1,076	19.2

[1] With cost-of-living allowance of 63.4%, as in January 1972.

5 FOREIGN EXCHANGE RATES

On the establishment of the State of Israel the Israel pound, which replaced the Palestine pound, was also linked to sterling and followed its devaluation both in October 1949 and in November 1967. The value of the Israel pound was determined by mass immigration, rapid economic development, and heavy defense expenditure, all of which led to rises in prices and wages. To adjust the rate of exchange to the changing price levels, the government introduced a number of devaluations (see table 72). From 1952 to 1955 a system of multiple rates was in operation, graded according to the importance of the transaction concerned. In 1955 the government returned to a single rate, modified however by export premiums, surcharges on luxuries, and

Table 72. Official Dollar Exchange Rates in Israel, 1948—71

	IL
December 1948—October 1949	0.248 (for certain purposes 0.333)
October 1949—February 1952	0.357
February 1952—May 1953	0.357—0.714—1.000 (multiple rates system)
May 1953—December 1953	0.357—0.714—1.000—1.800
January 1954—June 1955	1.000—1.800
July 1955—February 1962	1.800
March 1959—February 1962	1.800—2.200 (tourist rate)
February 1962—November 1967	3.00*
November 1967	3.50
August 1971	4.20

The Israel pound was divided into 1,000 perutot until 1962 and, from then, into 100 agorot.

subsidies for essential consumer items, intended to offset the increased price of imported commodities from devaluation. Apart from the official exchange operations, regulated by the controller of foreign exchange at the treasury and carried out by the banks acting as official dealers, an unofficial market exists, on which rates fluctuate approximately 10–20% above the official rate according to supply and demand.

6 FOREIGN TRADE

The most important key to the development of a strong and viable economy in Israel is the continued expansion of its foreign trade. This is due to the geographical and political situation. In the first place, the country is poor in natural resources. It possesses little fuel, metallic ores, or timber, and is largely dependent on imported grain, fodder, meat and sugar. On the other hand, the climate is ideal for citrus cultivation and the growing of fresh vegetables, fruit, and flowers, some of which may be marketed in Europe during the off-season. There are also deposits of potash and phosphates, now used as the basis for chemical and fertilizer industries. The second basic problem of Israel's economy is the small size of the local market. There are few branches of industry which can run economically and competitively without ready access to a very large and expanding market. For political reasons, moreover, Israel is cut off from its natural trading partners in the Middle East, so that both imports and exports are hampered by longer distances and greater transportation charges, as well as the necessity to keep large stocks. Thirdly, Israel is still an underdeveloped country, compared with industrialized nations such as the U.S. or Germany and, therefore, has to import capital. Hence, the present position and future prospects of the economy have to be such as to attract foreign investors, while sufficient foreign exchange must be earned to service foreign loans and investments. Furthermore, Israel is a country of immigration. In the long run, immigrants—particularly those with skills and professions—bring great economic benefit, but in the short run they necessitate heavy initial

Israel postage stamp dedicated to the export of diamonds,
1968. Designed by O. Adler. Jerusalem, B. M. Ansbacher
Collection.

investment in housing, education, and other services while
they are being absorbed into productive employment. A
substantial part of these initial investments have to be
financed from external sources, which is an additional
strain on the balance of payments.

For all these reasons, foreign trade is of vital importance
to the Israel economy. Through imports it obtains essential
raw materials, foodstuffs, and capital equipment, while the
opening up of export markets enables it to overcome the
handicap of the small local market. The necessity to
compete on foreign markets forces the Israel producer to

work efficiently and to keep abreast of the most modern methods of production, packaging, and marketing.

The central problem of Israel's foreign trade is the large and persistent deficit in the balance of trade. One of the primary aims of its economic policy has been to achieve economic independence, namely freedom from dependence on noncommercial capital transfers (such as contributions from world Jewry) to pay for imported goods and services. From Table 73 it may be seen that considerable progress was made toward this goal before the Six-Day War in 1967. In absolute terms, the trade gap remained relatively stable, at over $200 million a year, but exports rose from a mere 11% to over 70% of import value. In relative terms, Israel thus came a long way toward closing the trade gap. There was also a tremendous rise in the total value of trade in both directions: from $280 million in 1949 to $1,200 million in 1967. If trade in services is included, the deficit rose from approximately $230 million in 1949 to $440 million in 1967. This, however, also represented a considerable decline when viewed as a percentage of the total. After the Six-Day War of 1967, the increased imports required to meet the needs of defense and economic expansion swelled the trade deficit to unprecedented proportions, the gap being filled by much greater capital imports.

Table 74 shows that there has been a continuous increase in the share of manufactured goods (other than diamonds) in total exports: from 18% in 1949 to 50% in 1972, while the share of citrus and diamonds (the two most important exports) fell from 81% to 45%. Whereas the share of citrus has declined continuously since 1949, that of diamond exports increased to a peak of 36% in 1968, since when it has remained more or less stable. These percentage figures, based on total export value, mask the true relative importance of the two products to the economy, however. In terms of net added value (i.e., after deduction of the costs of imported raw materials) the value of citrus exports actually exceeded that of diamonds: $75 million added value as against $70 million in 1972. **139**

Table 73. Development of Israel's Foreign Trade (Goods), 1949–72 (in millions $)

	1949	1955	1960	1967[1]	1969[1]	1970[1]	1971[1]	1972[1]
Net imports	251	334	495	759	1,316	1,445	1,807	1,922
Net exports	28	89	211	532	757	807	984	1,101
Trade gap	223	245	284	227	559	638	823	821
Exports as % of imports	11%	27%	43%	70%	58%	56%	55%	57%

[1] Including trade with the occupied territories.

Table 74. Changing Structure of Israel's Exports 1949–72 (percentages)

	1949	1955	1962	1967	1968	1969	1970	1971	1972
Total exports	100	100	100	100	100	100	100	100	100
Total agriculture	64	38	24	19	18	16	18	17	15
Total industry	36	62	76	81	82	84	82	83	85
Citrus fruit	63	36	18	15	14	12,6	12	12	10
Diamonds (net)	18	23	30	28	36	35.1	27	29	35

Source: Israel's Foreign Trade (Annual) Central Bureau of Statistics.

Loading Jaffa oranges at Haifa port. Courtesy Ministry for
Foreign Affairs, Jerusalem.

Despite diversification, about 72% of Israel's export
earnings in 1972 are derived from ten major commodity
groups. These are: citrus fruit, polished diamonds, citrus
products, textile yarns, clothing, chemicals, fertilizers
(chiefly potash and phosphates), copper cement, metal
products, and tires. Israel's export policy is to achieve an
even greater diversification and to build up a larger number
of substantial export branches. There is increasing emphasis
on science-based industries, the fashion industry and, in
agriculture, the export of high-quality out-of-season produce.

Table 75 shows that over half of Israel's trade in both
directions is with Western Europe, while the United States
supplies some 25% of its imports and takes about 21% of its
exports. Western Europe and the U.S. together account
for nearly 80% of Israel's imports and close to 66% of its
exports. This trading pattern, which has remained more or   **141**

Table 75. Imports and Exports, By Area (1964–1971)

Area	1964	1965	1967	1968	1969	1970	1971
IMPORTS				Absolute Numbers			
Europe	*500,763*	*472,324*	*429,058*	*699,124*	*812,518*	*869,823*	*1,094,675*
Common Market	241,398	201,508	185,250	320,618	401,286	447,154	559,033
Free Trade Area (E.F.T.A.)	228,133	244,312	206,535	341,385	364,804	361,474	434,922
Comecon countries	17,332	16,530	19,793	22,046	25,317	34,672	33,224
Other countries of Europe	13,900	9,974	17,480	15,065	21,111	26,523	68,496
United States and Canada	*218,114*	*217,252*	*201,892*	*256,171*	*323,828*	*338,753*	*451,576*
Asia and Africa	*46,011*	*57,244*	*54,352*	*51,365*	*65,948*	*106,567*	*99,286*
Other countries	*72,603*	*85,424*	*92,572*	*114,124*	*128,299*	*139,832*	*162,083*
Total	837,491	832,244	777,874	1,120,784	1,330,593	1,454,975	1,807,620
				Percentages			
Europe	*59.8*	*56.8*	*55.1*	*62.4*	*61.0*	*59.8*	*60.5*
Common Market	28.8	24.2	23.8	28.6	30.2	30.7	30.9
Free Trade Area (E.F.T.A.)	27.2	29.3	26.6	30.3	27.4	24.8	24.1
Comecon countries	2.1	2.0	2.5	2.0	1.9	2.4	1.8
Other countries of Europe	1.7	1.2	2.2	1.3	1.6	1.8	3.8
United States and Canada	*26.0*	*26.1*	*26.0*	*22.9*	*24.3*	*23.3*	*25.0*
Asia and Africa	*5.5*	*6.8*	*7.0*	*4.5*	*5.0*	*7.3*	*5.5*
Other countries	*8.7*	*10.3*	*11.9*	*10.2*	*9.7*	*9.6*	*9.0*

EXPORTS

	Absolute Numbers						
Europe	*232,715*	*264,747*	*334,183*	*335,870*	*389,921*	*414,734*	*485,263*
Common Market	104,111	121,628	159,761	173,366	189,190	205,272	257,533
Free Trade Area (E.F.T.A.)	94,314	102,050	127,802	133,710	144,814	147,013	178,318
Comecon countries	14,895	16,890	18,099	18,609	22,654	22,654	16,183
Other countries of Europe	19,395	24,179	28,521	30,185	33,263	33,088	33,299
United States and Canada	*60,349*	*68,984*	*98,536*	*131,610*	*152,553*	*164,182*	*201,433*
Asia and Africa	*61,228*	*78,019*	*96,329*	*114,454*	*140,489*	*158,328*	*209,958*
Other countries	*18,048*	*17,841*	*25,405*	*37,285*	*46,347*	*41,491*	*60,595*
Total	372,350	429,591	554,453	639,219	729,310	752,028	957,319
	Percentages						
Europe	*62.5*	*61.6*	*60.3*	*55.6*	*53.5*	*53.3*	*50.7*
Common Market	28.0	28.3	28.8	27.1	25.9	26.4	26.9
Free Trade Area (E.F.T.A.)	25.3	23.7	23.1	20.9	19.9	18.9	18.6
Comecon countries	4.0	3.9	3.3	2.9	3.1	2.9	1.7
Other countries of Europe	5.2	5.6	5.1	4.7	4.6	4.2	3.5
United States and Canada	*16.2*	*16.1*	*17.7*	*20.6*	*20.9*	*21.1*	*21.1*
Asia and Africa	*16.5*	*18.2*	*17.4*	*17.9*	*19.3*	*20.3*	*21.9*
Other countries	*4.8*	*4.1*	*4.6*	*5.9*	*6.3*	*5.3*	*6.3*

less stable for the first twenty years of Israel's existence, stems from the basic facts of its geopolitical position. On the one hand, as we have noted, Israel is cut off from all commercial contact with its immediate neighbors. On the other hand, the products of its agriculture and industry (e.g., citrus, polished diamonds, textiles) are of a type which can be most readily marketed in the more sophisticated industrialized countries. A large part of its imports (e.g., machinery and components for industry) can also be obtained most readily from the Western Hemisphere.

Eastern Europe in 1966 provided about 2% of Israel's imports and purchased 2% of Israel's exports. With the rupture of diplomatic relations following the 1967 war, trade with these countries came to a standstill. Rumania, however, has remained on close terms with Israel, and trade has expanded considerably. Israel has made considerable efforts to expand its trade with Asia, Africa, and South America, in spite of the absence of regular shipping lines,

Fresh gladioli being sent from Lydda airport. Courtesy
Government Press Office, Tel Aviv.

the great distances involved, and the need to become familiar with these new markets. Israel's fertilizers and chemicals are in great demand in these areas and an expansion of Israel's exports to these countries is anticipated.

Free access to foreign markets is vital for the further expansion of Israel's foreign trade. One of the major problems confronting Israel is the emergence of regional economic groupings, which aim to reduce or abolish custom duties between members of the group while practicing discriminatory import policies toward countries outside. Such regional blocs now exist all over the world, in South America, in Africa and, more particularly, in Western Europe, Israel's principal export market. Israel does not belong to any of these regional groupings and consequently finds itself discriminated against in all markets—hence its application in 1966 for associate membership of the European Common Market. Under a five-year preferential agreement between Israel and the Common Market, signed in 1970, Market tariffs on Israel's industrial products, citrus, and certain subtropical fruits were lowered by up to 50% and Israel tariffs on imports from Common Market countries were reduced by 10–30%. Israel also tried to tackle this problem through active participation in GATT (General Agreement for Tariffs and Trade). The all-round reduction in duties achieved through the Kennedy Round Negotiations led to a lowering of the general level of discrimination.

For invisible exports see Tourism, page 289.

7 EXHIBITIONS

UNDER THE MANDATE (1917–48). The first country-wide exhibitions in Ereẓ Israel were organized by the British Mandatory government. Four agricultural exhibitions were held between 1926 and 1929, with considerable participation by Jewish farmers. On a suggestion by the Jewish institutions, special exhibitions devoted to citrus were held in Jaffa in 1926, 1927, and 1929, at which Jewish growers demonstrated new varieties previously unknown in Palestine such as grapefruit, the Valencia orange, and the clementine (a variety of mandarin). In 1932, at a fruit exhibition in Jaffa, bananas, apples, and plums were shown for the first time. Two modest exhibitions of home products were organized in Tel Aviv in 1923 and in 1924 by the Iggud le-Ma'an Toẓeret ha-Areẓ ("Association for the Promotion of Local Produce"); 16 factories and workshops took part in the first and 127 in the second.

At an exhibition site near Tel Aviv railroad station three exhibition buildings were erected in 1925, and three exhibitions were held in 1925 and 1926. In 1929 and 1932 international exhibitions and fairs were organized at the site under the patronage of the high commissioner for Palestine and a committee headed by Mayor Meir Dizengoff. Although 121 foreign firms participated in 1929, foreign governments were officially represented for the first time in 1932, among them Great Britain, the U.S.S.R., Egypt, Cyprus, Rumania, Turkey, Switzerland, Poland, Latvia, and Bulgaria. A new site, on the sand dunes in north Tel Aviv, was acquired in 1934 and transformed into a modern exhibition city, comprising 30 permanent buildings. From then on the exhibitions assumed the new name of Levant

The seventh Levant Fair, Tel Aviv, 1936. Courtesy Keren Hayesod, United Israel Appeal, Jerusalem.

Fairs, with a flying camel as their emblem. Thirty-six countries and 2,200 firms (700 Palestinian) participated in the Levant Fair of 1934, which was known as the sixth. It attracted 600,000 visitors, including many from the Middle East and overseas, and a seventh was held in 1936. The Arab revolt of 1936, the Ethiopian War, and the outbreak of World War II in 1939 led to a long interruption in the Tel Aviv exhibitions and fairs. However, in 1941, while the German army was pushing toward Palestine, a Palestine Industrial Exhibition was organized in Cairo for the Palestine government's War Supply Board, to show that the country's industry was capable of handling military orders, which until then had been placed in Europe or America.

AFTER INDEPENDENCE. The first important exhibition in independent Israel was the Conquest of the Desert International Exhibition and Fair, held at the Jerusalem Convention Center (Binyanei ha-Ummah) in 1953. Participants included UNESCO, the World Health Organization, the Food and Agricultural Organization, the International Labor Office, Israel government ministries, the Jewish Agency, the Jewish National Fund, PICA, and more than 500 organizations and private firms from Israel and 21 **147**

The Israel pavillion at the Conquest of the Desert International
Exhibition and Fair in Binyanei ha-Ummah, Jerusalem, 1953.
Courtesy Jewish Agency Photo Service, Jerusalem.

foreign countries. The exhibition was devoted to the
reclamation and settlement of arid regions and was visited
by over half a million people. In 1958 the Israel Tenth
Anniversary Exhibition was held at the same place, the
central theme being the ingathering of the exiles. Over 350
institutions and private firms participated and nearly
600,000 visitors attended.

In 1962, the Tel Aviv trade fair was revived, under a new
name, as the Eighth Near East International Fair. It was
held on an area of 75 acres; there were nearly 1,000
exhibitors from 33 states and 660,000 visitors came from
Israel and 56 other countries. The 1964 fair, now called the
Tel Aviv Trade Fair, attracted 1,000 exhibitors from 40
countries; in 1966 1,200 exhibitors came from 46 countries
(18 African). In 1968, after the Six-Day War, only 33
countries took part, but there were 1,350 exhibitors.
including 15 from areas occupied during the war. In 1970,
51 countries participated and all display space was taken.

The Israel Tenth Anniversary Exhibition, held in Binyanei ha-Ummah, Jerusalem, 1958. Courtesy Government Press Office, Tel Aviv.

During the 45 years following the first exhibition in 1923, more than 250 exhibitions were held in the country on various aspects of economic and cultural activity. Many of them, such as fashion shows and exhibitions of textiles and food products, were staged by the Israel Manufacturers' Association, while others, on construction, electrical equipment, and machinery, were sponsored by the Association of Engineers and Architects. In 1965 a House and Home Exhibition for building, construction, and home crafts was held in Tel Aviv with 430 exhibitors. From 1951, Haifa held an annual international flower exhibition: at the 17th in 1969, 23 countries from every continent were represented. An event that attracts widespread interest is the Jerusalem International Book Fair, which has been held biennially since 1963 and has been recognized as the second-most important of its kind, after that of Frankfurt. At the 1973 Fair, 720 publishers from different countries exhibiting 38,000 books were represented, 80% of whom sent their personal representatives. A notable feature of the Fair is the award of the Jerusalem Prize to distinguished writers, such as Bertrand Russell, Max Frisch, André

The Third Jerusalem International Book Fair in Binyanei ha-Ummah, 1967. Courtesy Government Press Office, Tel Aviv.

Schwarz-Bart, Ignazio Silone, Jorge-Luis Borges and Eugène Ionesco.

A special exhibition held in Tel Aviv in 1960 was devoted to the city's 50th anniversary. A number of cultural exhibitions have been organized by the Jewish National Fund, the Histadrut, and the kibbutz movement. There have also been exhibitions on such diverse subjects as health protection, adult education, woman's role in society, social security, the printing industry, food products, chemicals and plastics. The Israel Defense Forces Exhibition, held in 1968 in Tel Aviv, was part of Israel's 20th anniversary celebrations. After 1967, a number of agricultural exhibitions were held in Judea and Samaria.

ISRAEL EXHIBITIONS ABROAD. Israel exhibitions abroad, participation in international fairs, and Israel weeks in large foreign stores are of great importance for penetration of new export markets and the widening of existing ones. In 1957 the Israel Company for Fairs and Exhibitions Ltd. was established to publicize the "Made in Israel" label throughout the world. The government, the Jewish Agency, and the commercial and industrial organizations of the private and labor sectors are represented on its board of directors. The company organizes exhibitions, distributes publicity material, builds exhibits and pavilions, packs and dispatches goods, and advises exhibitors.

During the first ten years of its activity, 80,000,000 people saw Israel exhibits at some 300 fairs and exhibits, and 40,000,000 customers visited Israel weeks in large stores. In 1970 the company organized Israel's participation in 25 fairs and exhibitions in 16 countries, which were seen by some 6,000,000 people, and 20 Israel weeks were organized in ten countries. The general policy is now to participate in specialized trade fairs in the developed countries of Europe and America and in general exhibitions in the developing countries, especially in Africa, where Israel goods are less well known. As well as promoting exports, these displays are of importance in winning goodwill for Israel and exemplifying the work of her architects and designers who are responsible for them.

8 WATER AND IRRIGATION

IN THE PRE-STATE OF ISRAEL PERIOD (1880–1948). It was only some 25 years after the beginning of modern Jewish settlement that the Jewish farmers began to dig their own wells with modern pumping equipment, and that some villages, like Petaḥ Tikvah and Reḥovot, were provided with piped water. Each citrus grove generally relied on its own well; a central waterworks on the Yarkon River, built before World War I, which had a 75-hp motor pumping 300 cubic meters an hour through a sixteen-inch pipe, was the largest of its kind in the country. With the extension of Jewish settlement under the Mandate, and the arrival of water experts during the Third Aliyah, the Jewish national institutions helped to improve techniques: new wells were dug by more modern methods and larger quantities supplied. Development was further speeded up from the 1930s onward. Electric power was used; spring water was exploited in the Ḥarod area; water was discovered for the first time in the hill regions, and district water supply schemes were set up. In 1936, the Mekorot water company was established by the Jewish Agency and the Histadrut to develop resources on a larger scale. During World War II, the urgent need to increase agricultural production stimulated more vigorous and far-ranging efforts to expand water supply. Inspired by faith in the country's agricultural potentialities, the Zionist authorities made the first efforts to work out a national water plan, which an American engineer, G. B. Hayes, was commissioned to prepare on the basis of the principles laid down by Walter C. Lowdermilk[2]. Hayes outlined his plan, which provided for bringing

[2]U.S. land conservation and hydrology expert (1888–)

water from the Jordan to irrigate the Negev, in his book *Tennessee Valley Authority on the Jordan.* Three observation posts for the collection of water statistics were set up in the Negev, and temporary pipes laid to supply the 11 settlements founded there in October 1946.

PLANNING AND ORGANIZATION. It was only after the establishment of independence that it was possible to attempt a clear evaluation of national resources, or a definition of growth and production targets. The approach to development changed abruptly with the establishment of the State of Israel in 1948. Intensive effort was devoted to drawing up an inventory of resources, defining growth objectives, formulating methods, and determining planning strategies. In fact, the development of water resources, settlement on the land, and agricultural production were the first sectors of the Israel economy for which long-term plans were drawn up and approved. The need for comprehensive long-term planning in the development of irrigation was recognized from the outset in view of the limiting factors: scarcity of water and land and shortages of capital, of time, of data, and of the basic tools of development.

A first draft plan was adopted in 1950 and has been continually revised in keeping with changing needs and fuller information. It is based on maximum conservation of water, optimum management of resources, and carefully considered allocations. Preference has been given to irrigation installations that facilitate control of the amounts applied, minimize conveyance losses, and are economical in the use of labor. Since application technologies elsewhere have been based on low-cost water, an extensive research and development program has been carried out with a view to evolving approaches suitable to Israel's high water costs. In 1952, Tahal, the Israel Water Planning Corporation, was set up to plan the country's water, sewage and drainage systems, and supervise development. The government, which took over one-third of the shares in Mekorot, holds 52% of the stock in Tahal, the Jewish Agency and the Jewish National Fund holding 24% each. In 1959 the 153

Construction of the pipeline for the National Water Carrier at Hukok, early 1960s. Courtesy Government Press Office, Tel Aviv.

Knesset passed the Water Law, by which all rights in water are vested in the state and the Water Commissioner in the Ministry of Agriculture has the sole authority to issue licences for the exploitation of water resources, fix tariffs and allocate water among the various types of consumers.

NATIONAL WATER SYSTEM. Israel's climate is typically Mediterranean. Rainfall occurs only in the winter months, and decreases from north to south: from an annual average

Dam and water reservoir at Tel Yeruḥam in the Negev.

of about 1,000 mm. in Safed to 500 mm. in Tel Aviv, 200 mm. in Beersheba and only 30 mm. in Eilat; it is less than 180 mm. a year in the southern part of the country. There are considerable fluctuations from year to year. Development during Israel's first decade proceeded from local and, later, more extensive groundwater projects to regional projects utilizing groundwater, springs, storm runoff and reclaimed wastes—the latter designed, mainly, to spread available surpluses in such a manner as best to meet the needs. The Jordan Project, completed in the late 1950s and early 1960, conveys the surplus water from the north-east to the water-deficient areas in the center and, at the same time, integrates the local and regional water works into one national water "grid," which is operated according to an overall national plan.

THE WATER INVENTORY. The major water resources directly or indirectly interconnected by the national grid have a total average annual yield of about 1,400 million cubic meters. They include:

(1) The Upper Jordan and its tributaries, including Lake Kinneret and the Beth-Shean spring area (37%);

(2) The groundwater formations of the Galilee mountains and the Valley of Jezreel, subintegrated into the regional Kishon-Jezreel system, which also comprises spring flows, storm runoff, and reclaimed waste water from the greater Haifa area (9%);

(3) Coastal and foothill groundwater formations, also receiving recharge from the waste water of many coastal towns and villages—subintegrated into a number of regional systems (29.5%);

(4) The Yarkon River, subintegrated into the Yarkon regional system, extending from Tel Aviv to the Negev (14%);

(5) Storm runoff in the major coastal intermittent streams, mainly stored in the coastal unconsolidated aquifer (5.5%);

(6) Reclaimed waste water (also stored underground) from the Tel Aviv metropolitan area, numbering over one million inhabitants, subintegrated into the Greater Tel Aviv waste water reclamation project (5%).

Regulation of cyclical and seasonal fluctuations is achieved by two main storage facilities. Lake Kinneret, in the north, provides seasonal storage for the Jordan River, while the groundwater formations in the coastal area, with their great subsurface storage capacity, serve as the main cyclical hold-over storage of the national system. The potential energy of the system—which, in balance, is highly negative, since the main areas of demand lie higher than the main water resources—is regulated by two main pumping stations in the north, with an insulated capacity of over 100,000 hp, and a number of booster stations. Between 1949 and 1968 the utilization of proven water resources rose from 17%, mainly from local groundwater, to almost 90% (including the utilization of the Yarkon and Jordan rivers). The expansion of the irrigated area from 70,000 acres to 428,000 in 1970 was a major factor in raising agricultural **156** production to over $500 million—a sevenfold increase at

Israel's National Water System, 1971. Based on material supplied by Tahal.

constant prices over the period. At the same time, growth was maintained despite the fact that more than half of Israel's farmers have taken up agriculture only in the last 15   157 years, most of them with little education and no previous farming experience. Domestic and industrial water supply has been extended; today even isolated villages in the hill and desert regions have piped water.

PRICES OF WATER. The production cost of water varies according to the distance from the sources of supply, the most expensive sources being in Upper Galilee and the Central Negev, and the height above sea-level of the place of consumption. About 10% of the water supply costs up to 10 agorot (about 2½ cents) per cubic metre; 50% costs 10–30 agorot, and 30% costs up to 40 agorot. Water supply is subsidized according to the nature of its use: in 1971/72 farmers paid 5–10 agorot per cubic meter, industry up to 20 agorot and domestic consumers up to 30 agorot. Charges and subsidies are regulated by an equalization fund operated by the Water Commissioner.

DESALINATION. Since Israel in the late 1960s was using 90% of its limited natural water resources—about 1,500

A reverse osmosis unit for the desalination of brackish water at the Hydronautics Israel Company, Reḥovot, 1970. Courtesy Government Press Office, Tel Aviv.

158

million cubic meters yearly—future economic development, especially in agriculture, would depend on desalted water. About 100 scientists and engineers were involved in desalination research in 1972, and about $1,000,000 was spent up to 1973. The desalting plants in operation in the late 1960s used four different methods: flash evaporation, freezing, vapor compression, and electrodialysis. Projected larger plants were expected to use either flash evaporation or electrodialysis.

From 1965, a dual-purpose multistage flash distillation plant at Eilat used oil fuel to produce 6,000 kilowatts of electric power and 7,000 cubic meters of desalted seawater a day. The plant is operated by the Israel Electric Corporation and supplies water to the southern part of the country to supplement the local brackish water sources and improve its quality by blending. A plant for the desalination of seawater by an original Israeli process, with an output capacity of 40 million cubic meters per day, is in the planning stage and is expected to start production in 1978.

A large nuclear dual-purpose seawater desalting plant is planned at Niẓanim, on the coast south of Tel Aviv, to produce, by the 1970s, some 300 megawatts of net salable electricity and 120 million cubic meters of desalted water a year. A joint U.S.-Israel feasibility study conducted by Kaiser Engineers–Catalytic Construction Company concluded in January 1966 that the plant was technically feasible: the cost of water would be between 7.6 and 17.7 cents per cubic meter with a fixed charge rate of between 5 and 10%.

Freezing processes were developed by the Israel Desalination Engineering Co. Ltd. The Zarchin[3] compressor is the main Israel contribution to these processes. It is a simple and cheap radial centrifugal compressor with a flexible bladed rotor. Research into, and development of, direct freezing under vacuum conditions, including a small pilot plant, were conducted at the company's headquarters

[3] Alexander Zarchin (1897–   ), Israel engineer and inventor

Installation of machinery at the Zarchin desalination plant in Eilat, 1967. Courtesy Government Press Office, Tel Aviv.

at Tel Barukh. A demonstration plant is in operation at Eilat. As from the 1960s plants were built on a commercial basis with a full guarantee, and are regularly exported to different parts of the world. A pilot plant based on a secondary refrigerant process using butane operates at Tel Barukh. The vapor compression process uses the Zarchin compressor at ordinary temperatures. Plants up to a capacity of 500 cubic meters a day were designed and built in the late 1960s. A 90-cubic-meter-a-day plant was sold to Spain in 1967, and a 125-cubic-meter-a-day plant to the Canary Islands in 1968.

Ten years of research and development work (1956–66) at the Negev Institute for Arid Zone Research culminated in the design, construction, and operation of a pilot plant in **160** Ze'elim that desalts 500 cubic meters a day of brackish water through electrodialysis. A demonstration plant producing 5,000 cubic meters a day (the largest in the world) was established at Mashabbei Sadeh in the Negev, with the cooperation of the United Nations. Basic research into the functioning of both natural and artificial membranes has been pursued, with promising results, during the 1960s, at the Weizmann Institute of Science at Reḥovot, and at the Hebrew University of Jerusalem. Reverse osmosis research was started in 1967 at the Negev Institute and a demonstration plant built in the Arabah Valley at Yotvatah to produce 200 cubic meters of desalted water a day from brackish water. At the Technion in Haifa, research is directed primarily toward heat- and mass-transfer problems through direct-contact heat exchange, the mechanism of scale formation and corrosion, and the linking of nuclear reactors to distillation plants.

9 AGRICULTURE

UNDER OTTOMAN RULE—1870–1917. A small number of Jewish peasant communities which had remained from ancient times, such as those in Peki'in, Shephar'am, and Kafer Yasif, were still in existence in Erez Israel at the end of the 19th and the beginning of the 20th century, but the first pioneers of modern Jewish agriculture had to start completely afresh in the last part of the 19th century. At the beginning of the 20th century, there were some 5,000 Jews in the new villages, most of them farmers, with over 250,000 dunams (4 dunams = 1 acre) at their disposal. The initial agricultural achievements of these settlements were limited, both in quality and quantity, due to inexperience and difficulty in acclimatization. Most of the farmers could not support themselves, and were largely dependent on the philanthropy of Baron Edmond de Rothschild, who initiated and encouraged wine production, with prices guaranteed, which were generally higher than current world prices. These factors encouraged widespread cultivation of vineyards, resulting in overproduction and large surplus stocks of wine. A serious crisis occurred at the beginning of the 20th century, and many vineyards were subsequently uprooted and replaced by olive groves and almond trees. The Zionist Movement gave new impetus to the development of agriculture in the country. The budget of its Palestine Office, which was opened in Jaffa in 1908 under the directorship of Arthur Ruppin[4], expanded from 208,000 French francs in its first year to about 7,000,000 francs in 1913. The Palestine Office helped found new settlements,

[4]Sociologist, "father" of Zionist settlement in Erez Israel (1876–1943)

Plowing a vineyard, Reḥovot, 1912. Courtesy Central Zionist Archives, Jerusalem.

including the Kinneret Farm, Deganyah, Merḥavyah, Ben Shemen, and Ḥuldah, and started plantations financed by private capital, Aḥuzzot in Migdal, Poriyah, and Sharonah in Lower Galilee, and Kefar Uriyah, Ruḥamah, Karkur, and Ein Ḥai.

UNDER BRITISH RULE—1917–48. After World War I Baron de Rothschild's officials encouraged the cultivation of vineyards and olive groves in the early settlements, while the ICA introduced grain crops in their settlements—first, because grain crops yielded from the first year, thus necessitating less outside financial help for the farmer; second, because this type of farm was less dependent on outside markets; and third, because Galilee soil was suitable for field crops. Soil cultivation was extensive, each settler working 200–300 dunams. The settlements of the Zionist Organization, on the other hand, were based on the principle of self labor (no hired workers) and were divided into six types of cultivation: 1) intensive grain cultivation on areas of 200–250 dunams; 2) mixed farming, especially milk production, on areas of 100 dunams; 3) unirrigated plantations of fruit trees, on areas of 60–70 dunams; 4) mixed irrigated farming, based on vegetable crops, fruit trees, fodder, and dairy cattle, on areas of 40 dunams; 5) intensive farming based on vegetable crops, on areas of 20 dunams; 6) auxiliary farms of the agricultural laborers living in the settlements, for various supplementary produce.

An important development in farming progress was the improvement in cattle breeding. The local or "Arab" cow, a thin animal (weighing 200–250 kg.) with a low milk yield (600–700 liters per year), fed on pasture with the addition of a little fodder could, if necessary, be used to work the fields. The Damascus cow, introduced by the German (Templer) farmers during the latter half of the 19th century, had a higher yield (up to 2,000 liters per year, and even more under superior conditions). This cow, crossed with the Friesian and bred over a long period, produced cows with a yield of 5,000–6,000 liters per year, and more under better conditions of keeping. The local breed of chicken, fed on farm waste and laying about 50 eggs a year, was replaced by the Leghorn, which, although requiring more feed, laid about three times as many eggs.

Work cattle were gradually replaced by tractors, combined harvesters, forage harvesters, hay balers, and maize-picking machines. Chemical fertilizers were introduced, methods of soil cultivation and crop rotation were improved, and new crop varieties were cultivated, with corresponding increases in yield. The relative scarcity of land area at the disposal of Jewish agriculture necessitated the intensification of farming methods, mainly through irrigation. Introduced at first only for citrus fruit, irrigation was utilized later for other crops, including vegetables, green fodder, and fruit trees. Winter crops in areas of low rainfall also began to receive supplementary irrigation. At first, irrigation was only applied in areas where there was an abundant water supply (the Jordan Valley, the Beth Shean Valley, and the Coastal Plain), but when additional subterranean water supplies were located in other parts of the country, irrigation was expanded, resulting in the production of two or more crops per year. Special attention was devoted to hill settlement, mainly in Judea and Galilee, even before the end of World War I. These farms at first concentrated on fruit-tree cultivation, but later cattle breeding was introduced and reached a high standard. In the early 1930s middle-class immigrants, particularly from Germany and Central Europe, started private mixed farms, concentrating on laying hens, fruit trees, and vegetables.

IN THE STATE OF ISRAEL—1948–72. Significant changes took place in agriculture with the establishment of the State of Israel (1948). There were increases in the area of land, both irrigated and unirrigated, in the amount of livestock per farm, and in crop and livestock production. Mechanization also increased; the use of chemical fertilizers and pesticides became widespread; agricultural exports grew; industrial crops were introduced; and a large number of new agricultural settlements were founded.

From the 1950s, Israel agriculture consistently tended toward greater specialization. The new agricultural settlements were no longer planned for mixed farming, as formerly, but were classified into two types: crop farms, growing industrial crops and vegetables on an area of 45 to 50 dunams of irrigated land per farmer; and citrus farms, with an allocation of 30 dunams per farmer, of which between a third and a half was to be devoted to citrus groves, and the rest to field crops. This latter type was to have no cattle, but each would have a hen run. Most of the veteran settlements bred dairy cattle.

In the 1950s and 1960s efforts were made to increase exports of other agricultural products, in addition to citrus. Cultivation of vegetables grown in hothouses and under plastic increased, with continuing extensive research and practical experience. There was also an increase in industrial crops, e.g., sugar beet, cotton, and groundnuts. The cultivation of flowers for export was introduced successfully. Although flower cultivation in Europe had increased, it was unlikely to meet the winter and spring demand because of the necessarily large investments in 165

Table 76. Land Under Cultivation in Israel (in thousand dunams)

	Total			Under irrigation		
	1948/49	1969/70	1971/72	1948/49	1969/70	1971/72
Field crops						
All farming	1,094	2,685	2,735	66	637	642
Jewish farming	877	2,153	2,180			634
Vegetables, potatoes and melons						
All farming	106	346	305	53	262	300
Jewish farming	66	267	301			263
Fruit-tree plantations						
All farming	355	855	865	150	678	694
Jewish farming	275	725	735			684
Fishponds						
All farming	15	54	56	15	54	56
Jewish farming	15	54	56			56
Miscellaneous						
All farming	80	180	184	16	96	98
Jewish farming	75	155	158			97
Total						
All farming	1,650	4,120	4,145	300	1,727	1,790
Jewish farming	1,310	3,354	3,430		1,681	1,734

Table 77. Local Food Production and Demand (in metric tons)

Commodity	1968/69 Production	1968/69 Consumption	1970/71 Production	1970/71 Consumption	1971/72 Production	1971/72 Consumption
Wheat	155,000	299,943	199,500	503,000	255,500	523,000
Potatoes	144,600	93,532	133,500	110,000	134,100	141,400
Sugar	22,630	99,915	26,000	175,000	23,700	180,000
Pulses, edible, dry	3,300	3,720	4,000	4,200	3,500	3,700
Vegetables	452,250	331,850	479,900	342,000	503,000	356,000
Bananas	53,000	48,000	56,600	39,590	41,800	30,146
Grapes	80,400	25,319	66,600	18,509	81,300	23,500
Miscellaneous fruit and deciduous	148,200	129,374	172,250	150,000	175,000	152,000
Meat	143,000	158,000	176,400	187,000	191,000	200,000
Eggs	1,115	930	1,303	995	1,298	960
Fish	21,900	22,200	26,100	22,949	26,100	24,063
Milk	470,666	201,077	476,000	160,000	498,900	180,000

Table 78. Cultivated Area and Production of Field Crops,
Vegetables and Orchards (1970 — 71)

Crop	Area in 1,000 (dunams)	Production in 1,000 (tons)
A. *Field crops*		
unirrigated—total	2,043	
Wheat	1,129	200
Barley	158	34
Pulses for grain	75	11
Hay	279	
Silage	37	
Sorghum	50	14
Cotton lint	45	2
Tobacco	19	1
Sunflowers	25	3
irrigated—total	618	
Sugar beet	40	237
Cotton lint	293	35
Groundnuts	56	19
Green fodder	156	
Silage	14	
B. *Vegetables and Potatoes*		
Total	277	765
Potatoes	55	142
Tomatoes	50	141
Cucumbers	30	38
Carrots	14	31
Onions	19	29
Eggplants	9	15
Marrows	10	11
Peppers and Gambas	17	26
Cabbage and flower	15	12
Artichokes	10	5
C. *Orchards*		
Total	855	
Citrus	426	1,513
Grapes	100	67
Stone fruit	92	147
Olives	103	13
Bananas	19	56
Subtropical fruits	31	23
Nuts and Almonds	31	3

Table 79. Israel Agricultural Produce, 1948—70 (in millions of Israel Pounds)

Fiscal year	1948	1949	1954	1959	1962	1964	1966	1970
All farming	44.4	56.3	307.4	749.5	1,161.3	1,355	1,623	2,509.9
Arab farming	2.8	5.1	24.2	40.6	58.3	78.7	129.5	116.7
Arab percentage of total	6.2	9.0	7.9	5.3	5.1	5.8	8.0	4.6

Cultivation of roses for export in a greenhouse at kibbutz
Mizra, northern Jezreel Valley. Courtesy Government Press
Office, Tel Aviv.

greenhouses and heating equipment. Israel's advantage in
this field is a short, warm growing season, insuring cheap
production, as the flowers may be grown with little or no
protective covering, and even in the open. Flowers raised
include gladioli, roses, irises, anemone, gerbera, and
carnations. Flower exports for 1972 were valued at
$9,400,000.

Following the decrease of grape production in the early
20th century, vineyards were again widely cultivated after
1948. In 1970/71 vineyards occupied an area of 100,000
dunams, of which 59,000 dunams were wine grapes, and
41,000 were table grapes. Overall grape production was
67,000 metric tons of which 30,000 metric tons were table
grapes, 37,000 metric tons wine grapes. Some of the table
grapes also went to the wine presses, so that a total
of 49,500 tons went for wine. In 1971 wine production,
170 including brandy and liqueurs, reached 23,000,000

Loading grapes for transport to the wine cellars in Zikhron Ya'akov. Courtesy Government Press Office, Tel Aviv.

Sheep being milked in a roundabout at kibbutz Sarid in the Jezreel Valley. Courtesy Government Press Office, Tel Aviv.

liters, of which 14,000,000 was table wine. Overall wine export for 1971 was 2,930,000 liters, almost all in table wines and sweet wines, with a value of $1,900,000. Half the exported wine went to the United States. After 1948 the cultivation of citrus fruits was greatly expanded, as was the cultivation of deciduous fruit trees and, during the latter 1960s, of sub-tropical fruits. The varied climates found in Israel permit the cultivation of a wide variety of fruit types, including citrus, grapes, bananas, apples, pears, plums, apricots, peaches, olives, almonds, mangoes, avocadoes, guavas, dates, pomegranates, quinces, and persimmons. About 80% of the fruit crop, including citrus, is raised on irrigated land.

Livestock breeding expanded, so that in 1971 the number of dairy cattle on Jewish farms reached 91,500 head, yielding over 520,000,000 liters of milk, 66,600 head of beef cattle, 105,000 sheep, 22,500 goats, and about 7,300,000 chickens laying 1,410 million eggs. Fishing also expanded. The total catch for 1970/71 was over 25,500 tons (see page 183).

Spraying fields with pesticide at kibbutz Ḥanitah, 1963. Courtesy J.N.F., Jerusalem.

172

Greater mechanization in all types of farming developed as a result of increased production and the rise of labor costs. In 1971 there were 18,535 tractors employed in agriculture, 980 hay balers, 570 combine harvesters, and 347 mechanical cotton pickers. The number of mechanical sprayers rose. Modern milking machines and packing plants came into use. Chemical fertilizers used in 1971/72 were the equivalent of 32,600 tons of nitrogen, 15,850 metric tons of phosphoric acid, and 11,500 metric tons of potash. The use of pesticides and herbicides was also greatly increased. Scarcity of water is the greatest problem in Israel agriculture. Irrigation farming is a necessity, and the water supply comes from internal water sources only, which collect quantities of from zero to 900 mm. precipitation per year. Since the establishment of the State of Israel, water consumption in agriculture rose from 257,000,000 cu. m. in 1948–49 to 1,335,000,000 cu. m. in 1970/71, out of a total quantity of 1,655,000,000 cu. m. of water consumed that year. Over 90% of the total water sources in the country are fully utilized; the other sources are technically and economically marginal. The amount of soluble salts in the water is an important factor in agriculture because of the sensitivity of certain crops to these salts. About 117,000,000 cu. m. of salt water were used, however, in 1970/71 for fishponds and industrial purposes.

At the beginning of 1972, the rural population (without the administered areas) totaled 538,000 in 807 villages—17.4% of the population. For Jews the figures were 275,000 in 707 villages—10.5% of the Jewish population. Over half the Jews living on the land were new immigrants who arrived after the establishment of the state, and two-thirds of the Jewish villages were established after that date. As in all developed countries, the number of agricultural workers is diminishing. In 1958 they constituted 15.7% of the labor force: in 1963, 11.5%, in 1969, 8.9%, and in 1972, 8%. Israel agriculture supplies the total domestic demand for vegetables, potatoes, fruits, milk, eggs and poultry: more than one-quarter of the demand for wheat and legumes; about 40% of the meat; about 70% of the fish; and over one-third of the demand for sugar.

Agricultural Education and Research. Agricultural training in Erez Israel preceded actual settlement, though the first agricultural school, Mikveh Israel, founded by Charles Netter in 1870, was the only such school for over 50 years. In 1924 the Meir Shefeyah Youth Village was founded; followed by the Ben Shemen Youth Village in 1927, the Kadoorie School in 1934, and the Pardes Ḥannah School in 1935. During the 1930s training farms for women (*mishkei po'alot*) were founded, which eventually became coeducational agricultural schools.

By the end of the 1960s there were 30 agricultural schools, sponsored by the state and by Zionist women's organizations (Pioneer Women, WIZO, Mizrachi Women), public bodies, and regional and local authorities. There is a state agricultural school at Rama to serve the non-Jewish population. The agricultural educational network numbered 29 schools in 1972, with 263 classes and 7,200 pupils. Agricultural schools, all of which have boarding facilities, provide students with both technical agricultural knowledge and a general academic education of matriculation standard, in addition to practical agricultural work on the school farm. Most of the pupils come from towns and development areas; girls constitute 30–40% of the enrollment. Graduates of the schools generally settle in agricultural communities, serve as village instructors, continue studying agricultural techniques, or study for a university degree in agriculture.

Higher education in agriculture is offered at the Faculty of Agriculture of the Hebrew University in Reḥovot, with an academic staff of over 100, some 550 students, and 70 research students in 1972, and at the Haifa Technion's Department of Agricultural Engineering, which had a staff of 42, some 235 students, and 11 research students in 1970/71. The Ruppin College in the Coastal Plain is also a center for education in various branches of agriculture.

Local agricultural extension, training and guidance, which was started in 1924 as a special department of the agricultural experimental station of the Zionist Organization, became a special service of the Ministry of Agriculture, and in 1968 maintained 11 regional offices. These offices deal with all branches of agriculture, including auxiliary fields like plant protection, mechanization, irrigation, home economics, and farming economics. The service employed some 550 instructors in 1970. In addition, the Jewish Agency gives instruction to new moshavim through local instructors who usually live in the moshavim themselves and are constantly in touch with the Ministry of Agriculture.

The first agricultural experimental station in Erez Israel was set up by Aaron Aaronsohn [5] at Athlit, before World War I, but was shut down with the outbreak of war. In the first decades of the 20th century the Mikveh Israel Agricultural School also played an important role in agricultural research. In 1921 Yizhak Elazari-Volcani (Wilkansky)[6], in conjunction with the Zionist Organization, started to set up experimental farms: at Ben Shemen, Deganyah, and Merhavyah, later at Gevat, and still later, the Mordekhai farm, all sponsored by an agricultural experimental station at Rehovot and Bet Dagon, which was eventually named the Volcani Institute for Agricultural Research. In 1970 the Institute had a staff of 1,210, of whom 283 were research scientists and assistants. The Mandatory government also established research stations at Acre, Jericho, Farouana, Beth-Shean, Beersheba, Majdal, and Fardieh near Safed. The Institute for Agricultural Studies was established by the Hebrew University in 1942, and later became the Faculty of Agriculture (1952). It carries out basic research in most spheres of modern agriculture. Agricultural research was also undertaken by

[5] Agronomist and natural historian (1876–1919)
[6] Agronomist, one of the planners of agricultural settlement in Erez Israel (1880–1955)

other research departments of the Hebrew University, by the Technion in its department for agricultural engineering, by the Institute for Arid Zone Research at Beersheba, and by the Veterinary Institute and Meteorological Service at Bet Dagon. The major research problems in Israel agriculture during the late 1960s included the need for water saving through development of more efficient irrigation systems, raising the yield and quality of crops, increasing production and reducing agricultural imports by developing suitable agricultural products, reducing output costs, and market research.

The Volcani Institute for Agricultural Research is organized in the following sections and divisions: soil and water, garden and field crops, fruit-tree plantations, livestock, plant protection, mechanization, food technology, and afforestation. The institute has three large research farms—the central farm at Bet Dagon, the Neveh Ya'ar farm for agrotechnical problems in the western Valley of Jezreel, and the Gilat farm for Negev farming problems. A number of other regional farms are sponsored by the institute, mostly in conjunction with regional councils and other public bodies, at Karei Deshe (for the improvement of natural pasture in Upper Galilee), Ein Dor (for research on grain crops in Lower Galilee), Gat (for research on grain crops in the south), Mivtaḥim (for research on problems of export crops in the sandy soil of the western Negev), and a study farm in Jerusalem, operated jointly with the Hebrew University (for finding methods of more efficient and profitable hill farming). The institute publishes a journal entitled *Ketavim,* offering the results of its research, which are also published in international scientific journals. In 1972, the Institute employed 860 workers.

Arab Sector. During the period preceding Jewish settlement, there was little difference between Arab agriculture in Erez Israel and that in neighboring countries. The same was true of the Mandate period, when a sharp contrast developed between Arab and Jewish agriculture, which existed side by side but were completely independent of one another. After World War II, and particularly after the establishment of the State of Israel, significant changes took place in the Arab economy. Branches of agriculture were altered and expanded; working methods were modernized; and the amount of land under irrigation was increased. In addition, mechanization was intensified and more chemical fertilization, pesticides, and weed killers utilized.

A significant factor was the labor market boom in the State of Israel, which drew Arab workers from the villages and offered them work in the citrus groves, in industry, or as construction laborers. This, together with increased agricultural mechanization, brought about a breakup of the traditional Arab village society and a considerable drop in the number of agricultural workers. An additional factor was the breaking up of some Arab farms into smaller units which, if not irrigated, could hardly assure the owner a reasonable livelihood. Nearly half the adult labor force in the Arab villages (including women) do not work the land, and some landowners lease their land in order to be free for more profitable non-agricultural work. In 1971 there were 23,200 Israel Arabs working in agriculture, forestry, and fishing (22% of Arab employees—about three times the percentage among Jews). Despite modernization, old and new still existed side by side on the Arab farm in the late 1960s: the ox-drawn wooden plow was worked beside the tractor-driven plow; the sickle and threshing sledge stood beside the combine harvester; seed was sown by hand alongside a mechanical broadcaster; weeds were hoed manually, as well as destroyed by chemical means. The most important agricultural products grown by Arab farmers in Israel at the end of the 1960s were as follows:

Field crops were the most extensive (555,000 dunams—about 140,000 acres—in 1971/72) and most valuable crops. There were considerable differences in the types of grain cultivated by Arabs and by Jews: while most of the wheat cultivated in Israel in 1970/71 (800,000 out of 1,132,000 dunams) was grown by Jews, Arabs cultivated 109,000 out

Table 80. Arab Agricultural Produce, 1970—71
(in Millions of Israel Pounds)

	Field crops	Vege- tables and potatoes	Citrus	Other fruit	Milk	Eggs	Meat	Miscel- laneous	Total
	21,7	31,7	5,6	15,7	13,0	1,3	23,6	4,1	116,7
Percentage of total	18.6	27.2	4.8	13.5	11.1	1.1	20.2	3.5	100.0

Bedouin plowing in the Negev in the 1940s. Courtesy J.N.F., Jerusalem.

of 158,000 dunams of barley. Arab farmers played an even greater role in tobacco, of which they grew 16,000 out of 19,000 dunams in 1970/71. Arabs also grew muskmelons and watermelons (21,000 dunams) by non-irrigation methods that are unique to their farms, and they produced nearly the entire Israel sesame seed crop. Arabs produced little industrial crops: they cultivated only about 17,000 dunams of sugar beet in 1970/71—without irrigation.

Arab irrigated farming in Israel totaled 56,000 dunams in 1971/72, as against 8,000 dunams for 1948-49. The crops produced were mainly vegetables and potatoes (37,000 dunams) and fruit trees (10,000 dunams). The most typical vegetables were tomatoes, eggplants, cucumbers and marrows, onions, garlic, okra, and beans. The most commonly cultivated fruits were the olive (82,000 dunams in 1971/72), table grapes (18,000 dunams), and stone fruit, such as peaches, apricots, and plums (5,000 dunams). Relatively little citrus was grown (5,000 dunams). The total Arab-owned land under fruit production, both irrigated and dry, was 130,000 dunams for 1971/72.

An Arab graduate of the Ruppin Agricultural School plowing his land at Kafr Qasim in the Ḥefer Plain, 1954. Courtesy Keren Hayesod, United Israel Appeal, Jerusalem.

There were few cattle on Arab farms. The total for 1971 was approximately 28,000 head, with milk production reaching 9,700 kiloliters. There were 250,000 laying hens, which produced 14 million eggs. However, sheep-raising was widespread, and in 1971, there were 75,000 sheep, as well as 111,000 goats. The number of animals raised by Arabs fluctuated considerably, because there was no irrigated grazing, and the numbers were affected by drought more seriously than on Jewish farms. In drought years Arab shepherds took their flocks to wetter areas. However, the growing demand for meat, eggs, and milk in the evolving Arab community, and the opportunities for marketing these products outside the village, resulted in improving conditions for increased livestock-rearing. Local breeds of cattle, goats, and chickens, which need little feeding, gave way to breeds which, though they require better fodder and care, produced better meat and showed an increased profit. Work animals such as the horse, the mule, and the camel were gradually replaced by tractors and combine harvesters.

The cultivation of vegetables under plastic cover, a process initiated in Israel during the 1960s, was also developed on Arab farms, and in 1968 this method of cultivation covered about 3,000 dunams. Arab farmers have also adopted cultivation of vegetables for industry and export, in an area of about 7,000 dunams. The development of irrigation works also progressed considerably. In contrast to other Asian countries, Arab agriculture in Israel was characterized by the large amount of land owned by the farmers themselves: about 85% of Arab farmers worked their own land, and the government rented many tracts of land to peasants who owned little or no land. Almost a third (31.4%) of agricultural land worked by Arabs is divided up into farms of 30 dunams or less, and these farms constituted over 70% of the total.

Judea and Samaria (the "West Bank"). The Samarian hills are extremely exposed, but are intersected by valleys whose soil is fertile and produces grain crops. Fruit trees, vineyards, and olive trees are cultivated on the hillsides, and the western slopes are gentle and suitable for cultivation. The hills of Judea are eroded and produce little vegetation, but the small valleys are fertile. There is a relatively high rainfall in the Hebron area (500–600 mm. annually), and the same applies to the hills of Jerusalem, where fruit trees are cultivated on the terraced slopes. Agriculture was rather primitive, and methods differed little from those practiced during the British Mandate. Some progress has been made in methods of working the soil, the quality of the seed, improved plant varieties and livestock breeds, and in the use of chemical fertilizers and pesticides. Nevertheless, there was little mechanization and the yield was low (100–110 kg. of wheat and barley per dunam). Land under cultivation in 1966 amounted to over 2,000,000 dunams (500,000 acres).

In 1970/71 the cultivated area totaled 2,670,000 dunams, of which wheat was grown on 450,000 dunams, barley on

West Bank Arabs cultivating vegetables under plastic cover, 1969. Courtesy Government Press Office, Tel Aviv.

225,000 dunams, and pulses, such as lentils, vetch, broad beans, and chick-peas, on 108,000 dunams. The total value of grain crops and pulses amounted to 2,878,000 dinars (over $8 million) in 1966 and IL25,500,000 (some $7,300,000) in 1970/71. Vegetable produce amounted to 3,672,000 dinars (about $10,681,600) on an area of 250,000 dunams in 1966 and IL32,000,000 (some $8,100,000) in 1970/71, the main vegetable crops being muskmelons and watermelons, tomatoes, cucumbers, potatoes, onions, runner beans, and eggplant. The value of the fruit crop was 4,500,000 dinars (about $12,600,000) in 1966 and IL86,000,000 (about $24,600,000) in 1970/71. Fruit was grown in the latter year on 710,000 dunams (compared with over 500,000 dunams in 1966). Over two-thirds (520,000 dunams) was devoted to olives, 62,000 dunams to grapes, 47,000 to almonds, 40,000 to figs, 22,000 dunams to citrus, and 20,000 to other fruit. Only 13% of the 23,000 head of cattle were Friesians, the rest being local breeds whose milk and meat production is poor. As in the rest of the Middle East, sheep were the commonest form of livestock on Judean and Samarian farms (379,000 head in 1966), followed by goats (268,000), with donkeys, mules, horses, and camels, mostly employed as work animals. In 1970/71 meat production totaled IL45,000,000, milk IL25,000,000, and eggs and miscellaneous IL7,000,000.

Out of 117,000 persons employed in Judea and Samaria in 1971, almost 40,000 were employed in agriculture—34% of the total, as against 21% of Israel Arabs working on the land. The total income originating in agriculture in the area was IL192,000,000 and the total product IL227,400,000.

Gaza Strip: The total area of land under cultivation in the Gaza Strip in 1969 was 210,000 dunams, of which one-third was given over to citrus groves. Citrus produce in 1970/71 totaled about 175,000 tons, of which 105,000 tons were shipped overseas and 45,000 tons were sent to Judea and Samaria and to Jordan. Other fruit cultivated included watermelons and pumpkins (5,000 dunams) and grapes (11,000 dunams). The main grain crops were barley (22,500 dunams) and wheat (5,000 dunams). The yield was relatively high, due to the adequate water supply, reaching 150 kg. of wheat and barley and 750 kg. watermelons per dunam. Vegetables were grown on about 19,000 dunams, with tomatoes the most important crop, yielding about 1,000 kg. per dunam. The value of agricultural produce in 1970/71 totaled IL106,000,000, including IL57,000,000 from citrus, IL12,600,000 from other fruit, IL11,800,000 from vegetables, and IL21,700,000 from livestock and livestock products. The total income arising from agriculture in the Strip was IL72,000,000.

Fisheries. *Pioneer Efforts.* At the beginning of the 20th century, all the fishermen—with the exception of a few in Tiberias—were Arabs; the early pioneers showed no interest in fishing. Between 1920 and 1936, repeated but unsuccessful attempts were made by small groups of *ḥalutzim* to earn a living as fishermen in the Mediterranean and Lake Kinneret. Lacking expierience and familiarity with local conditions, as well as the support of the community, they could not overcome the opposition of the Arab fishermen and master the unaccustomed and difficult work.

An upward turn came in 1936, when the Arab revolt broke out and Jaffa Port was paralyzed. A wave of enthusiasm for seafaring and fishing spread among the Jews: a port was built at Tel Aviv and the Jewish Agency set up a maritime department. Up to the end of the 1930s, on the initiative of the department and with its assistance, ten fishing villages (eight kibbutzim and two moshavim) were founded on the shores of the Mediterranean. The villagers intended to combine agriculture with fishing, but it soon transpired that a modern fishing village could not maintain itself without a proper harbor. After 25 years of effort they gave up the struggle: the original fishing villages turned into flourishing agricultural settlements and the Jewish fishing industry was transferred to the port cities. Nevertheless, this pioneering effort established the basis of modern deep-sea fishing in Israel, providing its first trained fishermen. Fishing in Lake Kinneret by Jews started in earnest with the founding of two kibbutzim on its shores: Ein Gev (1937) and Ginnosar (1938), which still engage in this among other pursuits. Fishing in Lake Huleh was started by the villagers of Hulatah and came to an end only in 1957, when the Huleh reclamation project was completed and the lake dried out. In 1970/71 the catch from all types of fishing reached 26,000 tons.

Sea Fishing. The first trawler was acquired by the Jewish Agency in 1937 and Italian instructors were engaged. It was a successful venture and 30 modern trawlers were operating in the Mediterranean by 1958. Owing to their exclusion from the fishing grounds off Turkey, the fleet was reduced to 16 trawlers in 1971, with Ashdod as their base and a yearly catch of 1,200 tons of high-quality fish. From 1957, after the opening of the Straits of Tiran as a result of the Sinai Campaign, Israel trawlers operated in the rich fishing grounds off the Ethiopian coast (by agreement with the Ethiopian government), with Eilat, 1,500 miles

Fishing vessels at the Kishon harbor near Haifa. Courtesy Government Press Office, Tel Aviv.

away, as their home port. Two trawlers were operating there in 1968 and eight more were under construction in 1969.

Sardines are the most plentiful fish along Israel's shores, but the Arab fishermen, using primitive methods, had a catch of only 500 tons. Under the guidance of Italian instructors, Israel introduced modern purse seine fishing. The catch is used primarily for canning and is sufficient for the country's sardine requirements. About 30 groups, numbering 300 fishermen, are engaged in this type of fishing, which is seasonal work lasting from April to

Carp ponds in the Ḥuleh Valley. Courtesy Government Press Office, Tel Aviv.

November, and about 100 small boats are engaged in in-shore fishing. They employ time-honored methods (gill nets, hooks, and traps), but their equipment is modern. The total catch in 1971 was 1,500 tons.

In 1971 three Israel boats were engaged in deep-sea trawling in the distant Atlantic with a total catch of 7,100 tons, and two in the Red Sea, with a catch of 400 tons.

The total marine catch in 1971 was 10,000 tons.

Lake Fishing. Up to 1948, the 200 Arab fishermen and a few Jews from the kibbutzim on the shores of Lake Kinneret (Sea of Galilee) had an annual catch of 350 tons. The number of Jewish fishermen was limited to 30 by the Mandatory authorities, who opposed their efforts to introduce more up-to-date methods. In 1948, during the

War of Independence, the Arab fishermen left and the work was taken up by Jews from Tiberias and new immigrants. In the period 1948 to 1967, the Kinneret fishermen, by carrying on their daily work in spite of dangers and losses, maintained Israel sovereignty over the lake, in the face of attacks by Syrian soldiers entrenched at the northeastern corner, which is the richest in fish. The Six-Day War (1967) relieved them of this constant threat and they thereafter fished in all parts of the lake.

There are six fishing boats, equipped with modern apparatus, and 40 groups of fishermen engage in in-shore fishing, also using modern equipment. The catch in 1970/71 was 2,300 tons, with a value of about IL4.1 million. There is a steady drive to improve and develop Kinneret fishing. A revolutionary step was taken when pelagic fishing and the purse seine were introduced. This brings in about 1,800 tons of Kinneret sardines for canning, as well as "Kinneret fish." The Ministry of Agriculture also carries out an intensive program of stocking the lake. While the introduction of carp was a failure, the annual addition of some two million Tilapia, or St. Peter's fish, of which 400 tons a year are caught, has met with great success. So has the grey mullet. As this fish does not breed in sweet water, millions of the young fish are caught in the Mediterranean and transferred to the Kinneret. Within two years they grow to a weight of two kg., and eventually reached five kg. and over—among the highest growth-rates in the world.

Fish Ponds. This branch of fishery utilizes land and water unfit for ordinary agriculture. The first experiments were made in 1938; by now the ponds cover an area of 14,000 acres and have become an integral part of the landscape. Pond fish represent 3.6 kg. out of 10 kg. per capita consumed in Israel annually. The principal fish bred in the ponds is carp, which is not particular in its tastes and feeds on grain and food waste. St. Peter's fish and grey mullet are bred together with the carp. As they each require a different kind of food, a maximum use of land and water is achieved. As Israel's climate is suitable for year-round fish-breeding **187** and the most up-to-date methods are used, the yield is among the highest in the world—200 kg. per dunam as against 60 to 70 kg. in European ponds; some ponds achieve record crops of 350 to 400 kg. per dunam. Israel shares its know-how in this field with foreign countries. Fish ponds are mostly run by kibbutzim in Galilee, the valleys, and the Coastal Plain. The yield in 1970/71 was 12,800 tons, valued about at IL34 million.

Off the Gaza Strip and Northern Sinai. The Gaza Strip coast is the richest fishing ground on the shores of the Land of Israel. Fishermen operate mainly from Gaza, but also from Deir al-Balah, Khan Yunis, and Rafa. The main offshore fish are sardines, which are caught with purse seines, or, in the case of larger fish, with long lines. After the Six-Day War, the equipment was modernized and the cotton nets replaced by nylon ones with the aid of the Israel authorities. Lake Bardawil, a salt-water lake separated from the Mediterranean by a narrow bank, is rich in carp, mullet, and gilt-headed bream, which are caught mainly at the three gaps in the bank. Under Egyptian rule fishing was conducted by an Egyptian concessionnaire, as well as by local inhabitants and Bedouin using antiquated gill, drag, and trammel nets. A Nahal outpost, Nahal Yam, was established at the end of 1967 as a fishing village on the lake shore. In 1971 IL3,200,000 worth of fish were caught off the Gaza Strip shore and in the 1969/70 season 213 tons of fish were exported, as against 80 tons in 1968/69.

10 AFFORESTATION

HISTORICAL SURVEY. In biblical times when the Israelites took possession of the largely mountainous land of Canaan, they found there many forests, testified to by dozens of species of woodland trees and shrubs referred to in scripture such as: the oak, the terebinth, the cedar, the cypress, the acacia, the tamarisk, etc. It is known that the word *erez*, mentioned 70 times in scripture, refers also to other coniferous trees. Scripture indicates four regional forests: "the forest of the *negev*" (= south); "the forest of Ephraim" (similar to it being the forest of Gilead), the "forest of Carmel" and "the forest of Lebanon," as well as a local forest, "the forest of Hereth." The geographical boundaries of the forest of the *negev* and the forest of Lebanon are now obscure. This is not so in the case of the forests of Ephraim and Carmel which fell into the possession of the tribes of Ephraim and Manasseh. Their geographical borders are known. The forest of Ephraim on the Samarian hills extends over about a million dunams (250,000 acres) and was of the Tabor oak group. The forest of Carmel in the possession of the tribe of Manasseh extended over about one and a half million dunams (375,000 acres), and was composed of the oak group in the hills and the group of Jerusalem pines on Mt. Carmel.

The majority of these forests were cut down to develop the land on which they grew for economic agriculture (Josh. 17:18), and a minority during Israel's war of conquest (Deut. 20:19–20) and in the course of the First and Second Temple periods, for building fortifications and bastions. The forests declined and their place was taken by the lowly wood, which through supplying timber for building, for furniture, and for all manner of objects, was also used for grazing flocks, especially goats, and given no protection to preserve it. New forests were not planted and they continued to decline.

The forests were ravaged by the Arab conquerors, who brought with them flocks of sheep in abundance. The condition of the forests at the time of the Crusades was described as poor in comparison with the biblical era, when most of the mountains were covered. The impoverishment of forest and woodland continued also afterward and only wretched remnants remained here and there as is testified by Conder[7] in his report to the Palestine Exploration Society in the last quarter of the 19th century: "According to the indications scattered throughout the whole country it is apparent that recognizable changes took place in the wild vegetation leading to a decrease in the trees. Man, not nature, has destroyed the quality of the soil. Hence only by man's labor can the land be revived and restored to its previous agricultural fertility." Only a few years elapsed and that man, in the guise of the pioneering Jew returning to his homeland, appeared. With him began the improvement of the land.

Modern Period—1870–1970. Of the State of Israel's 20,255,000 dunams (5,063,750 acres), 3,600,000 dunams (15%) have been classified as forest terrain unfit for agricultural use. These areas have thin topsoil, or are rocky, sandy, or steep and eroded. Of the forest terrain, 47% is in the hills, 44% in the northern Negev, and the rest in the Plain of Sharon and other lowlands. Before 1870 the forest terrain consisted solely of ancient indigenous vegetation that had regenerated naturally after destruction by felling, burning, or grazing. At the end of the 19th century this natural forest still extended over 750,000 dunams, although a large part had been depleted with the increase in population and subsequent clearance of land for agriculture, grazing, and fuel. By the late 1960s natural forest

[7] British army officer in charge of the survey of Western Palestine (1848–1910)

covered an area of 570,000 dunams, of which 210,000 dunams were in Upper Galilee, 140,000 in Lower Galilee, 80,000 in Samaria (mostly on the Carmel Range), and 140,000 in Judea. These natural forests consist of Jerusalem pine *(Pinus halepensis Mill)*, common on the Carmel Range; Tabor oak *(Quercus ithaburensis Boiss.)*, common on the Coastal Plain, the hill regions of Samaria, and Lower Galilee; oak and terebinth, of which the dominant species are the common oak *(Quercus calliprinos Webb)* and the Palestine terebinth, which are most abundant in the hill regions; and carob and pistachio, which are common on the coastal sands and foothills up to a height of 400 meters. In the Negev and the Arabah Valley, tamarisk acacia, and zizyphus may still be found.

In the 1870s Charles Netter introduced the eucalyptus tree, a native of Australia, into the Mikveh Israel agricultural school grounds, and this tree was propagated in the Jewish settlements founded on the Coastal Plain after 1880. Between 1880 and 1890, the farmers of Petaḥ Tikvah planted a eucalyptus forest over hundreds of dunams of swampland to the northwest of their village. In the 1890s the settlers of Ḥaderah planted 3,000 dunams of eucalyptus. Its satisfactory acclimatization, rapid spread, and usefulness in draining malaria-breeding swamps also popularized the eucalyptus in the Galilee settlements. Many dunams were planted at Yesud ha-Ma'alah near Lake Ḥuleh and in an extensive belt north of Rosh Pinnah. Groves were also planted in the deep sandy soil of Reḥovot in Judea. Casuarina and strains of acacias, also from Australia, were planted to form avenues and windbreaks. Members of the German Templer movement reforested the slopes and central heights of the Carmel, supplementing the growths of Jerusalem pine with stone pine *(P. pinea)* grown from seeds obtained from the Lebanon. They sowed directly instead of using the then customary method of transplanting saplings. At the end of the decade, the hill areas of Ben Shemen and Ḥuldah were planted with pine and cypress.

Jewish National Fund afforestation projects near Kiryat Gat, 1966. Courtesy J.N.F., Jerusalem.

The technique of planting in varying formations—forest, grove, or belt—adopted by the new Jewish settlements was increasingly utilized after World War I. The Mandatory government promoted forest conservation and afforestation of wasteland. In 1920 a department of agriculture and forests was set up. Legislation to preserve forest trees from despoliation was enacted, forest tree nurseries were established, and many forests were planted in the hill regions and along the sandy coast. A separate department of forestry was established in 1936. By 1945, 30,000 dunams had been afforested. The Palestine Jewish Colonization Association (PICA) also sponsored afforestation, generally restoring the natural forest. Many eucalyptus groves were planted by individual landowners. From 1919 the Jewish National Fund (J.N.F.) undertook a systematic program of afforestation. The program was financed by a tree fund established by the Zionist Organization after the death of Theodor

Herzl to plant Herzl forests and groves around new

settlements. Many of the J.N.F. forests commemorate personalities such as Balfour, Einstein, and George V of England, or communities and historical events. Up to the establishment of the state in May 1948, the area thus afforested covered 62,000 dunams. A further 24,000 dunams of eucalyptus plantations were privately financed.

The Israel government recognized the importance of afforestation for amelioration of wasteland and for providing work for new immigrants preparatory to agricultural settlement. Forests and belts were planted for protection along the frontiers of the country and for both protection and shade along the highways. The J.N.F. also extended its own activities, especially in the northern Negev, and planted windbreaks in this arid zone at set intervals to protect the settlers, farm animals, and crops from the prevailing strong east winds which erode the soil and dry out the natural moisture. These projects included plantations of carob, the pods of which serve as foodstuff. Large nurseries were established where millions of saplings were grown annually. The acclimatization of new trees, experiments to develop better techniques in the nurture of saplings, and research into various branches of forestry were also undertaken. New strains of pine (*P. brutia* and *P. canariensis*) and eucalyptus *(gomphocephala)* have been successfully introduced. The latter, of Australian origin, has flourished in chalky soils and in the torrid areas of the northern Negev. Attempts have been made to introduce the Atlantic cedar in hilly areas.

Through the J. N. F. and the Israel government, up to 5,000,000 saplings have been planted annually, and by the late 1960s totalled 85 million over an area of 350,000 dunams, excluding trees used for avenues and private groves.

An agreement between the government and the J.N.F. gave the latter, in 1959, the authority to carry out all afforestation work. Forestry research, however, is conducted by the Institute of Agricultural Research of the Ministry of Agriculture. The total afforested area in Israel, **193**

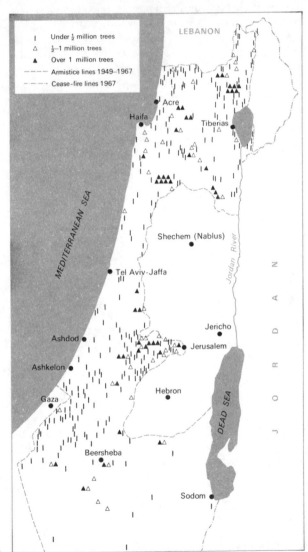

	Under ½ million trees
△	½–1 million trees
▲	Over 1 million trees
---	Armistice lines 1949–1967
·--·	Cease-fire lines 1967

LEBANON

MEDITERRANEAN SEA

Acre

Haifa

Tiberias

Shechem (Nablus)

Jordan River

Tel Aviv-Jaffa

Jericho

Ashdod

Jerusalem

Ashkelon

Hebron

Gaza

DEAD SEA

J O R D A N

Beersheba

Sodom

194

including various private groves, covered over 550,000 dunams in 1970/71 and a further 1,500,000 dunams were scheduled for afforestation.

11 ENERGY SOURCES

ELECTRICITY. There was absolutely no supply of electricity in the country under Ottoman rule. The first generating stations for adequate supply of electricity were established during the early Mandate period by the Palestine Electric Corporation (incorporated in 1923), which was founded and directed by Pinḥas Rutenberg[8], in connection with a comprehensive scheme for utilizing the country's water resources for electric power generation and irrigation. One of the main features of this scheme was the conservation of the abundant winter flow by creating storage reservoirs. In September 1921 the Crown Agents for the Colonies entered into an agreement with Rutenberg for granting of a concession for the utilization of the rivers Jordan and Yarmuk and their affluents with exclusive rights to generate and supply electric energy in the entire territory of Palestine including Transjordan, except the Jerusalem area. In pursuance of this agreement a concession was granted to the Palestine Electric Corporation Ltd. From the early years the main object was to facilitate the growth of the economy of the country and the expansion of its capacity to absorb immigration. The first Tel Aviv power station was erected in 1922–23, with an initial capacity of 1,000 hp. Diesel plants were installed in 1924–25 at Haifa and Tiberias, while the capacity of the Tel Aviv plant was gradually extended to 4,000 kws.

Construction work began in 1928 on a hydroelectric power scheme on the river Jordan and the plant was commissioned in 1932. The basic feature of the project was

[8] Yishuv leader and pioneer of modern industry in Israel (1879–1942)

Electric power plant across the Jordan at Naharayim, built in 1928 under the direction of Pinḥas Rutenberg. Courtesy Jewish National Fund, Jerusalem.

the use of Lake Kinneret as a storage reservoir. The power station was located a short distance below the junction of the Yarmuk and Jordan rivers, the waters of which were diverted by means of two dams and two canals to the headrace of the powerhouse. A regulating dam, with large sluice gates, built across the Jordan below its outlet from Lake Kinneret, facilitated the retention of the winter flow of the Upper Jordan in the lake, as well as the regulation of the outflow from it. The power station was built for four turbines of 8,500 hp each, of which three units were installed. The turbines were directly coupled to the electric generators, which supplied current via transformers to the high-tension transmission lines.

The first steam-driven power station was built in 1934 at Haifa and has since been extended several times. It is situated on the shore of the Mediterranean, assuring unlimited supplies of cooling water and, thus, the possibility of unrestricted expansion. The present generating

The Reading power station in Tel Aviv in 1969, with Reading D under construction in the foreground. Courtesy Government Press Office, Tel Aviv.

capacity is over 500,000 kws. The second steam-power plant, named after the first Lord Reading[9], who was chairman of the board of directors of the corporation until his death in 1936, was built in 1937 near Tel Aviv, also directly on the Mediterranean shore. The basic features of the Reading station were the same as in Haifa. Originally built for three turbogenerators of 12,000 kws., it was later extended to house two more units of 50,000 kws. each, and

[9] British statesman (1860–1935)

Table 81. Electricity Development

	1948	1958	1969	1971	Index 1948=100
Generating capacity (mw)	70	360	1,012	1,410	2,014
Peak demand (megawatts)	65	320	944	1,285	1,977
Power output (million kwh)	314	1,720	5,903	7,330	2,344
Consumers (end of year in thousands)	129	491	882	949	735
Annual Consumption (millions of kwh)					
Industry	70	466	1,715	2,119	3,027
Water pumping	75	472	1,187	1,428	1,904
Domestic consumers, etc.	101	513	2,166	2,781	2,753
Total consumption	246	1,451	5,068	6,328	2,570
Consumption per capita (kwh)	366	710	1,760	2,077	567

was extended in 1970 by another unit of 215,000 kws. (Reading D) and a second, similar unit was under construction. The third steam-power plant was erected in 1955–56 further south on the Mediterranean shore, where a few years later the town and harbor of Ashdod were established. This station has a capacity of 300,000 kws. and is to be further extended by 450,000 kws.

For the supply of electricity in the Jerusalem area, a separate concession, granted by the Turkish authorities before World War I, was acquired by a British firm, the Balfour-Beatty Company, which formed in Palestine the Jerusalem Electric and Public Service Corporation in 1928. The company erected a diesel power station in Jerusalem, but with the development of the city and the growth of its population, the local company could no longer meet the needs of the area. (After the occupation of East Jerusalem by Transjordan (1948) a separate company was formed for that part of the city.) From 1951 the Israel Electric Corporation supplied electricity to Jewish Jerusalem and its water-supply network. At the end of 1954 it acquired all the shares of the Jerusalem company, which then became its subsidiary. A high-tension transmission line to Jerusalem was erected together with a large transformer station on the outskirts of the city. The supply of electricity to Jerusalem thus became a component part of the overall supply to the entire country.

The capacity of the power stations in Israel has been increased twentyfold since 1948 to 1,410,000 kws. in 1971. All power stations are connected to the high-tension transmission system which covers the entire country; a separate plant installed at Eilat has also been linked to the national grid. The Corporation has always endeavored to assist the active advancement of agriculture and industry; this policy finds expression in intensive rural electrification and low charges for electricity used for irrigation and for industry. In 1955 the ownership of the Corporation was transferred to the State; its name was changed to Israel Electric Corporation in 1961. The Ministry of Development is responsible for planning the expansion of electric generating capacity and the regulation of the production, distribution, and utilization of electricity.

OIL AND GAS. *Exploration and Production.* A petroleum product that was known in ancient Erez Israel was asphalt, or bitumen, which was found in natural seeps in the Dead Sea region. The material is mentioned by Strabo [10] (*Geography*, 16, 2:44), Josephus [11] (Ant., 1:171ff.), and Pliny the Elder as *"Bitumen judaicum."* It was natural therefore that the first oil explorations in the country, which were undertaken before World War I, centered on the Dead Sea.

A comprehensive geological survey of western Palestine was first carried out by F. J. Fohs in 1919 for the Zionist Organization, but a detailed report, mentioning 23 potential oil-bearing structures, was published only in 1927. During 1922–23, an expedition of the Turkish Petroleum Co. (subsidiary of the Anglo-Iranian Oil Co.) carried out a survey of the southern Jordan Valley and the Dead Sea region and a report by B. K. N. Wyllie (see bibliography) was published. In 1939 Petroleum Development of Palestine (P.D.P.), a subsidiary of the Iraq Petroleum Company, obtained from the government of Palestine 24 licenses for oil exploration, covering most of the country. The company prepared some geological maps of the Negev and a gravity map of the Coastal Plain. The P.D.P. also did wildcat drilling near Ḥelez (then Ḥuleiqat). In 1940 the government granted two licenses south of the Dead Sea to the Jordan Exploration Company, but its operations were terminated with the establishment of the State of Israel in 1948.

The Petroleum Law adopted by the Knesset in 1952 and amended in 1952 and 1965 divides the country into four areas, in each of which individual licenses are restricted to 400,000 dunams (100,000 acres) for a period of three years, extendable to seven. A company may hold no more than

[10] Greek historian and geographer (1 cent. C.E.)
[11] Jewish historian (c. 38–after 100 C.E.)

three licenses in each of the areas and not more than 1,000,000 dunams in all. If oil is discovered, the holder of the license may obtain a production lease for a 250,000-dunam area. The government takes 12.5% in royalties on production. Nine companies were formed and spent several years in oil exploration; several are still in operation.

The main oil field is at Ḥeleẓ, some 35 mi. (55 km.) south of Tel Aviv and 7 mi. (11 km.) east of the coast. Drilling was started in 1947 by P.D.P. but was terminated early in 1948, due to the outbreak of hostilities, at a depth of 3,600 ft. (1,105 m.) It was resumed in 1955 by Lapidoth Israel Oil Prospecting Co., which struck oil at 5,000 ft. (1,500 m.) in lower cretaceous sands. Thirty-seven wells have been drilled in the field since, and 22 were in operation in 1970. Up to January 1968 the field yielded 7,770,000 barrels of crude oil, remaining reserves being estimated at 7,000,000 barrels. The Bror field is a southern extension of the Ḥeleẓ field. The first producing well was drilled in 1957. Of 11 wells, four were productive until January 1968, producing 700,000 barrels, and one was in operation in 1970. Oil was struck at the Kokhav field, a northern extension of Ḥeleẓ, in September 1962. Eleven out of 24 wells are productive and, up to January 1968, produced 2,700,000 barrels; in 1970, 16 wells

Table 82. Total Production of Crude Oil and Gas in Israel

| Year | Crude Oil | | Gas | |
	Tons	Barrels	Cu. m.	Fuel Equiv. in Tons
1956	22,280	160,648	—	—
1961	133,945	970,300	5.5	5,000
1963	150,667	1,089,300	13.2	12,000
1965	202,000	1,455,000	77.0	70,000
1967	130,000	932,626	110.0	100,000
1969	101,381	725,000	145.2	132,000
1970	75,965	538,953	134.0	122,000
1971	62,153	444,471	124.0	113,000

were in operation. Oil was struck at the Negbah field, northeast of Ḥeleẓ, in 1960. Only one of the six wells drilled is productive. The license is owned by Lapidoth.

The gas fields of Zohar, Kidod, and Kanna'im are near Arad, approximately at the border between the Judean Desert and the Negev. Gas was encountered at Zohar for the first time in July 1958. Five of the seven wells drilled are gas producing. The field covers some 4 sq. mi. (10 sq. km.) and its reserves are estimated at 55 billion cu. ft. Gas was found at the Kidod field, which covers about 2 sq. mi. (5 sq. km.) in 1960, and in 1970, two wells were in operation. Reserves are estimated at 8–15 billion cu. ft. The Kanna'im field, some 4.3 mi. (7 km.) west of the Dead Sea, was opened up in November 1961. Of its three wells, only one is in operation. Exploratory drilling has been carried out in the areas of Ashkelon, Gurim (east of the Zohar field where signs of oil have been found), Revivim-Lahav, south of Beersheba, Netanyah, Caesarea, and other places. The first offshore well was drilled in 1970 by Belco at Barbur, 10 mi. (16 km.) west of Ashkelon, in 260 ft. (80 m.) of water. Offshore exploration is also carried out by Lapidoth, Naphtha, Israel National, Mayflower, and others.

CONSUMPTION, REFINING, AND MARKETING. The consumption of petroleum and its products in the country has been continously on the rise, reflecting the steady expansion of the economy. Until World War I the only petroleum product marketed was kerosene, which was used for domestic purposes and in the pumping engines of the citrus groves; the demand did not exceed a few thousand tons. With increased Jewish immigration and settlement, consumption of petroleum products increased notably, as seen from Tables 83, 84. Since the construction of the Haifa Refineries in 1939 by the Anglo-Iranian Oil Company, only crude oil has been imported. After expansion and modernization, the refineries, which were acquired by the Israel government in 1958, produce 6,000,000 tons a year (120,000 barrels per day). They have facilities for cracking, plateforming, desulfurization, and the manufacture of lubri-

Table 83. Consumption of Petroleum Products in Metric Tons

Year	Metric tons
1866	466
1910	8,000
1913	10,000
1937	200,000
1948	350,000
1951	859,000
1961	1,978,900
1969	4,151,300
1971	5,510,000

Table 84. Consumption of Petroleum Products in Israel
(in thousands of metric tons)

	1951	1961	1968	1969	1971
Gasoline	172.9	212.9	393.2	437.4	565.0
Kerosene	111.5	192.9	374.5	444.0	632.0
Gas and diesel oil	126.8	330.0	640.8	719.3	1,020.0
Fuel oil (light and heavy)	422.9	1,149.8	2,127.9	2,216.2	2,815.0
Bitumen	22.8	41.4	114.7	126.1	160.0
L.P.G.	2.1	45.4	104.1	112.9	192.0
Others	–	5.7	90.8	94.4	126.0
Total	895.0	1,978.1	3,846.0	4,151.3	5,510.0

cants. To meet rising local demand and export possibilities, a second plant, planned to start production in 1973 and reach an output of approximately 3,000,000 tons per year (60,000 barrels per day), is under construction at Ashdod.

Among the products manufactured by the Haifa Refineries are liquefied petroleum gases (L.P.G.), gases for the petrochemical industry (e.g., butane and ethylene), 83 octane and 94 octane benzine, domestic kerosine, jet fuel, gasoil, mazut, asphalt, and lubricating base oils. Polyethylene and carbon black are manufactured in subsidiary petrochemical plants. Until 1948 the Haifa Refineries obtained their crude oil via the Kirkuk-Haifa pipe line. After the establishment of the state, this line was disused and crude oil was brought by tankers to the Haifa port terminal. Since 1957 oil has been brought to Eilat and piped to Haifa via a 16-inch pipeline. Since 1970 a 42-inch pipeline has been in operation from Eilat to Ashkelon. In 1973 the pipeline had a capacity of some 40 million tons a year, and it was planned that this would grow to 60 million tons. The local market is supplied by Paz (formerly Shell Oil), Sonol (formerly Mobiloil), and Delek, the Israel Fuel Corporation, established in 1957, which have central installations at Haifa Bay and numerous supply stations and depots throughout the country. "White" products (gasoline, kerosene, and solar oil) are distributed via the "white pipeline," which has terminals near Tel Aviv, Ashdod, Beersheba, and Jerusalem.

ATOMIC ENERGY. Development of atomic energy in Israel was initiated even before the War of Independence (1948–49) was over, and by the late 1960s research and development in all fields of atomic energy represented one of the major national research efforts. Successive Israel governments recognized the importance of atomic energy to a small developing country with limited natural resources and continued support for research and development has thus been assured.

The initial phase of atomic energy development in Israel consisted of two enterprises. The first was a survey of the natural resources of the country, particularly with respect to the nuclear raw materials uranium and thorium. The survey, which took about three years and was executed jointly by the army and the Weizmann Institute of Science, failed to discover any rich deposits of these materials. However, low-grade deposits, primarily associated with phosphate rocks, were located. In the course of the survey, other mineral deposits were discovered, some of which were commercially exploited (for example, copper at Timnah and phosphates at Oron).

The second enterprise was the initiation of a training program to provide the necessary scientific and technical staff for possible application of atomic energy to the national economy. This training program, which is still in operation, initially consisted of sending groups of scientists to study in various countries abroad (primarily the U.S., U.K., and France). Gradually more and more of the training was provided in Israel, and for this purpose research was initiated at existing institutions and special facilities were set up for the study of various aspects of atomic energy.

As a natural follow-up to the resources survey, research and development work was initiated in the early 1950s on the extraction of uranium from phosphate rock. Another research project which was launched at about the same time related to the production of heavy water. Since there was, at the time, no special atomic energy research center in Israel, these projects were carried out at facilities provided by the Weizmann Institute of Science. Not only were they valuable for their potential practical application, but they also provided the first opportunity to gather together in Israel a professional team for research in atomic energy problems.

The next phase was the establishment of the Israel Atomic Energy Commission in 1952. Its first chairman was the chemist Ernst David Bergmann and its director of research was the physicist Israel Dostrovsky. After reorganization in 1966, the prime minister became the chairman of the commission, and Professor Dostrovsky was appointed its director-general. The members of the commission include men prominent in science, technology, and industry, as well as senior civil servants. The commission advises the prime minister on nuclear research and development and supervises the execution of policy decisions. It functions through a number of subcommittees for research, power and water, and applications of radiation and
radioisotopes.

Inserting neutron detection apparatus in the core support bridge at the Naḥal Sorek Atomic Reactor, 1960. Courtesy Government Press Office, Tel Aviv.

One of the first acts of the commission was to recommend the establishment of research centers specifically for atomic energy development. The first such center was located in temporary quarters near Reḥovot, and later moved to its present site at Sorek. The major facility at the Sorek Research Center is a 5 Mw swimming-pool-type reactor acquired with the assistance of the U.S. under the 1955 Atoms for Peace program. This reactor became operational in 1960. Other facilities at Sorek include hot laboratories, and research laboratories for physics and chemistry, as well as health-physics, electronics, and 207 mechanical services. A Radioisotope Training Center, a joint Weizmann Institute–Israel Atomic Energy Commission venture, was also established at Sorek to provide basic training in the techniques and applications of radioactivity. In the course of time, these subjects became part of the regular syllabus in Israel's educational institutions, and the special training program was discontinued. A second nuclear research center was established at Dimonah, some 40 km. S.E. of Beersheba. It was designed to provide better facilities for technological research in nuclear power and desalting as well as more extensive laboratories for basic research and training. The main facilities there include a 24 Mw natural-uranium heavy-water reactor with extensive experimental facilities. In addition, the center has hot laboratories, and engineering, chemical, and physical research laboratories.

The aim of the research and development program is to acquire the technology and fundamental knowledge of nuclear science and to apply these as early as possible to the advancement of the country. The research program covers, therefore, a broad spectrum of activities extending from basic research to technological development. The commission also supports research at various institutions of higher learning in the country. Research is carried out in nuclear, solid state, and reactor physics; physical and inorganic chemistry (particularly of the actinides); reactor and chemical engineering, metallurgy and radiation biology. The commission's nuclear safety committee recommends safety practices to be followed in nuclear work, and approves sites for nuclear installations.

National services provided by the Commission include film-badge service and a radioactive waste disposal service for hospitals and other institutions. Radioactive isotopes are produced and distributed throughout the country for application in medicine, industry, agriculture, and hydrology. Both the irradiation of a number of agricultural products with a view to prolonging storage life, and the radiation sterilization of medical supplies, are being exploited commercially. An important application of radiation is in the possible eradication of the Mediterranean fruit fly, a major pest in Israel, by the sterile male technique.

Israel is a member of the International Atomic Energy Agency (Vienna) and participates actively in various international programs. Her experts have been sent to various countries (Brazil, Costa Rica, Formosa, Greece, Kenya, Rumania, and Uganda) to help in establishing atomic energy programs or to help in various applications. International courses held in Israel àt the Sorek Nuclear Research Center have included: the effects of radiation in biological systems; a radioisotope training course for high school teachers; an advanced interregional course on cellular and molecular aspects of radiobiology; and a training course in radiation biology. Israel has agreements with the following countries for cooperation in atomic energy research and development: Argentina, Brazil, Chile, Mexico, Peru, the Philippines, Thailand, and Uruguay.

12 MINERAL RESOURCES

HISTORICAL SURVEY. The natural resources of Erez Israel have been exploited since ancient times. The country is rich in flint strata, which supplied raw material for artifacts in prehistoric times, and large numbers of flint tools are found throughout the land, particularly in the Negev. Iron and copper are known from the Bible, where the country is described as "A land whose stones are iron and out of whose hills thou shalt hew copper" (Deut. 13:9), and asphalt was known in the Dead Sea area in the days of the Patriarchs—"The Valley of Siddim was dotted with bitumen pits" (Gen. 14:10; the "clay" or "slime" of these pits is traditionally interpreted as bitumen). There is archaeological evidence of copper production in the Arabah in ancient times, although archaeologists disagree as to the exact period (surveys by Glueck [12] 1937, Tylecote et al. 1967). Iron and copper crucibles were found at various sites in the country (Tell Jamma', Timna, etc.). Glass was manufactured by the Phoenicians of Tyre and Sidon, on the northwestern border of Erez Israel; the manufacture of ceramics was extensively developed; and much pottery has been found in archaeological excavations. Building was based mostly on the raw materials available in each area: stone masonry in the mountainous regions and mud brick for the houses on the Coastal Plain.

Clay quarries for the pottery industry, lime kilns, and primitive stone quarries were common before the modern Jewish settlement in the 19th and 20th centuries. The first modern industry to use local mineral resources, including

[12] U.S. archaeologist (1900–1971)

gravel pits and modern lime kilns, was that of building materials. In 1925 the first chalk quarry for the production of cement was opened at the foot of Mt. Carmel. Salt from Mt. Sodom was mined even in ancient times, and in 1911 research was undertaken to determine the possibilities of exploiting the Dead Sea salts. Production of these salts began at the northern end of the Dead Sea in 1931 and at the southern end in 1937.

After 1948 natural resources and the industries based upon them became among the most important sources of employment and livelihood in the Negev. Among the larger projects there are the Timna copper mines, the Dead Sea Works at Sodom, and the phosphate works at Oron, Zefa Efeh, and Ha-Makhtesh ha-Katan.

TIMNA COPPER DEPOSIT. It is believed that the Timna copper deposits are a syngenetic sedimentary formation, which occurs in the sandstones and silts of the Nehushtan Formation and in the shales of the overlying Mikhrot Formation (Bartura 1966), both of Early Cambrian Age. Locally the lowermost part of the overlying Lower Variegated Nubian Sandstone is also mineralized. In 1949, in the course of the geological mapping of the Negev, Professor Ya'akov Bentor discovered the deposit that is now being exploited. In the Timna and Punon (Wadi Faynan, Transjordan) areas, copper was manufactured even in early historic periods, and Nelson Glueck believed that copper was used in Solomon's time. Benno Rothenberg (in Tylecote et al. 1967) believes that copper was exploited during at least three periods: the early Chalcolithic period (4th millennium B.C.E.); the earliest Iron Age (1200–1100 B.C.E.); and the Roman-Byzantine period (3rd–7th century C.E.).

The copper-bearing strata that were worked in those periods are not the same that are mined today. Formerly, copper nodules associated with fossilized trees within the Middle White Sandstone were exploited. This layer appears near Timna about 330 ft. (100 m.) above the copper-bearing Cambrian rocks that are now worked. The texture of the

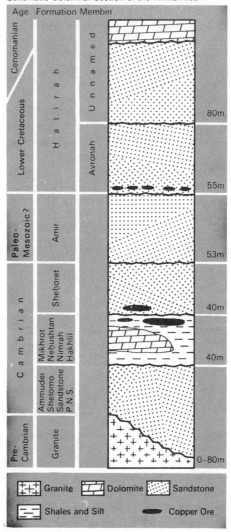

Schematic Columnar Section of the Timna Area

Age	Formation	Member	
Cenomanian		Unnamed	
Lower Cretaceous	Hatirah	Avronah	80m / 55m
Paleo-Mesozoic?	Amir		53m
Cambrian	Shehoret		40m
	Mikhrot Nehushtan Nimrah Hakhlil		40m
	Ammudei Shelomo Sandstone P.N.S.		
Pre-Cambrian	Granite		0–80m

Granite   Dolomite   Sandstone

Shales and Silt   Copper Ore

212

wood is clear in the fossilized remains. The organic material was first substituted by pyrite (FeS_2), which was then replaced by chalcocite (Cu_2S), precipitated from acid solutions by the reducing effect of organic material on copper-bearing solutions (Slatkine 1961, Tylecote et al. 1967). The nodules seem to consist of sulphides (chalcocite—Cu_2S, covellite—CuS), and their products of oxidation, chrysocolla ($CuSiO_3 \cdot 2H_2O$), azurite ($2CuCO_3 \cdot Cu(OH)_2$), malachite ($CuCO_3 \cdot Cu(OH)_2$), and occasional small particles of oxidized pyrite. Despite a 20–40% copper concentration in the nodules, they cannot be profitably worked because of their dispersion throughout the sandstone and their limited quantity.

In the early 1950s the Cambrian deposit was prospected, and in 1955 a state-owned copper plant was established, starting production in 1958. The initial intention was to use both open-cast and underground mining during the first years and, after a while, to transfer to underground mining only. The planned output was for 7,000 tons of copper per annum in the form of copper cement. During 1963–68 comprehensive surveys were carried out in the Timna area that resulted in the discovery of additional reserves suitable for open-cast mining. Through improved methods of mining, it was possible to continue with both open-cast and underground mining on an extended scale. In 1971/72 annual copper production at Timna has reached 11,000 tons, accomplished mainly by extending the mining area and the increased efficiency of the machinery. Since 1965 Timna Copper Mines Ltd. has taken over the operation of Timna from Israel Mining Industries (I.M.I.).

Description of the Deposit. Today, copper-bearing strata are known to exist over an area of 8 sq. mi. (20 sq. km.) around the granite complex of the Timna Massif. The sediments dip toward the north, west, and south and are faulted by the Rift Valley faults on the east. Mineralization occurs only in the upper part of the marine Cambrian sequence (Neḥushtan and Mikhrot Formations). The Neḥushtan Formation, varying in thickness up to 46 ft. (14 m.)   **213** is composed of soft, fine-grained sandstone with thin layers of shaly siltstones and scattered lenses of dolomite; the Mikhrot Formation, varying in thickness from 1 to 10 ft. (.03–3m.), is composed of a contorted sandy clay that may be subdivided in places into a pale yellow lower part and a red upper part.

Copper minerals occur in fissures and joints and as thin bands, concretions, and disseminations. Disseminations and, locally, concretions of manganese minerals occur in the same formations. The average concentration of copper in the deposit is about 1.4%, but mining conditions and economic circumstances sometimes enable profitable exploitation of ore containing only 1% copper or even less. In some restricted zones, ore of 2.5–3% copper is found. The thickness of the ore body varies approximately up to 33 ft. (10 m.) but mining varies mostly in a bed 10–18ft. (3–6 m.) thick. The main minerals forming the ore are chrysocolla ($CuSiO_3 \cdot 2H_2O$) and malachite ($CuCO_3 \cdot Cu(OH)_2$). In addition there are plancheite ($3CuSiO_3 \cdot H_2O$), bisbeeite ($CuSiO_3H_2O$), dioptase (H_2CuSiO_4), brochantite ($CuSO_4 \cdot 3Cu(OH)_2$), pseudomalachite ($Cu_5(PO_4)_2(OH)_4H_2O$), paratacamite ($Cu_2(OH)_3Cl$), CU-montmorillonite, and others. No sulphidic minerals were found so far. The main gangue minerals are: quartz, illite and other clay minerals, calcite, dolomite, and apatite.

Table 85. Average Chemical Composition of Timna Ore

		Per Cent
Copper	(Cu)	1–2
Silicon Dioxide	(SiO_2)	77
Phosphorus Pentoxide	(P_2O_5)	2
Manganese Dioxide	(MnO_2)	2.5
Ferric Oxide	(Fe_2O_3)	2
Aluminum Oxide	(Al_2O_3)	7
Calcium Oxide	(CaO)	3
Water	(H_2O)	5

The sediments are considered a first-cycle deposit directly derived from the weathering of the nearby igneous massif and deposited in a shallow marine lagoon, together with the copper minerals (Bentor 1966).

Mining. In the early years of open-cast mining at Timna, it was customary to strip away the ore with the overlying alluvium and sandstone at a 1 : 3 ore overburden ratio. With the improvement in mining methods and the acquisition of heavier equipment, the ratio 1 : 11 was reached and a ratio of 1 : 18 or more may be reached in the future. Open-cast mines of various size are scattered around the Timna Massif, including downfaulted blocks toward the east, in the direction of the Rift Valley. The underground mine has so far been developed in a layer dipping southward at an angle of 7°, and thus the overburden above the ore thickens toward the south. As opposed to open-cast mining, which has exceeded the planned quantity, underground mining has not yet reached capacity output. Underground mining is largely dependent on manual work, whereas open-cast mining is entirely mechanized.

Throughout the world mining is considered a profession, often inherited from generation to generation. There was not a strong Jewish, nor an Israel, tradition in mining, and it is therefore difficult to develop this specialized profession. In addition to the human element, several other unexpected difficulties were encountered in the course of underground mining, such as many more faults than were expected and underground water, which weakens the roof during mining. Therefore the undergound output has not yet reached the planned target. Despite the limitations of underground mining, the general output of the Timna copper mines has exceeded the planned quantity by 50%. According to the surveys made so far, the reserves available for open-cast mining are limited to a number of years; if additional open-cast reserves are not found by 1974, the total output of ore will have to be obtained from underground mines alone. Underground mining is carried out at a depth of about 500 ft. (150 m.) beneath the surface, and ore is carried 215

Sulfuric acid plant at Timna.

out via a conveyor belt through a tunnel. The available known reserves for open-cast and underground mining amount to about 21,000,000 tons of ore.

Processing and Beneficiation. After mining, the ore undergoes primary and secondary crushing. The final stage is wet milling in a ball mill, after which the ore slurry is transferred to extractors. Extraction is done by means of sulfuric acid, produced at Timna from imported sulfur. The total capacity of two sulfuric acid plants in Timna is 250 tons per day. The sulfuric acid consumption per ton of ore varies from 110 to 165 lb. (55–75 kg.). In the extraction of the copper by sulfuric acid, copper sulfate is obtained, from which the copper is reduced by scrap iron ($3CuSO + 2Fe^{+++} \rightarrow 3Cu^{++} + Fe_2(SO_4)_3$). The iron used is salvage from the local industries. The final product is copper cement, containing about 80% metallic copper. Data on annual copper production at Timna are summarized in Table 88.

Research is in progress to find the most suitable method for refining the copper cement in Israel, which will replace the present arrangement of exporting copper cement and importing copper metal for the country's needs. In addition, the possibilities for manufacturing by-products such as phosphate and manganese dioxide, which are present in small quantities in the ore and are presently disposed with the waste, are being investigated. A by-product already under exploitation is aggregated copper minerals such as chrysocolla and malachite, which are polished and used as semi-precious stones for jewlery. Although the hardness of these stones is relatively low, they are in great demand because of their blue-green and black patterns, which give them a unique local flavor. Copper production at Timna is the largest metallurgical industry in the country that is based on local raw materials. In addition to its commercial value as a full-scale exporter, Timna is of great importance for the general economic development of the Eilat area.

THE DEAD SEA MINERALS. The most saline of the world's lakes, the Dead Sea covers an area of 393 sq. mi. (1,020 sq. km.) and contains 136 cubic kilometers of water. It occupies the lowest of a series of depressions along the floor of a long, narrow, rift valley. The lake is divided into two basins: the North Basin, which accounts for about 73% of the area and which is about 1,300 ft. (400 m.) deep, and the South Basin, which occupies 27% of the area and reaches only 16 ft. (5 m.) in depth. The Lashon ("Tongue") Peninsula and its straits divide the two basins. The waters of the Dead Sea are a concentrated brine of various salts. The average salt concentration is 28–31%, which is nearly ten times greater than the average of oceans and open seas. The estimated salt content of the Dead Sea is about 44 billion tons (see Table 86). The concentration of ions dissolved in the Dead Sea water is not homogeneous. Neev and Emery (1967) gave figures for the different depths (see Table 87).

The combined influence of high year-round temperatures and low rainfall explains the tremendous rate of evaporation in the area. The strong evaporation is utilized to obtain Dead Sea salt in evaporation pans. The deep North Basin contains two water bodies: a fossil Lower Water Mass, extending from 130 ft. (40 m.) beneath the surface to the bottom at about 1,300 ft. (400 m.), and an Upper Water

Table 86. Estimated Composition[1] of Salts Dissolved in the Dead Sea (in million tons)

Magnesium Chloride	(MgCl$_2$)	21,410
Sodium Chloride	(NaCl)	13,430
Calcium Chloride	(CaCl$_2$)	6,240
Potassium Chloride	(KCl)	1,870
Magnesium Bromide	(MgBr$_2$)	810
Calcium Sulfate	(CaSO$_4$)	90
	Total	43,850

[1] In ionic equivalents, not the actual composition of Dead Sea precipitates.

Table 87. Quantities of Ions Dissolved in the Dead Sea (after Neev and Emery, 1967) (tons × 10^9)

Water body		Upper water mass	Transitional member	Deep member	Entire Dead Sea
Volume Km^3		28	32	76	136
Depth m		0–40	40–100	100–400	0–400
Calcium	Ca++	0.459	0.531	1.306	2.296
Magnesium	Mg++	1.012	1.298	3.225	5.535
Sodium	Na+	1.078	1.231	3.017	5.326
Potassium	K+	0.182	0.229	0.577	0.988
Chlorine	Cl$^-$	5.514	6.741	16.663	28.918
Bromine	Br$^-$	0.129	0.165	0.400	0.694
Sulfate	SO$_4^=$	0.016	0.016	0.032	0.064
Bicarbonate	HCO$_3^-$	0.006	0.007	0.017	0.030
	Total	8.396	10.218	25.237	43.851

Mass, between 130 ft. and the surface. Most of the physical and chemical processes in the lake are limited to the Upper Water Mass. The differences in the chemical composition of the two water masses are given in Table 87.

The Dead Sea area was famous in ancient times for its natural resources, particularly as a source of rock salt (sodium chloride). Salt mines are known in Mt. Sodom from the Early Bronze Age. From ancient times there have also been reports of asphalt blocks floating occasionally on the lake surface (Jos., Wars, 4:8). The first vision of modern industry connected with Dead Sea was presented by Theodor Herzl in his utopia *Altneuland* (1902). He was aware of the existence of potassium, bromine, and magnesium in the Dead Sea and saw their exploitation as a great political and technological goal. (Herzl also mentioned the possibility of producing electricity from a canal linking the Mediterranean Sea to the Dead Sea.) The first step toward the use of the Dead Sea resources was made by Moshe Novomeysky[13], who drew up practical plans for industrial installations on the sea's shores in 1911, and in 1921, after long negotiations, was finally given a licence to exploit the Dead Sea resources. In 1931 the first potash and bromine works were established by the Palestine Potash Co. Ltd., which was founded by British and Jewish investors, on the northwestern shore of the Dead Sea close to the inflow of the Jordan River. In 1937 the company founded another plant at the foot of Sodom on the southwestern shore of the sea. The raw potash was transported in barges to the northern plant and from there via Jerusalem to Haifa for export. During Israel's War of Independence the northern plant was destroyed and only the plant at Sodom remained, although it did not operate because of the lack of road connections. In 1952 a new company, the Dead Sea Works Ltd., was founded, with most of its shares in the hands of the Israel Government. Production began in 1955, after the construction of the Beersheba–Sodom road and a new factory. Only in 1958–59 did production again reach the level of 1947–48 (see Table 88).

In 1962 large-scale expansion of the works began, projected to reach production of 600,000 tons of potash in

[13] Industrial pioneer in Erez Israel (1873–1961)

Table 88. Production and Exports of Minerals in Israel
(in metric tons, with value of exports in thousands $ U.S.)

	Potash			Bromine
1937	36,467			510
1946	90,571			50
1947/8	103,000			
1951/2				
1954/5	17,997			
1955/6	24,036			
1956/7	50,472			
1957/8	85,481	**77,978**	**2,600**	916
1958/9	104,482	**92,346**	**3,154**	1,580
1959/60	113,800	**101,830**	**3,540**	1,920
1960/1	135,500	**118,652**	3,620	2,870
1961/2	139,962	**129,000**	**4,327**	4,000
1962/3	150,670	**134,000**	**4,000**	2,565
1963/4	188,000	**192,000**	**6,030**	5,400
1964/5	319,800	**267,800**	**9,999**	8,000
1965/6	498,300	**357,000**	**12,300**	10,500
1966/7	514,000	**492,000**	**15,500**	9,200
1967/8	495,900	**330,000**	**8,500**	8,200
1968/9	602,262	**600,000**	**13,287**	9,414
1969/70	605,063	**607,367**	**14,064**	11,097
1970/71	909,266	**853,559**	**20,579**	12,114
1971/72	947,613	**860,161**	**25,220**	13,552

Phosphates			Copper		
4,100					
58,500					
85,500					
114,025					
184,860	55,695	564			
209,900	39,353	375	662	360	163
221,198	109,700	790	5,469	5,470	4,238
224,491	96,800	676	5,713	5,240	3,919
231,601	125,396	927	6,142	6,142	4,121
202,700	90,334	625	5,389	4,544	2,714
300,500	156,550	1,176	7,755	8,004	4,986
232,000	180,000	1,550	9,500	10,100	9,800
526,000	370,000	4,000	8,479	8,079	8,184
669,600	460,000	4,800	10,000	9,300	9,600
738,800	480,000	5,300	9,519	9,800	11,365
840,000	768,000	7,847	10,087	10,000	10,900
1,026,311	847,867	8,423	10,685	10,499	16,018
939,147	793,147	7,861	10,963	10,232	11,228
594,824	591,725	6,890	11,002	11,923	11,494

Table 88 (cont.)

Flint Clay			Glass Sand	Portland Cement	
				157,770	
				259,480	
				323,694	
				439,200	
			13,750	563,099	
695			13,000	663,548	
1,300			15,800	612,837	
1,727			18,400	718,300	201,005
3,300	843	11	19,800	712,941	143,702
12,784	8,672	100	22,200	780,978	246,460
14,648	9,294	123	26,900	805,507	214,243
22,588	10,255	141	26,794	846,284	180,592
40,150	6,300	104	38,800	953,601	169,175
10,010	14,300	165	42,890	1,023,622	120,757
24,700	16,700	180	42,000	1,098,300	115,350
32,100	6,889	141	39,500	1,258,300	159,943
65,300	–	–	34,700	1,152,769	175,224
46,600	1,892	57	35,400	800,018	253,163
–	8,517	50	53,281	1,107,015	174,394
4,572	2,380	40	53,228	1,312,400	–
7,440	–	–	62,963	1,384,150	–
23,500	8,000	70	57,298	1,395,217	–

the first stage and an eventual capacity of 1,000,000 tons in the late 1960s. This great expansion was made possible by loans from the World Bank and other foreign banks and by the sale of shares in Israel and abroad. The actual output in 1969/70 was over 600,000 tons and in 1971/72 was about 950,000 tons (see Table 88). The company's recent difficulties were due mainly to marketing, as a result of increased potash production by Canada and strong competition in the West European markets on the one hand and the closing of the East European market on the other. With the cessation of dumping by Canadian producers, world prices of potash almost doubled and the company regained its profitability.

Potash Production. The salt concentration of the Dead Sea is not constant; it changes with depth and with the season. The composition of water in the South Basin is given in Table 89 (Kenat, 1965). The water contains only 1% (by weight) of potassium chloride (potash), which must be

Potash works at the Dead Sea, 1970. Courtesy J.N.F., Jerusalem. Photo Dafnai, Jerusalem.

Table 89. Average Composition of Water in South Basin
of the Dead Sea (in grams/liter)

Magnesium	Mg ++	33 – 41
Calcium	Ca++	14 – 17
Sodium	Na++	32 – 40
Potassium	K+	6 – 7.5
Chlorine	Cl-	173 – 212.5
Bromine	Br-	4 – 5
Sulfate	$SO_4^=$	0.65 – 0.8

separated from large quantities of calcium, magnesium, and sodium salts. In order to remove most of the calcium sulfate and sodium chloride, the Dead Sea water is channeled into large evaporation pans, which cover an area of about 50 sq. mi. (130 sq. km.). Almost all of this area was separated from the Dead Sea by dikes built into the shallow South Basin. The intense, almost year-round solar radiation supplies the heat necessary for evaporation. Calcium sulfate precipitates almost immediately after the sea's water is conveyed into the pans. When the sodium chloride concentration in the pans reaches about 9% it begins to precipitate. The precipitation of sodium chloride (NaCl) continues until approximately half the water has evaporated. At this stage about 90% of the sodium chloride and more than 95% of the calcium sulfate have precipitated. The brine continues into a second system of pans in which carnallite ($KMgCl_3 \cdot 6H_2O$) precipitates, as well as an additional amount of sodium chloride. The carnallite mixture is pumped by dredgers (floating pumps) in a 10–20% solid slurry to the factories and there the carnallite crystals are separated from the brine by filtration. The carnallite is then decomposed by water. The magnesium chloride (MgCl) is dissolved whereas the potassium chloride (KCl), which is also dissolved at the beginning, crystallizes again from the magnesium chloride solution. The remaining solids, a mixture of potassium chloride with sodium chloride, is called sylvinite. The sylvinite contains 50–65% potassium chloride on a dry weight basis, the rest being sodium chloride. The sylvinite is filtered and goes through either the "cold process" (flotation, which is used in the old plants) or the "hot process" (hot leaching), which is used in the new plant.

In the cold process this sylvinite goes through a flotation process, as a result of which potassium chloride is separated from sodium chloride. The froth containing the potassium chloride is washed in order to remove remaining sodium chloride impurities. The potassium chloride is filtered and dried in a rotary kiln and is then ready for shipping. The sodium chloride obtained from the flotation process is directed to the table salt factory for the production of table salt of various crystal sizes. In the hot process the potassium chloride is leached out of the sylvinite by a hot liquid saturated with sodium chloride and unsaturated with potassium chloride. The last saturated solution of potassium chloride is separated from the sodium chloride by centrifugation and is then cooled in vacuum crystalizers. The potassium chloride crystals produced by this crystalizing process are separated from the mother liquor by centrifugation and are dried in a rotary kiln. Various crystal sizes of potassium chloride are obtained after screening. The remaining sodium chloride is centrifuged, washed, and heaped for sale as industrial salt.

Production of Other Materials. Bromine is produced from concentrated brine after the precipitation of carnallite. The concentration of bromine salts in the brine is 50–60 times higher than in open sea water. The principal use of bromine is in the form of ethylene dibromide, used as an anti-knock in gasoline. Bromine is also used in agriculture, photography, pharmaceuticals, and other industries. Magnesium oxide (MgO) is an important raw material for refractory products, and plans provide for its production to be connected with an Aman reactor, in which magnesium 225 chloride will be the raw material for the production of magnesium oxide and hydrochloric acid. In agriculture magnesium in the form of magnesium chloride, sulfate, or chlorate and other compounds has a number of different uses as a plant nutrient, defoliant, etc. Research is aimed at discovering the most profitable exploitation of the Dead Sea resources.

PHOSPHATE FIELDS OF THE NEGEV. The Negev phosphate fields are part of the Mediterranean phosphate belt that stretches from Morocco in the west to Jordan in the east and Turkey in the north. The phosphorite (phosphate-bearing rock) is a marine sediment that was probably deposited in elongated, shallow bays during the Late Cretaceous period. The sea was rich in phosphoric oxide (P_2O_5), as testified by fish remains that are abundantly preserved within the phosphorite. The phosphorites of the Negev are always found in synclines in the uppermost part of the Mishash Formation and are overlaid by marl or bituminous chalk of the Ghareb Formation.

The existence of phosphorites in Ereẓ Israel has been known since the beginning of geological exploitation in the country, about 100 years ago (Lartet 1869). It was only in 1950, during the geological mapping of the Negev by Bentor and Vroman, however, that the first economic deposit was discovered at Oron (Bentor 1952). Following the detailed investigation and operations at the Oron fields in 1951, 18 other phosphate fields were discovered in the northern and central Negev, differing from each other in their phosphoric oxide concentration and other prospects for mining and enrichment. Apart from Oron, mining has begun at the Ẓefa-Efeh (Arad) and Ha-Makhtesh ha-Katan fields. The main phosphate mineral in the Negev fields is calcium-fluor-apatite $(Ca_{10}(PO_4,CO_3)_6 F_{2-3})$, also known as francolite. The main gangue mineral is calcite ($CaCO3$), with small amounts of gypsum ($CaSO_4 \cdot 2H_2O$). Chemical analyses of the phosphorites resulted in the values given in Table 90(although the true variability is probably greater). Phosphorite is used mainly for producing fertiliz-

Table 90. Chemical Composition of some Negev Phosphorites (per cent)

		Zefa-Ef'eh		Oron	Makhtesh Katan
Phosphorus Pentoxide	P_2O_5	32.85	25.40	28.50	31.73
Calcium Oxide	CaO	50.02	50.00	52.10	49.68
Aluminum Oxide	Al_2O_3	0.95	1.65	0.30	0.22
Ferric Oxide	Fe_2O_3	0.07	0.03	0.25	0.15
Magnesium Oxide	MgO	—	traces	0.35	0.06
Sodium Oxide	Na_2O	1.25	1.06	1.35	1.77
Potassium Oxide	K_2O	0.09	0.12	0.01	0.08
Silicon Dioxide	SiO_2	0.86	1.31	0.85	0.08
Chlorine	Cl	0.43	0.44	0.55	2.03
Fluorine	F	3.75	3.43	3.10	3.96
Carbon Dioxide	CO_2	4.66	11.20	10.95	3.85
Sulfite	SO_3	3.16	3.02	1.85	2.91
Crystalline Water	$+H_2O$	1.92	1.94	—	1.52
Humidity	$-H_2O$	1.74	1.42	1.30	3.86
Organic matter		0.03	0.13	—	0.26
		101.78	101.15	101.46	102.16
Halogen Corrections		1.58	1.44	1.46	2.13
Total		**100.20**	**99.71**	**100.00**	**100.03**

Sources: Shiloni (1966), Würzburger, Lasman (1963).

ers such as super-phosphate and triple-phosphates. The fact that Israel produces both potash and phosphates gives the country an advantage among the world's fertilizer producers.

The Oron Field. There are three layers of phosphorite in the Oron Field each 3–6 ft. (1–2 m.) thick, separated by chalk, marl, or limestone layers about 3 ft. (1 m.) thick. The phosphorite contains 23–27% phosphoric oxide (Axelrod 1966). The field extends for about 12 mi. (20 km.) along a syncline southeast of the Ha-Tirah anticline and is between $\frac{1}{2}$–3 mi. (1–5 km.) wide. The ore body is covered by the Ghareb marl of Maostrichtian Age, up to 260 ft. (80 m.) thick. To date, exploitation has been restricted to opencast mining in areas where the overburden does not exceed 33 ft. (10 m.). Extraction of the phosphorite at Oron was begun in 1951 by the Negev Phosphate Co. Ltd. Mining is done by heavy equipment that strips away the overburden and the sterile intercalations between the phosphorite layers. The raw phosphorite is transported to beneficiation installations situated at the northern end of the Oron field. At the first stage a mechanical beneficiation plant was installed, based on the milling of the rock and the removal of fine and coarse fractions, which are poorer in phosphoric oxide than the medium fragments (.2–.6mm.). The enriched rock (29–30%) was then transported to fertilizer plants in Haifa Bay, where the phosphorite was converted to super-phosphate and other phosphate fertilizers, intended mainly for use in Israel. Since 1963 the materials nave been transported by railroad from Dimonah.

In 1957–58 phosphate began to be exported to the international market, and the amount has increased steadily since (see Table 88). Parallel with increased production, better methods of beneficiation were sought. A large calcination kiln was brought into operation at Oron in 1964/65, but has since been closed owing to heavy losses incurred. There is also a defluorination plant in operation at Oron for the production of phosphate suitable for chicken feed.

Phosphate beneficiation plant in Oron.

Phosphorite reserves with up to 66 feet (20 m.) overburden known today at Oron amount to about 70,000,000 tons of variable quality. There are larger reserves lying deeper than 20 m. In 1963 the Negev Phosphate Co. Ltd., which has operated the Oron field since 1951, merged with Fertilizers and Chemicals Ltd. of Haifa. The new company is known as Chemicals and Phosphates Ltd., whose shares are owned by the government.

The Ẓefa-Efeh Field. In 1961, during a detailed survey in the Arad region, the Ẓefa-Efeh field was discovered by the Mineral Resources Division of the Geological Survey (Wuerzburger and Lasman 1963). In this field, phosphate with an average content of 28–29%—sometimes even reaching 30–33%—of phosphoric oxide was found, placing the field among the richest phosphate deposits in the world. In the new Ẓefa-Efeh field there is one phosphorite layer, varying in thickness between 8–15ft. (2.5–4.5 m.), but the overburden thickens over a short distance. This field may yield 15,000,000–20,000,000 tons by open-cast mining, after which underground mining may be used. During 1963–66 small amounts of phosphorite were extracted from **229** this field by Chemicals and Phosphates Ltd. Thereafter, mining ceased and a new project was planned instead. The discovery of the Żefa-Efeh field brought about a change in the concept of phosphate production in Israel and in the prospects for a chemical industry in the Negev. For the purpose of continued mining and chemical industries at the Żefa-Efeh field, the government established Arad Chemical Industries Co. Ltd., affiliated with the government and with a foreign company, the Madera Corporation, which, however, later withdrew. During the first stage, the company will erect a plant for the manufacture of phosphoric acid for export by means of hydrochloric acid produced from residual Dead Sea brines, according to an original process developed in Israel by A. Baniel of the Israel Mining Industries Laboratories. Manufacture of phosphoric acid has the advantage that products of 70% phosphoric oxide concentration can be transported and marketed.

Ha-Makhtesh ha-Katan Field. During phosphate surveys by the Geological Survey, another field of mining quality was discovered in 1964 southeast of the Ḥaẓerah anticline (Shiloni 1966). The phosphorite from this field is similar to that of the Żefa-Efeh field and in part reaches a 32–34% phosphoric oxide content. Mining from this field was begun in 1966 by Chemicals and Phosphates Ltd. However, known reserves are small and only amount to 10,000,000 tons. The overburden over most of the field does not exceed 66 ft. (20 m.). In the northern part of the field there is one layer of phosphorite similar to that at Żefa-Efeh, whereas in the southern part there are three layers separated by sterile chalk and limestone intercalations. Phosphate mined at this field does not undergo calcination, but instead undergoes some mechanical enrichment at the mining site, after which it is directly shipped for export.

Future of the Phosphate Industry. Phosphates are one of the most important natural resources in the Negev, and the world demand for them is always increasing. The economics of phosphate mining and preparation are a function of the mining and beneficiation methods on the one hand and of transport distances to the plants, ports, and export countries on the other. It is difficult to estimate the total phosphate reserves available in the Negev. The figure is of the order of 500,000,000 tons, only part of which can be mined by the open-cast method. At the Ein Yahav fields, investigated by the America-Israel Phosphate Co. Ltd., underground mining was also considered. Recently the Israel government has founded Israel Chemicals Ltd., to include all the government-operated industry in this field. This company has organic and inorganic chemistry divisions, the latter including all the companies that utilize phosphates and Dead Sea resources as their main raw material.

CLAYS AND SANDS. Clay minerals are hydrous aluminosilicates with special physical qualities such as plasticity, swelling in contact with water, refractivity, and so on. Because of these characteristics, clay is used extensively in the manufacture of ceramics, refractory materials, and cement, and as a filler in the paper, rubber, and other industries. The use of clay in Erez Israel dates from the dawn of history when earthenware vessels were household utensils. Pottery has been found in almost all archaeological excavations, and earthenware has remained in domestic use to the present day. The sources of these clays were marls and clay beds in Upper Cretaceous Formations in the northern and central part of the country. The modern ceramics industry requires white clay with a low percentage of iron oxide, to enable color control of the products. Today, locally mined clay is mainly used for the production of sanitary plumbing and in the refractory industry. The clays are quarried by the Negev Ceramic Materials Co. Ltd. in Makhtesh Ramon and Makhtesh ha-Tirah by open-cast mining. They occur at lenticular bodies within the Lower Cretaceous and Jurassic Sandstones exposed in the cores of the eroded anticlines. The main mineral composing these deposits is kaolinite ($Al_2O_3 \cdot 2SiO_2 \cdot 2H_2O$) and the main accessory mineral is quartz (SiO_2). The flint clay of Makhtesh Ramon is a special type of deposit (Slatkine and   231

Heller 1961); it lies unconformably upon Triassic lagoonal limestones (Mohilla Formation) and also fills pockets or sinkholes in the limestones. The clay sequence varies from 10–60 ft. (3–18 m.) in thickness; however, only 3–6 ft. (1–2 m.) are low in ferric oxide. The clay is hard and brittle, with a conchoid fracture. The color varies with the amount of ferric oxide from white to red, and very dark violet. The flint clay is particularly suitable for the manufacture of refractory products such as bricks and fireproof linings. In addition to kaolinite, it contains boehmite and diaspore ($Al_2O_3 \cdot H_2O$). As the percentage of these aluminous minerals increases, the refractory properties of the clay become better. The limiting factor in its industrial use is the percentage of Fe_2O_3, which must not exceed 1.5%. During 1956–65, white flint clay, low in iron content, was quarried at the Ramon deposit. In 1965–66 a magnetic separation plant to separate clay of high iron content from that of low content and a calcination kiln to bring the raw clay up to the industrial standard were established on the site.

In addition to these clays, a layer of bentonite clay is exploited in small-scale underground mining in Makhtesh Ramon. This clay, which is exposed in the Cretaceous sequence in the northern cliff of the Makhtesh, serves as a binder in the production of animal feed. Subrecent alluvial clays from the Zebulun Valley near Mt. Carmel and from the Coastal Plain near Ramleh are quarried and used in the cement industry. Many of the roof tiles used in Jerusalem are manufactured from the Cenomanian Motsa Marl, quarried near Moẓa. Production has dwindled, however, and roof tiles are now produced mainly from cement. White quartz sand containing only about .06% ferric oxide is quarried in the Makhtesh Ha-Tirah from Lower Cretaceous Sandstone of the Kurnub Group. It is used in the manufacture of glass at Haifa (Phoenicia), and at the Tempo and Phoenicia factories at Kefar Yeruḥam. Today, mainly white transparent glass is produced, for which white sands are required. Dune or shore sands are unsuitable.

Table 91 Chemical Composition of Ramon Clays (per cent)

	Bentonite	Kaolin clay S/5	Flint clay
Aluminum Oxide Al_2O_3	14—20	30—32	38—65
Silicon Dioxide SiO_2	38—54	52—54	20—43
Ferric Oxide Fe_2O_3	3—6	0.58—2	0.7—1.7
Titanium Dioxide TiO_2	0.8—1.2		3—4.5
Water & Humidity $H_2O\pm$	9.14	11—12	14—15

BUILDING MATERIALS. For the building material industry, which occupies a much more prominent position in Israel than in other countries, the following raw materials are provided by the local natural resources:

Quarries of dolomite and hard limestones, which are used for crushed aggregates, are scattered throughout the mountainous parts of Israel (Galilee, the Carmel, the Hills of Judea, and the Negev). The main geological units quarried for this purpose are of Cenomanian Age; in places Turonian and Eocene rocks are also quarried. The largest company in this field is Lime and Stone Production Co. Ltd. The Arad Company, which is affiliated with Rassco, operates a number of quarries near Jerusalem, and other public and private companies operate quarries in various parts of the country.

Limestone is quarried in large blocks for the manufacture of commercial marble and building stones. The quarries are found mainly in Galilee, Judea, and Samaria, though there are a few quarries in other regions such as Arad and Makhtesh Ramon. There is a steady demand for building stone in Jerusalem due to the local regulation that requires the use of natural stone in most parts of the city. Commercial marble is quarried mainly from the Turonian Bi'na Formation (Shadmon, 1965). In Peki'in, Upper Galilee, a brecciated Cenomanian Limestone is quarried along a fault plane and used in the marble industry.

Sand and sandstone are used as fine aggregates in concrete. Sand is mainly quarried from dunes along the Mediterranean coast. Calcareous Eolian Sandstone (*Kurkar*) of Plio-Pleistocene Age is used as a fill material in roadbeds and is quarried at various localities from lithified dune ridges along the coast.

The cement industry is one of the basic industries for any developing state. The first portland cement plant in the country, Nesher, was erected at Yagur, in 1925. In the following year, production reached 50,000 tons (see Table 88), and in 1963 it was 650,000 tons. The fluctuations in the cement-production curve are closely tied to the history of Jewish settlement in Erez Israel. A second Nesher factory was founded at Ramleh and began production in 1953. A third factory, Shimshon, was established by foreign investors during the 1950s at Beth-Shemesh. Its operation was discontinued in 1966 because of financial difficulties, and the plant was eventually bought by Nesher. Cement or cement grog is exported by the Nesher Co. to various countries via Haifa and Eilat. The two plants now in operation quarry their chalk and clay close at hand. Nesher Yagur now obtains its chalk from quarries on Mt. Carmel; the material is transported to the plant by cable car. The gypsum needed for the cement industry was initially quarried from a Tertiary lake deposit at Gesher in the Jordan Valley. It is now also quarried from the Triassic Mohilla Formation at Makhtesh Ramon. Today, large quantities of gypsum are obtained as a by-product from the manufacture of phosphoric acid at the Chemicals and

Phosphates Plant at Haifa.

OTHER MINERAL RESOURCES. Various deposits of other minerals and materials have been investigated during recent years. Their economic value is still unclear but may be influenced by variable factors such as new technology in ore dressing, changes in the road system, prices on the world market, and national economic policy. Among such resources are the Lower Cretaceous iron deposits at Manara, Upper Galilee (Boskovitz 1961), hydrothermal iron deposit in the Negev (Shraga 1967), oil shales of Maastrichtian age found near Arad (Shaḥar et al. 1967), Ein Bokek, and other places, and peat of the Ḥuleh Basin.

MINERAL DEPOSITS IN SINAI. Minerals have been mined in the Sinai peninsula since the beginning of recorded history. Turquoise ($CuO \cdot 3Al_2O_3 \cdot 2P_2O_5 \cdot 9H_2O$) has been mined, although on a limited scale, since the days of the early Pharaohs and continues in use to the present day as an ornamental material. It is mined by the local Bedouin, and the techniques used are very primitive. During the last decades other minerals have been exploited in Sinai, especially in the Umm Bugma-Abu Zenima region, where manganese-iron ore, kaolin, glass-sand, and gypsum are mined. The only mine worked outside this area is the coal mine in the Jebel Maghāra region, northern Sinai.

Manganese. Within the Carboniferous Sandstone and dolomite near Umm Bugma is a shaly layer that is rich in manganese or mixed manganese and iron minerals. The ore bodies are irregular and mostly lenticular in shape. The chief manganese minerals are pyrolusite and psilomelane (MnO_2), and those of iron are goethite and hematite ($Fe_2O_3 \cdot H_2O$, and Fe_2O_3). Manganese mining in this region began in 1918, and some 4,000,000 tons of ore have been extracted since. For many years iron ore and manganese have been mined together, although the percentage of manganese in the ore has dropped from 39% manganese, 19% iron in 1919, to 33% manganese, 25% iron in 1935, and 22% manganese, 35% iron in 1954 (Attia 1956). Moreover, throughout the years small amounts of rich manganese ore were extracted in selective mining. The operations were 235 discontinued in 1967. Difficulties in the marketing of ore rich in iron and poor in manganese stimulated the founding of a smelting plant by the Sinai Manganese Co. Ltd. (S.M.C.) at the port of Abu Zenima, some 12–19 mi. (20–30 km.) west of the mines. A cable car links the mining area to the port. The smelting plant was at an advanced stage of construction at the time of the Six-Day War (June 1967). No further activities were undertaken since to complete the plant.

Copper. Although the existence of copper is known, no mining works on a commercial scale operate in this field in Sinai. Copper was found in the Umm Bugma region within Cambrian sediments, where prospecting was done in recent years by the S.M.C. In a few places in central and eastern Sinai, traces of copper mineralization were found in igneous rocks, in dykes, and along fault lines. Ancient mining, as well as some prospecting by Egyptian companies, was carried out on a limited scale, but no commercial exploitation was attempted.

Kaolin. The kaolin mined near Umm Bugma is found at two stratigraphic levels: kaolin lenses within the Carboniferous sequence (Umm Bugma Formation) associated with coal, and kaolin in more continuous layers within Nubian Sandstone of Lower Cretaceous Age. Both types of kaolin were exploited during the years 1957–67 by underground mining, using primitive methods. The kaolin was sold mainly to European markets via the Abu Zenima port.

Glass Sand. At Jebel Nakhul, near Umm Bugma, there are glass sand quarries within the Lower Cretaceous Nubian Sandstone. Before 1967 this sand was filled into sacks on the spot and thus marketed.

Gypsum. Layers of gypsum and alabaster 66–100 ft. (20–30 m.) thick were found in the Ḥammām Farʿūn region, near the Gulf of Suez, in rocks of Miocene Age. Before June 1967 this gypsum was shipped in crushed form from a jetty near the quarry.

Coal. In the Jebel Maghāra region, northern Sinai, coal
was mined underground in strata of Middle Jurassic Age.

Mining started in 1964, and two beds 25–40 ft. (8–12 m.) apart were exploited, the upper one about 75 m. thick and the lower one 1.35 m. thick. The calometric value of the coal is about 7,000 cal./gm. and the ash percentage is 6.5%. The mine was operated by the Egyptian Coal Project, affiliated with the Egyptian General Organization for Geological Research and Mining. Operations were discontinued after the Six-Day War.

MINERAL RESOURCES OF JUDEA AND SAMARIA. Most of the quarries in Judea and Samaria (the West Bank) are for building materials. Unlike in areas of Jewish settlement, where most buildings are of ferro-concrete, building there is based mainly on local building stone from Upper Cretaceous Formations. Ornamental glass is made in Hebron from local sand of Turonian Age. A barite ($BaSO_4$) deposit has been discovered near Zuatra in the Judean Desert. The barite is found in Senonian rocks of the Mishash Formation, and a possible hydrothermal origin is suggested by Beyth (1968).

13 INDUSTRY

Modern industry made its first important strides in Palestine during World War II, when it emerged as a major branch of the economy, largely in response to the needs of the British forces and the Allied war machine in the Middle East. After the war, however, it could not maintain its high share of the national product and it declined nearly to its pre-war level (see Economic Development, page 47). Industry remained more or less at the same stage almost throughout the first decade of Israel's independence. It was only when the serious social and economic pressures on the state were lightened that the government could begin to create more encouraging conditions for its expansion.

EXPANSION OF INDUSTRY. The rapid development of industry in Israel is even more outstanding than of the economy as a whole. Between 1950 and 1972 industrial output increased more than 9 times—by an average of more than 10% a year, reaching IL15,750 million (1971 prices) in 1972. (Lacking reliable data for the first two years of independence, statistical series generally begin with 1950.) Industrial exports grew from $18 million to over $920 million in 1972—an average annual growth of 20%: approximately IL12,000 million (in terms of 1971 prices) were invested in industrial fixed assets, and the gross stock of capital expanded at an average rate of 17% a year, reaching almost IL9,500 million in 1972. Industry provided 170,000 additional jobs, raising industrial employment at a rate of 4.7% per annum from 90,000 in 1950 to over 248,000 in 1972, and output per worker rose on the average by more than 5.8% a year.

Table 92. Major Indications of Industrial Development, 1950 and 1972

	1950	1972	Average Annual Growth %
Output (IL million)	1,800	15,750	10.8
Exports ($ million)	18	920	20.0
Stock of capital (IL million)	865	9,500	11.7
Employees (thousands)	90	248	4.7
Output per worker (IL thousands)	20.3	63.5	5.8
Capital stock per worker (IL thousands)	9.6	38.3	5.6

Factors in Industrial Expansion. This rapid industrial development, which is still continuing, was influenced by a number of factors. First, local demand for industrial products grew fast, owing to the growth of population and the rise in the standard of living, especially during and after the latter half of the 1950s. Then there was a steady increase in exports, which accounted for 20% of the rise in industrial output during the period. Still another cause was the enhanced development of the entire economy, which stepped up the demand for semi-finished products and industrial investment goods. A fourth factor was the flourishing construction activity, which led to a remarkable expansion of demand for industrial intermediate products. Last, but not least, industry enjoyed a high degree of protection against competitive imports and most of the increase in domestic demand for industrial products was channeled to local industry, enabling it to replace imports.

During most of these years industry also enjoyed an expanding supply of production, factors which enabled it to meet the rising demand. Much of the heavy investment in the economy—made possible by the extensive import of capital, even without a sufficiency of local savings—found its way to industry, which also received a great deal of machinery and equipment through the Reparations Agreement with West Germany. By means of intensive vocational training programs, problems connected with the supply of highly trained manpower were solved with remarkable success—especially in view of the lack of skills, previous industrial experience, or sufficient educational background among the new immigrants.

The government played a decisive role in the development of industry, especially during the 1960s. Among the reasons for its considerable influence on the process was the fact that a high proportion of capital imports was carried out through it. Economic development policy gradually began to change during the second half and toward the end of the 1950s: the emphasis shifted from agriculture to industry, as agriculture was already highly developed and could no longer provide additional jobs or make a significant further contribution to the dispersal of population.

LIMITATIONS ON INDUSTRIAL DEVELOPMENT. The main limitation confronting Israel's industry is the scarcity of raw materials and sources of energy. The country is poor in natural resources, sources of energy, such as oil and gas, facilities for generating cheap electricity, and important agricultural raw materials. Another limitation lies in the limited size of the local market. Apart from limiting future industrial growth, this factor is also thought to be the cause of many structural deficiencies: small plants, fragmentation of production, and insufficient competition. In addition, there is the distance from export markets and the sources of imported raw materials. Due to political circumstances, the natural markets for Israel products—the neighboring Arab countries—are closed to them because of the Arab boycott. Owing to the serious social and economic difficulties which faced Israel in its early years, rapid physical development was achieved, in many instances, only by sacrificing

considerations of economic profitability and relative advantages, so that most industrial production developed in a somewhat haphazard fashion.

OUTPUT. During the early 1950s industry was primarily concerned with the final processing of semi-finished products and the manufacture of basic consumer goods, such as food, clothing, and footwear, so that locally added value constituted only a small proportion of output. In response to the growth of local demand, due to the rising standard of living, there was an increase in variety of output. As a result of government protection by tariffs and administrative means, the growing demand was supplied mostly by local production, which, in many instances, was of low profitability to the national economy.

Today industry is engaged in all stages of production, from the primary stage to the final product. The share of intermediate products, for the use of industry and other branches of the economy, has risen owing to the vertical "deepening" of production and import substitution. Most of the consumers' goods which used to be imported during the early years are now manufactured in Israel. The production of machinery and equipment has developed from practically nil.

In 1971 total industrial production could be classified, by final demand, as follows: about 42% went to meet private consumption; 15% was for public consumption; 16% served for investment in industry and other branches of the economy; 27% were exported. Of the output in 1971, the biggest single share—19% came from the food industry. Next came metal products—9.5%, chemicals—9.3%, textiles—9.2% and diamonds—8.3%.

INVESTMENTS. As late as during the first half of the 1950s Israel industry was still technologically backward. Most plants were small and used outdated equipment, part of it dating back to the 1930s. The rapid growth of industry was made possible by a high level of investment. Between 1949 and 1972 some IL12,000 million, in terms of 1971 prices—about one quarter of the total investments exclusive of housing, and some 16% of the total including housing—

Table 93. Output, Employment, and Exports by Branch of Industry, 1971 (in IL million and %)

Branch	Output		Employment		Exports	
	IL millions	%	in thousands	%	IL millions	%
Mining and quarrying	339	2.4	4	1.8	41.9	5.6
Food (including beverages and tobacco)	2,705	19.1	32	14.2	81.2	10.7
Textiles	1,309	9.2	22	9.8	49.4	6.6
Clothing and made-up textiles	751	5.3	22	9.8	69.8	9.3
Wood, wood products, and furniture	447	3.2	11	4.9	9.6	1.3
Paper, printing, and publishing	624	4.4	13	5.8	13.7	1.8
Leather and leather products	132	0.9	4	1.8	4.8	0.7
Rubber and plastic products	612	4.3	9	4.0	27.4	3.7
Chemicals and petroleum refining	1,316	9.3	10	4.4	63.7	8.5
Non-metallic mineral products	550	3.9	9	4.0	3.7	0.5
Diamond industry	1,175	8.2	9	4.0	268.0	35.6
Basic metal industry	392	2.8	5	2.2	9.1	1.2
Metal products	1,348	9.5	25	11.0	44.6	5.9
Machinery	560	3.9	11	4.9	9.2	1.3
Electric and electronic equipment	915	6.5	17	7.6	25.3	3.4
Transport equipment	839	5.9	18	8.0	14.0	1.9
Miscellaneous products	171	1.2	4	1.8	15.2	2.0
Total	14,185	100.0	225	100.0	750.6	100.0

were invested in manufacturing, mining, and quarrying. To a large extent these investments were made possible by the extensive import of capital. The Reparations Agreement was of considerable importance in this respect: it stimulated many industrialists to make new investments and replace old equipment. Between 1954 and 1962 industrial machinery worth about $68 million was imported to Israel under the agreement. It is estimated that about 22.5% of investments was used to replace discarded equipment. The rest went to increase the stock of capital, almost doubling it every five to six years.

The Law for the Encouragement of Capital Investment, 1950 (amended a number of times subsequently) was designed mainly to attract foreign, but also local, capital to develop the productive capacity of the national economy—first and foremost industry, which would increase exports and reduce reliance on imports. Various benefits, including grants (of up to one-third of outlay on machinery and equipment) and low-interest loans (of up to 55% on fixed assets) are given to approved investors according to the zone where the investment is made and the rate at which foreign currency is saved. Other benefits are concessions on property, income and indirect taxes, deferment of fees, and special rights to repatriate profits and principal in foreign currency.

EMPLOYMENT AND OUTPUT PER WORKER. While employment in industry rose at an annual average rate of 4.7% (see above), output went up even faster, by 10.8% a year. In other words, industrial development was accompanied by increasing productivity, output per worker going up on the average by 5.8% annually. There were many ups and downs in the rate of growth of industry through the years: in 1966 and 1967, for example, the trend was downward owing to the economic recession, but this was fully compensated for by a rise of 18.6% in 1968. Some 25% of the total additional employment in Israel between 1950 and 1972 was absorbed by industry. Since it only employed 21% of the total in 1950, the percentage of industry in total employment thus rose 243 steadily, reaching 24% in 1972. Many of the new workers in industry, especially those absorbed during the 1950s, were new immigrants without industrial training, experience, or tradition, and their general educational standards were low, but the level of skill rose considerably, thanks to training programs sponsored by the government and the Histadrut. Management also improved through practical experience and advanced training at home and abroad, though the shortage of managers with professional qualifications in administration and marketing, on a level suitable for modern enterprises, is still a problem. Thus, although the output per worker declined during the early years, there was an annual rise of 6% between 1954 and 1970, making an average increase of 4.4% per annum over the entire period.

PROTECTION OF INDUSTRY AND LIBERALIZATION OF IMPORTS. These two economic tools, which apparently work in opposite directions, have been applied to Israel's industry at different stages of its development. Until 1962 import policy was designed to give a high level of protection to local industry, primarily by administrative restrictions on the import of goods that were, or could be, produced in Israel, but also by protective tariffs.

One of the main provisions of the new economic policy proclaimed together with the currency devaluation of 1962 was the withdrawal of administrative protection and the subjection of industry to competition by imports, while maintaining high protective tariffs. When it became apparent that local producers were taking undue advantage of tariff protection, the policy was changed, in order to compel industry to increase its efficiency. Thus a plan was drawn up, under which tariffs have been reduced annually since 1967, aiming at the stage when, in the long run, only the efficient and competitive enterprises will remain in business, to the benefit of the economy as a whole.

STRUCTURE OF INDUSTRY. High costs in comparison with those prevailing in international markets constitute one of Israel industry's basic problems, reducing competitive capacity on both local and export markets. This problem is closely linked to the structure of industry: small plants, fragmentation of production and limited competition. These are due to the fact that output is mainly aimed at local consumption, which is limited and covers a large variety of products. Industrial development, however, has led to an enlargement of plants. Older establishments have expanded production: new ones were on the average larger than those existing before 1948; and the most modern ones larger than those built in the late 1950s and even the early 1960s. A tendency toward amalgamation is also beginning to be apparent.

In most fields a large share of production is concentrated in a small number of plants. The greater the capital necessary for technological reasons to start a new enterprise the more restricted will competition in the field be. Most of Israel industry operates under conditions of oligopoly, with a small number of firms controlling most of the output in their field. The oligopolistic structure of industry led many companies to form cartels, limiting competition through agreed prices, allocation of production quotas, etc. At times, such arrangements enjoyed government support, primarily in order to expand exports, and until 1960 there was no legal limitation on the formation of cartels. In that year, however, the Restrictive Trade Practices Law went into effect, making the existence of cartels subject to approval by a special public council, and in 1963 the law was strengthened. In 1969, 33 cartels, more than half of them in the food and chemical industries, had the approval of the public council. In addition, there were believed to be a number of unofficial agreements between firms to limit competition, which the council had not been able to track down.

ECONOMIC SECTORS. Like economic development in general, industrialization has been characterized by the coexistence of private, Histadrut, and public initiative, with various forms of initiative and ownership within these sectors. The Histadrut sector, for instance, includes cooperatives, kibbutz-owned enterprises, and firms wholly 245 owned by Ḥevrat ha-Ovdim, the economic arm of the Histadrut, while the public sector comprises undertakings owned by the government, the Jewish Agency and its subsidiary institutions, and the local authorities.

The non-private sector has, especially when considering the product data, a comparatively high share of industry—as of other branches of the economy. The reasons are mainly historical. Much of the economy was established during the first third of the century by public bodies since most of the Jewish immigrants arrived with little or no financial resources. After independence, moreover, many of the new enterprises in heavy industry required more outlays—and were involved in greater risks—than local, and even foreign, private enterprise was prepared for. Then, some privately owned businesses, like the Electricity Corporation or the Dead Sea Potash Works, had to grow faster—along with the economy as a whole—than the original owners could manage. In addition, the leaders of the pre-state *yishuv* were inspired by socialist ideologies and attached great importance to the building of a collective economy. This explains the almost unique phenomenon of the labor federation being the biggest single owner of economic concerns in the country.

According to the most recent data available, for 1967, the lion's share of industrial enterprises—90%—belonged to the private sector. These employed 75% of all industrial workers and accounted for 70% of the total industrial product. The Histadrut sector owned 8% of the enterprises, with 16% of the total employment and 21% of the product, while the public sector had only 2% of the plants, with 9% of industrial employment and 9% of the product. As the years pass the trend is toward a relative growth of the private sector and, though at a much slower rate, of the public sector—although recent government policy is to sell its profitable enterprises to obtain capital for further development.

MAJOR INDUSTRIES. Israel's most important industrial export product in 1972 was diamonds, of which she

Diamond cutting at Netanyah, the center of Israel's diamond industry. Courtesy Ministry of Commerce and Industry, Jerusalem. Photo Signon, Tel Aviv.

Oranges being delivered at a bottling plant in Ramat Gan.
Courtesy Government Press Office, Tel Aviv.

The grain silo in Haifa. **Courtesy Dagon**, Batey Mamguroth le-Israel, Ltd., Haifa. **Photo Erev**, Haifa.

Spinning division of a textile factory at Kiryat Gat. Courtesy Government Press Office, Tel Aviv.

exported $385 million worth in 1972. She was thus responsible for more than 35% of the international trade in polished diamonds, and as much as 80% of the trade in medium-size stones, in which she specialized. Israel was thus second only to Belgium as an international diamond center.

The largest industry was food, beverage, and tobacco manufacture, which accounted for about 19% of manufactures and employed some 32,000 persons in 1971. About 90% of its output was sold on the local market; the rest, such as juices, wines, chocolate, and coffee, went abroad.

The textiles and clothing industry, which was developed chiefly because of its low capital-labor ratio, produced about 15% of the total and employed some 44,000 workers, in 1972 it exported about $119 million worth—25% of its production.

Chemicals and petroleum refining covered about 9.3% of industrial output, with 10,000 employees and exports of about $63 million.

Electric and electronic equipment, a new industry for Israel, developed rapidly, with government encouragement, from the late 1960s onwards. Exports in this industry reached $25 million in 1971. Among other products, the industry made electronic equipment for telephones and military uses.

Israel Aircraft Industries Ltd., with its headquarters at Lydda, and the country's largest industrial enterprise, manufactured the Arava passenger cargo plane, the Fouga Magister jet trainer, and a twin executive aircraft (formerly the Jet Commander). Subsidiary and integrated plants made electronics, fiberglass, precision instruments, and ground-support equipment.

INVESTMENT POLICY. The first law for the encouragement of capital investment in Israel, passed in 1950, created favorable conditions for both Israel and foreign investments helping to increase exports or reduce imports. The law was amended in 1955, 1957, 1959, and 1967 to extend the scope of the benefits. These measures helped to maintain a growth in the gross national product averaging 10% a year (except in 1966 and 1967), the highest rate in the world, and an annual investment averaging 25% of total resources, which is also one of the world's highest. Of the total resources at the disposal of the economy in 1972—IL353 billion—IL89 billion was used for gross investment:

An oriental gown by Maskit Home Crafts Development
Company, modeled in Old Jaffa, 1970. Courtesy Government Press Office, Tel Aviv.

about 18% in industry and construction, 5% in agriculture
and irrigation, 20% in transportation, communications, and
electricity, 18% in commerce and services, and 35% in
250 housing.

A section of the automobile assembly plant in Nazareth.
Photo Keren-Or, Haifa.

Under the law as amended in 1959, a project is granted
the status of an "approved enterprise," entitling it to benefit
from certain concessions, if it improves the balance of payments by lowering imports or increasing exports, or
contributes to population dispersal, immigrant absorption,
and the creation of new sources of employment
by establishing a plant in a development area.

Overhaul of transport planes in an Israel Aircraft Industries' hangar at Lydda. Courtesy Government Press Office, Tel Aviv.

The main benefits are: a five-year exemption from property tax; a 50% reduction on income tax for the first five years in which the enterprise shows profit; double depreciation allowance on machinery, equipment and buildings; exemption from estate duty (granted only to foreign investors); exemption from customs duty and purchase tax on the import of capital goods for the establishment of the enterprise; the right of non-residents to take profits derived from the enterprise out of the country without limitations.

Further amendments, which came into operation in April 1967, provide for government grants to cover from one-fifth to one-third of the cost of machinery and other equipment, as well as 10–20% of the value of the buildings, to approved enterprises established before June 30, 1972, the size of the grant depending on the location of the

Beth-Shemesh turbo engines on exhibit at the International Trade Fair, Tel Aviv, 1970. Courtesy Government Press Office, Tel Aviv.

enterprise. In 1972, the rate of grants for machinery was reduced to 15–30%, with an additional grant of 15% for the purchase of machinery made in Israel. The government also assists investors by placing low-rental buildings at their disposal in development areas, and by participating in the cost of training workers. A further benefit is the grant of government loans in addition to the grants for the establishment of the enterprise, the amount depending on the location. Interest rates have also been decreased. The ceiling for grants and loans is 70% in A areas, 60% in B areas, and 50% in the rest of the country. The government also helps to finance part of the working capital.

Seventeen branches of industry which have been selected as worthy of particular government encouragement include **253** furs, clothing, leather goods, electronic equipment, irrigation and agricultural equipment, machinery, die casting, medical equipment, and light chemicals. In all these, the labor component is relatively high and the product is not manufactured in large quantities.

Israel economic representatives abroad are in contact with the Investment Authority in Israel, which is the central body dealing with foreign investors. The Authority publicizes investment programs, maintains contact with investors, and advises those visiting Israel to examine investment prospects. The potential investor is accompanied on his tours by a member of the Authority's staff, and if he decides to establish an industrial concern, the Authority assists him in submitting the request for recognition of the concern as an approved enterprise and in finding managerial staff. The request for approval is submitted to the Investment Center, a body established by law, which decides whether the concern meets with the specified criteria and can be recognized as an approved enterprise.

14 BANKING AND COMMERCE

BANKING. Under the Ottoman rule, in the mid-19th century, a few private banks were opened in Erez Israel. Later, some of the recently established European joint-stock banks set up branches in the country, but their activities were restricted to foreign exchange and foreign trade finance. In 1903, with the formation of the Anglo-Palestine Company Ltd., the foundation was laid for a modern banking system capable of serving the expanding Jewish population.

The first phase of the country's modern banking history, which opened with the inauguration of British rule in 1918, was marked by the reopening and gradual expansion of the Anglo-Palestine Company (later the Anglo-Palestine Bank), which became the central financial institution of the *yishuv*, and the founding of several other financial institutions such as the General Mortgage Bank Ltd., the Workers' Bank Ltd., the Palestine Corporation Ltd., the Central Bank of Cooperative Institutions Ltd., the Mizrachi Bank Ltd., the Kupat-Am Bank, and other cooperative credit societies. These institutions were established by groups primarily interested in the economic development of the *yishuv*, and helped the *yishuv* to expand and to withstand the economic and political setbacks of the period. The sources of their capital and the policy of their managements gave the banking system a national character. At the same time, several international joint-stock banks, Barclays Bank D.C.O., the Ottoman Bank, and the Banco di Roma, opened offices in the principal towns of Palestine. Barclays Bank, as banker to the Mandatory government, enjoyed a prominent position.

In the early 1930s large-scale immigration from Germany

and Central Europe was accompanied by a mushroom growth of more than one hundred banking institutions. This unsound expansion led, in 1937, to banking legislation requiring a minimum paid-up capital for opening a bank and providing for the appointment of an examiner of banks. As a result, the number of banks was reduced to about 30, of which some had been established by German Jewish private bankers. On the eve of World War II, a few more small banks were eliminated by a short-lived run on the banks, which the banking system successfully weathered. Most of the banks had been able to strengthen their resources and to cope with expanding business. They withstood the dislocations of the postwar disturbances and the War of Independence.

Palestine was excluded from the sterling bloc on February 22, 1948, and three months later the establishment of the State of Israel was accompanied by the introduction of new currency. The Anglo-Palestine Bank (from 1951 Bank Leumi) became banker to the government and bank of issue while remaining the leading commercial bank. It was relieved of its official functions as central bank in December 1954 upon the establishment of the Bank of Israel, which increasingly became an instrument of monetary and economic policy. In December 1972 the bank supervised 21 commercial (deposit) banks with 769 branches; 13 co-operative credit institutions with 57 branches; 20 mortgage and investment credit banks (most of them affiliated to commercial banks); and 13 other financial institutions. Open investment trusts, most of them affiliated to commercial banks, were also active.

The Israel banking system shows a high degree of specialization, while the commercial banks are, on the whole, restricted to short-term business. Medium- and long-term transactions are handled by institutions established to service agriculture, industry, housing, tourism, and shipping. These institutions are either fully government-owned or owned jointly by the banks and the government. Government development funds are directed through both the commercial and the credit banks. The Association of Banks in Israel represents the interests of all banking institutions and encourages the professional training of bank staff.

The Bank of Israel, established by law in 1954 as Israel's central bank with the sole right to issue currency; its specific tasks, as stated in the law, are: "to administer, regulate, and direct the currency system, and to regulate and direct the credit and banking system, in accordance with the economic policy of the government, with a view to promoting by monetary measures (1) the stabilization of the value of the currency in Israel and abroad, and (2) a high level of production, employment, national income, and investment in Israel." The capital of the bank, IL 10 million ($2.854 million), and an identical amount in reserves, were provided by a government loan which was repaid by the bank out of its annual profits. The bank is presided over by a governor (Heb. *nagid*) appointed by the government, who also serves as chief economic advisor to the government. From 1954 to 1971 the post of governor was held by David Horowitz who was replaced by Moshe Sanbar in November 1971. The governor is assisted by an advisory committee whose seven members also serve on the advisory board, together with eight other representatives of various economic interests and parliamentary parties. The governor is obliged to report to the government and the Knesset when the total means of payment exceed by 15% or more the amount in circulation at any time during the preceding 12 months, indicating the causes for this increase and the countermeasures required. Within five months of the end of every fiscal year, the governor must submit an annual report on the bank's operation and an analysis of the country's economic and financial situation.

As a banker's bank and as the ultimate credit resource, the bank, by its rediscount policy, may impose quantitive and qualitative credit and liquidity restrictions on the banking system. It also fixes the level of deposits which 257 commercial banks are obliged to maintain with the central bank. These measures are designed to control the quantity of money in circulation and to direct the flow of credit to economically desirable sectors. The bank's authorization is required for the establishment of new banks and for the opening of additional branches. Its periodic examination of bank operations prevents unsound practices and protects the public's interests. The supervision is extended to credit banks and other financial institutions. The bank and its branches serve as clearing centers for the clearing banks. As government banker, the Bank of Israel is entrusted with the administration of state loans. It also represents the state at the International Monetary Fund, the International Bank of Reconstruction and Development, and affiliated bodies. The assets of the bank on Dec. 31, 1972 totaled IL12.71 million, of which IL5,722 million was in foreign currencies and IL161 million in gold. The bank maintains an economic research department which prepares its annual report and bulletin. It also publishes occasional volumes of special studies and provides the government with much of the material required in economic planning.

Bank Leumi Le-Israel B.M., Israel's leading commercial bank, was incorporated in 1951 to take over and continue the business of the Anglo-Palestine Bank Ltd., which was registered in London in 1902 under the name of the Anglo-Palestine Company as a subsidiary of the Jewish Colonial Trust Ltd. and opened its first office in Jaffa in 1903. The Anglo-Palestine Bank soon became the principal financial institution of the young *yishuv.* In 1908 it was active in the financial arrangements for building Tel Aviv. In 1910 its original capital of £40,000 had increased to £100,000 and by 1914 deposits had reached £400,000. Soon after the outbreak of the war, the Turkish authorities ordered the bank to be liquidated, but it managed to survive clandestinely and by the end of the war its deposits stood at £700,000.

The Anglo-Palestine Bank was able to maintain its leading position under the British Mandate. Its board was transferred from London to Tel Aviv in 1931. In 1934 it arranged a loan of £500,000 from Lloyds Bank for the Jewish Agency, and the next year it launched an issue of £250,000 in 4% redeemable preference shares. The capital influx which had started with the German *aliyah* around 1933 was reflected in the steady growth of the bank, which in 1934 helped to set up the Haavara Trust Co. to enable German Jewish immigrants to transfer some of their capital in kind. By 1936 the bank's capital had increased to £860,000, with £218,000 of reserves. Deposits rose from £1,550,000 in 1932 to £6,150,000 in 1939. In anticipation of independence in 1948, the bank prepared its own currency notes. With the declaration of the State of Israel, the Anglo-Palestine Bank became government banker and bank of issue, until the establishment of the Bank of Israel in December 1954. Among the specialized institutions established by the bank, in cooperation with the Jewish Agency, were: the General Mortgage Bank (1924); the Oẓar le-Ta'asiyyah (Industry Fund, 1944); and the Oẓar le-Ḥakla'ut ("Agricultural Fund," 1944; merged in 1960 into Ya'ad Agricultural Development Bank). In 1934 a securities clearing house was set up, the forerunner of the Tel Aviv Stock Exchange. The Bank Leumi le-Israel Investment Corporation, the first in the country, was formed in 1945.

In 1961 Bank Leumi acquired the majority of the shares of the Union Bank of Israel, the country's fourth largest commercial bank, specialist in diamond-industry financing. In 1966 it bought the large cooperative bank Kupat Milveh la-Oleh ("Immigrant Loan Bank"). In 1972 the bank had 208 branches in Israel. Bank Leumi has a subsidiary in New York, Leumi Securities Corporation, and in 1968 converted its branch into the First Israel Bank & Trust Company of New York. Other subsidiaries abroad are the Anglo-Israel Bank in London and the Cifico Bank in Zurich and Geneva. Bank Leumi's capital at the end of 1972 stood at IL90,000,000 ($21,450,000) with reserves at IL120,200,000 ($28,600,00) and total assets at IL11,439,000,000 ($2,723,500,000). The director general of Bank Leumi le-Israel

Table 94. Israel's Commercial Banks (at the end of 1971)

Name of Bank	Founded in	Branches Israel	Branches Abroad	Capital and Reserves	Balance Sheet Total (in thousand IL.)
Arab Israel Bank Ltd.[1]	1959	18		890	57,047
Bank Hapoalim B.M.	1921	198	1	113,498	6,679,378
Bank Lemelacha Ltd.	1953	12		8,679	102,277
Bank Leumi Le-Israel B.M.	1902	194	3	127,353	8,608,370
Bank Otzar Hachayal B.M.	1946	12		5,718	73,745
Barclays Discount Bank Ltd.[2]	1971	48		22,000	880,579
Export Bank Ltd.[3]	1955	5		12,470	293,780
The Foreign Trade Bank Ltd.[3]	1955	30		19,485	684,333
Israel Agricultural Bank Ltd.[4]	1951	1		121,677	597,835
Israel-British Bank Ltd.	1929	8		20,733	434,258
Israel Discount Bank Ltd.[5]	1935	130	3	77,168	6,259,435
Israel Finance Bank Ltd.	1936	1		6,713	31,974
Israel General Bank Ltd.	1964	3		6,442	205,639
The Israel Industrial Bank Ltd.	1933	7		9,610	101,679
Japhet Bank Ltd.[6]	1933	12		7,520	346,790
Kupat-Am Bank Ltd.	1918	14		9,860	172,180
Mercantile Bank of Israel Ltd.[7]	1924	1		5,783	108,702
Trade Bank Ltd.	1937	1		2,036	19,167
United Mizrachi Bank Ltd.	1923	41		24,837	806,234
Union Bank of Israel Ltd.[1]	1951	14		11,887	1,062,925

1 Subsidiary of Bank Leumi Le-Israel B.M.
2 Jointly owned by Barclays Bank International Ltd. and IDB Bankholding Corporation Ltd.
3 Amalgamated in 1972 as First International Bank of Israel Ltd.
4 Government institution for financing agricultural investments (balance sheet date, 31.3.72).
5 Subsidiary of IDB Bankholding Corporation Ltd.
6 Subsidiary of Bank Hapoalim, B.M.
7 Subsidiary of Barclays Discount Bank Ltd.
(In addition to the above, two foreign banks operate branches in Israel: Bank Polska Kasa Opieki S.A. – Israel branch opened in 1930; Exchange National Bank of Chicago – Israel branch opened in 1970.)

enjoys a position of authority on national financial and economic problems. Noted directors general of the bank were Zalman Levontin (1903–19), Eliezer Siegfried Hoofien (1924–47), Aharon Barth (1947–57), Yeshayahu Foerder (1957–70), and from 1970 E. I. Japhet.

Israel Discount Bank Ltd., which was established in 1935 by Leon Recanati with a capital of £60,000, became Israel's largest private bank and the third largest banking institution in terms of both total assets (in 1972 IL8,070,625, or $1,920,000) and deposists (IL7,473,000,-000, or $1,780,000,000). In 1972 its total capital funds exceeded IL117,000,000 ($27,850,000). It operates a network of 129 branches in Israel, and two in New York City. In addition, the Mercantile Bank of Israel (est. 1926), its partly owned subsidiary, has three offices, will total assets of IL135,000,000 ($33,100,000). The Mercantile Bank absorbed the local business of the Ottoman Bank in 1953. The Mercantile Bank merged in 1971 with Barclay's Bank D.C.O., Israel. Long-term credits and investments are handled by the bank's subsidiaries: the Israel Development and Mortgage Bank Ltd. (est. 1959, total assets IL401,700,000, or $47,430,000), and the Discount Bank Investment Corporation Ltd. (IL838,700,000, or $199,700,000). Overseas affiliates are Discount Bank (Overseas) Ltd., Geneva (est. 1952); Overseas Discount Corporation, New York; Discount Bank (France), S.A., Paris; and other banks in London, Marseilles, Lima, Madrid, Milan, and Santiago. In the late 1960s a controlling interest was acquired in I.E.C. (Israel Economic Corporation), New York. The Israel Discount Bank Trust Company was opened in New York as a wholly owned subsidiary with a capital of $1,500,000. The Discount Bank Group is directed principally by the members of the Recanati family.

Bank Hapoalim B.M. (until 1961 known also as the Workers Bank Ltd.), third largest commercial bank in Israel, Bank Hapoalim was established in 1921 by the Histadrut with the aid of the World Zionist Organization, 262 as a central credit institute for its cooperative and settlement enterprises. In 1972 it had 198 branches, with total assets of IL9,962,000,000 ($2,372,000,000). The original capital of LE (Egyptian pounds) 30,000 (about $150,000) was gradually increased, largely with the aid of the American Friends of the Histadrut and particularly in 1957, when the bank merged with 25 workers' savings and loan associations. In 1972 its capital and reserves were IL178,600,000 ($42,500,000). Between 1962 and 1968 the bank opened representative offices in New York, Buenos Aires, and Zurich. For long-term credit and investments the bank operates through specialized subsidiaries and affiliates, such as the Israel-American Industrial Development Bank Ltd., Nir Ltd. (agriculture), Bizur Ltd. (public works), the Housing & Mortgage Bank Ltd., Public Buildings Ltd., and Yahav (the civil servants' fund). Locally, it mobilizes investment funds through the Workers' Bank Investment Corporation and retirement and pension funds, and, in the U.S., through the Ampal American-Israel Corporation, New York. It also controls the Industrial & Commercial Bank (Israel-Latin America) Ltd., Tel Aviv.

CHAMBERS OF COMMERCE. The first chamber of commerce in Erez Israel was founded in 1908 in Jerusalem. It was a mixed Arab-Jewish chamber, without official status, formed to settle commercial disputes and sometimes to intervene with the Turkish authorities. In 1919, the British military administration set up mixed Jewish-Arab chambers of commerce in Jaffa and Haifa and reconstituted the Jerusalem chamber to represent the business community and advise the government. The political conflict between Arabs and Jews, however, soon led to splits within the chambers.

After the 1921 disturbances the Arabs founded their own Jaffa National Chamber of Commerce, which existed until 1948. After the 1929 riots the Jewish members transferred the offices of their Jaffa and district chamber of commerce to Tel Aviv, changing its name to the Chamber of Commerce, Tel Aviv-Jaffa, and Eliezer Hoofien was its president from 1922 to 1943. In Haifa, the Jews left the mixed chamber over Arab refusal to recognize Hebrew as one of the official languages, and a Jewish chamber was established. It was headed by Nathan Kaizerman, followed (from 1928 till 1954) by Zalman Nathanson, both of the Anglo-Palestine Bank Ltd. In Jerusalem, Edgar P. Shelley, a retired businessman, and later A.P.S. Clark, manager of Barclays Bank were presidents of the chamber. The Jewish vice-president was Yiẓḥak Eliachar, followed by his son Menasheh (president from 1948). It stayed bi-national until the 1936 riots, when the Arabs established their own chamber, which continued to exist in East Jerusalem (there are eight other Arab chambers on the West Bank and at Gaza).

During and after World War II, the presidents of the three Jewish chambers frequently called on the high commissioner and other senior officials to submit representations, or were invited for consultation, warning, exhortation, or invitations to cooperate. Thus the informal but firmly established joint representation of the chambers of commerce in Palestine came into being, continuing its activities in the State of Israel, each chamber keeping its autonomous identity. Chambers of commerce in Israel are independent and non-party, though adhering to the policies of free trade and private enterprise. Among their almost 2,000 members (Tel Aviv 1,000; Haifa 650; Jerusalem 250) are firms concerned with all branches of commerce, industry, and ancillary services, excluding retail trade. The Israel chambers are affiliated to the International Chamber of Commerce (I.C.C.) in Paris. During the 1950s and 1960s, about 20 independent bi-national chambers of commerce, with representation both in Israel and abroad, came into being. Their special aim is to foster trade between Israel and the respective countries, stressing Israel's need for investment and exports.

STOCK EXCHANGE. In 1923, the city of Tel Aviv floated a £75,000 loan at 6½ per cent in New York and three years later the General Mortgage Bank issued the first securities in Palestine, which were also traded abroad. Public utilities and primary industries such as the Palestine Electric Corporation, the Jerusalem Electric Corporation, and Palestine Potash, as well as the Anglo-Palestine Bank, (succeeded by the Bank Leumi le-Israel) found a ready source of capital in London, where the Jewish Colonial Trust had sold some £400,000 worth of its shares as early as 1899.

Regular trade in Palestinian securities started in Palestine itself only after 1933, when middle-class immigrants from Germany, accustomed to the various forms of indirect investment, established a number of companies which raised capital by selling stocks and bonds to the public. Representatives of banks and brokers began to meet regularly to fix the prices of the handful of securities available, and in 1935 they established the Tel Aviv Securities Clearing House, which functioned until 1953, when the Tel Aviv Stock Exchange Ltd. was registered as a privately owned limited company. Its members meet five times a week to buy and sell stocks and bonds registered at the Exchange, which is Israel's only recognized capital market. The quotations published after each day's trading fix the prices of transactions in these securities. In 1972 the Exchange had 32 members: 22 banks and 10 brokers or financial corporations. It operates its own securities clearing agency.

In the early years of the state, a desire to ensure the value of the investor's pound against inflation made "linked" bonds popular. The capital and interest on these bonds were linked either to the dollar or to the consumers' price index; in most cases the buyer could choose between these two forms of linkage. (Linking to the dollar was discontinued after the devaluation of the Israel pound on Feb. 9, 1962.) After 1959 the public interest in common stock grew rapidly. There was a constant upsurge of prices and, although there was also a rapid increase in the number of stock issues, most of the issues were oversubscribed. During the second half of 1964, prices of stocks began to fall. The

The Stock Exchange in Tel Aviv. Courtesy Government Press Office, Tel Aviv.

decline was attributed in part to the competition of government securities and in part to a proposal to impose a capital-gains tax, from which listed stocks had hitherto been exempt.

Trading on the Tel Aviv Stock Exchange is based on the European call system. Members bring to the floor only those orders which they cannot settle from their own accounts. Prices are quoted according to the European system: as a percentage of the nominal value. Two remarkable features are the predominance of the banks as brokers, investors, and issuing houses, and the extent of the Israel government's association, directly or indirectly, with many of the securities traded on the Exchange.

INSURANCE. The first Jewish insurance company in Palestine was established in 1923. In 1939 there were eight domestic insurers with total own resources of less than **266** $1,000,000, but they accounted for only a small part of the business; the rest was still in the hands of foreign companies, mostly British, which operated through local general agents. After the establishment of the State of Israel in 1948, the rapidly growing economy resulted in a dynamic expansion of insurance. By the end of 1971 some 28 domestic companies were operating in Israel, with own resources of around IL24,000,000, total assets exceeding IL1,000,000,000, and premium income reaching IL650,000,-000, of which 25% related to life insurance. Israel's companies handled 81% of the insurance, Lloyd's Underwriters 7% and a considerable number of foreign companies shared the remaining 12%. Including reinsurance abroad placed by domestic companies, the total risk carried by foreign insurers covered insurances corresponding to over IL 290 million of the premium income.

The social values of Jews in Palestine, in particular the emphasis placed on the superiority of manual labor, were not conducive to the development of an efficient sales organization. However, with the gradual acceptance of western social and economic patterns, this psychological handicap was overcome. By 1971 a sales force of some 3,000 licensed insurance agents and brokers, most of them fairly well trained, served as the link between insurers and their customers. As yet, the insurance consciousness of the Israel public, measured by the proportion of total premiums to gross national product, is low compared with that of more advanced industrial economies.

The industry is regulated by the Insurance Business Law of 1951, administered by a superintendent in the Ministry of Finance. Rules are laid down for the licensing of insurers and agents, minimum capital, technical reserves, investment of funds, and the publication of accounts. Tariffs must be filed and the general conditions of policies have to be approved by the superintendent. The regulations are largely on the Continental pattern and are much less elaborate than those usual in the United States. Insurance contracts are formally still subject to an outdated Ottoman law of 1904, but in practice they are governed largely by common law. **267**

15 COMMUNICATIONS

Transportation. The donkey and the camel have been very widely used for transport in the Land of Israel since biblical times; donkeys, horses, and mules are still used for short-distance haulage and, in the Arab villages, in agriculture, while the camel is the principal carrier for the Bedouin tribes in the Negev. In the 19th century public interurban transport was provided by stagecoaches (diligences), which also connected the country with some of its neighbors.

Railroads. In 1892 a railroad line from Jaffa to Jerusalem was constructed by a French concessionary company, shortening the traveling time between the two cities from three days to four hours. Its original narrow gauge of one meter (3.3 ft.) was converted in 1920 by the British authorities to standard gauge of 1.435 m. (4'8½"). In 1914 the Turks, with the help of the Germans, built the special-gauge Hejaz Railroad connecting Damascus with the Muslim holy places in Medina through Amman, with a branch via Ẓemaḥ and Afulah to Haifa and a spur to Acre. During World War I the Turks extended the line southward from Afulah through Jenin to Nablus and Tulkarm. A further extension via Beersheba reached Quseima in 1916. Also during the war, the British built the standard-gauge Sinai Military Railroad from Qantara on the Suez Canal to Haifa. Under the British Mandate this system, up to the Suez Canal, belonged to the Palestine Railroads and linked up in Qantara with the Egyptian Railroad. In 1942 it was extended from Haifa to Beirut and at the end of the Mandate there were 290 mi. (470 km.) of railroad in Palestine.

The first locomotive in Palestine, 1893. Courtesy Central Zionist Archives, Jerusalem.

Only 75 mi. (121 km.) could be brought into operation in the State of Israel after the War of Independence. The southward line had been cut at Yad Mordekhai on the Gaza Strip border and the lines to Beirut and to Zemaḥ had also ceased to operate. New standard-gauge lines were laid from Ḥaderah to Tel Aviv in 1953 and from Na'an to Beersheba in 1956. The latter was extended to Dimonah in 1965 and later extended to reach the Oron phosphate mines, with a branch line to the Arad chemical works. By 1971/72 the railroad system had about 425 mi. (over 760 km.) of standard-gauge line. Heavier rails allowed the standard axle load to be raised from 15 to 21 tons and the installation of a semiautomatic signal system between Tel Aviv and Haifa in 1957 permitted the speed to be raised to 60 mi. (96 km.) an hour, so that express trains cover the distance between the two cities in one hour. In 1958 the system's 105 steam locomotives were replaced by 30 airbraked diesel locomotives. Most of the freight wagons (average capacity 25.6 tons) and the 97 passenger cars (averaging 90 seats) were acquired through German reparations between 1954 and 1956. The railroad carried 4.3 million passengers and 3.2 million tons of freight in the fiscal year 1971/72. About 20% of the annual inland haulage goes by rail, the main commodities carried being minerals, fuel, cereals, and citrus.

Motor Transport. During the Ottoman regime there were few truck roads in the country, and those that existed were lightly constructed. Under the British Mandate, the first motor roads were built from Jaffa to Jerusalem and from Tel Aviv to Haifa. These were supplemented by a network of security roads built by the British and the Jews. The numbers of buses, commercial vehicles, and private cars increased. Jewish cooperative bus services were founded and gradually expanded to meet the defense and economic requirements of the *yishuv.*

In 1949 there were 15,800 motor vehicles of all kinds; by 1972 the number had grown to 331,000, including some 89,000 trucks, 196,000 private cars, and 5,100 buses, and there were 493,000 licensed drivers, as compared with 140,000 in 1959. Most of the urban and interurban passenger traffic is carried by the bus cooperatives: Egged covers the entire country, with the exception of greater Tel Aviv, where the Dan cooperative operates, and Beersheba, which runs its own buses. Services were controlled by the Ministry of Transport through the issue of licenses and the approval of fares and timetables. Fares are kept low by state subsidies.

The growth of traffic resulted in congested roads, considerable road damage, and a high accident rate. In 1962 a loan was granted by the International Bank of Reconstruction for a five-year highway construction program, which had cost over IL160 million by the end of 1967, and in 1966/67 and 1967/68 a further IL80 million was allocated. By 1972 the road network covered over 2,000 mi. (3,300 km.), mostly about 23 ft. (7 m.) wide, of which 100 mi. (166 km.) were for separated

traffic with double or triple lanes. The maximum weight

The Haifa–Tel Aviv highway near Athlit. Photo Werner Braun, Jerusalem.

on all interurban roads is 13 tons per axle.

Harbors. Israel's three modern deep-water harbors—Haifa and Ashdod on the Mediterranean and Eilat on the Red Sea—are managed, maintained, and developed by the Ports Authority. The lighter harbor at Jaffa, which had served the country since the second millennium B.C.E. and was the only port of entry for the early Jewish immigrants, and the one at Tel Aviv, which was built during the Arab riots of 1936–39, were closed in 1966 when Ashdod came into use. The decision to build this new deep-water harbor, with an annual capacity of 2.5 million tons, was taken in 1961, as the deep-water port of Haifa, built by the British in 1934, was rapidly becoming saturated with the expansion of commerce in both directions. The Red Sea deep-water port of Eilat, opened in 1965, has an annual capacity of half a million tons.

In 1972 the volume of cargoes (excluding fuel) loaded and unloaded at the three ports totaled 8.4 million tons, as against 3.2 million tons in 1961: Haifa handled 51% of the total, Ashdod 40%, and Eilat 9%. The Ports Authority forecast a volume of 10 million tons in another decade after the completion of the Ashdod extension program and the extension and improvement of Haifa port. The number of passengers through these ports declined from 256,500 in 1961 to 174,000 in 1972, due to the ever-increasing share of air traffic, a common tendency the world over. Since the establishment of the state, more than IL250 million were invested in Israel's harbors—69% on the construction of Ashdod, 17% on Eilat, and 14% on Haifa. The improvement of port facilities and the training of port labor by the Ports Authority has resulted in a speedier turn-round of the 9,145 ships which touched at Israel's harbors in 1972. Extensive investments have been made to prepare the ports for the inception of the container era.

Unlike the ports of Haifa and Ashdod, Eilat is not linked with the railroad system. It was handicapped by the imbalance between exports and imports, but in 1972 from 710,000 tons, 56% were export and 44% import.

Shipping. The modest beginnings of shipping go back to 1921, when an attempt was made to establish a shipping service between Palestine and the neighboring countries with the 250-ton *He-Ḥalutz.* The vessel ran aground and nothing was done until 1928, when the *Ḥeẓ* (150 tons) sailed in the Mediterranean for a short time, and then a coastal cargo service was maintained for a year and a half with another small ship, the *Carmel.* In 1933 the Orient Shipping Line was established, and its ships, the *Carola* and the *Dora,* sailed between Haifa and Egypt, Lebanon, Syria, Cyprus, and Greece. The Palestine Maritime Lloyd was established in 1934 and until 1939 ran a regular service between Haifa and Constanta with the 2,500-ton *Har Zion* and *Har*

Carmel. In the same year the Atid freight company was founded.

The increase in Jewish immigration heightened awareness of the need for maritime knowledge and experience, since the sea was the natural means of communication with the rest of the world, as well as an important source of income. Between 1924 and 1928 the maritime section of the workers' sport organization Ha-Po'el and the Zevulun Seafarers' Society (Agudat Yoredei Yam Zevulun) were established to provide youngsters with maritime training. Through the initiative of David Remez, later Israel's first minister of transport, the Palestine Maritime League (Ḥevel Yammi le-Israel) was established in 1937 to provide information and training. In 1938, together with the Jewish Agency, the League founded a nautical school affiliated with the Technion, which was moved to Acre and greatly expanded after the establishment of independent Israel. Another was founded in 1934 at Civitavecchia, Italy, by the Betar movement. The 800 survivors of the 1,200 Jewish volunteers who served in the British Royal Navy during World War II gained valuable experience that was later used in the Israel navy. The experience gained at sea, under the most difficult conditions, in bringing in "illegal" immigrants between 1939 and 1948 also helped to develop Israel shipping.

The foundation was laid for the large-scale development of Israel shipping in 1945 with the establishment of Zim Israel Navigation Company, Ltd. by the Jewish Agency, the Histadrut and the Palestine Maritime League. Progress was slow at first; the *Kedmah* (3,500 tons) was purchased, but in 1948 Israel's entire merchant fleet consisted of four ships, with a deadweight of 6,000 tons. In view of the complete closure of land frontiers, shipping was of vital importance for the transport of supplies and the carriage of hundreds of thousands of immigrants. A serious beginning was made with the expansion of the fleet, and by the end of 1953 it comprised 31 ships with a total capacity of 119,000 tons. Most of the vessels were old, however, and it was not until 273

Ships in harbor at Ashdod, 1968. Courtesy Government Press Office, Tel Aviv.

the conclusion of the reparations agreement with Germany that it was possible to build up a modern merchant fleet. At the beginning of 1973, there were 129 ships with a deadweight of some 3.6 million tons.

In 1965 most of Zim's shares were taken over by the government, but in 1970 a controlling interest was sold to the Israel Corporation, an investment corporation founded after the Jerusalem Economic Conference in 1968. At the beginning of 1972 it operated 60 vessels, with a total deadweight of 1,600,000 tons divided almost equally between cargo ships, bulk carriers, and tankers. In view of the declining profitability of passenger shipping, this branch of its business was transferred to a separate company, Israel Passenger Lines. In 1952 El-Yam (Cargo Ships), Ltd., a subsidiary of the Israel Discount Bank, was founded. It bought three 10,500-ton Liberty ships and successfully developed tramp shipping. In 1972 El-Yam and its affiliated companies operated almost a million tons of shipping, including bulk carriers, tankers, and refrigerated vessels for the transport of fruit, meat, and dairy products. Other important shipping companies are Fruit Carriers, Ltd., (Ḥevrah Yammit le-Hovalat Peri), which in 1972 operated almost 200,000 tons of shipping, Tarshish, Mediterranean Lines (Kavvei ha-Yam ha-Tikhon), and Gadot.

Auxiliary services have been expanded parallel to the growth of the fleet. Repairs and shipbuilding up to 20,000 tons are carried out by Israel Shipyards (Mispenot Israel) at Kishon port. The training of more Israel seamen is of considerable importance; out of some 4,000 employed in Israel shipping, about 40% are foreign. In addition to prevocational training in Haifa, Acre, Netanyah, Herzliyyah, Tel Aviv, and a number of kibbutzim, there are nautical schools at Acre (for officers), Haifa, Mikhmoret, Tel Aviv, and Ashdod.

Air Transport. Civil aviation has made no small contribution to tourism, exports, rapid internal communications and economic development. This is due to a number of factors. Israel's location at the junction of Europe, Africa, and Asia makes it a convenient focus for air transport. Due to the political situation, this advantage is not, however, exploited to the full. As Israel has been surrounded by enemies, her air links bring her closer in terms of traveling time to distant lands, sources of supply, and markets. Regular air services enable Israel to maintain close contact with world Jewry, and the Israel national air carrier is widely used by Jews everywhere. The aircraft industry is a source of employment for skilled labor and a valuable economic asset.

Airports and Airfields. Lydda (Lod) airport, the international airport for passengers and freight, began to operate in 1936 and was taken over by Israel in 1948. In 1950 some 115,000 passengers passed through Lydda airport; in 1960, there were still only 220,000; but the number grew to 660,000 in 1966 and over 1,700,000 in 1972. Considerable investments were also made in Eilat airport, which served some 350,000 passengers in 1972. Jerusalem's airfield at Atarot (Kalandia) which served internal traffic after the 275

Six-Day War, was closed for repairs and reopened in 1973. In 1972 30,000 passengers passed through the airfield at Rosh Pinnah which serves Upper Galilee, and 400,000 through Sedeh Dov, near Tel Aviv, which serves as a transit point for passengers bound for Eilat and Rosh Pinnah.

International Traffic. In 1972, 17 foreign airlines were operating to Israel: Air France, Alitalia, Austrian Airlines, BEA, BOAC, Canadian Pacific, Cyprus Airways, KLM, Lufthansa, Olympic Airways, Sabena, SAS, Sterling Airlines, Swissair, Tarom, Turkish Airlines, and TWA. Table 95 shows the progress of international air traffic.

About half the passengers are carried by El Al. El Al was founded in November 1948 and began operating flights to Paris in August 1949, with one Douglas Skymaster. In 1969 its fleet consisted of nine standard Boeings, and one Boeing manufactured in accordance with the company's specifications. In 1971, it began to operate two jumbo jets. Over the years, it has flown about 50–55% of the total passenger traffic to and from Israel. El Al operates flights to Addis Ababa, Amsterdam, Athens, Brussels, Bucharest, Copenhagen, Frankfort, Geneva, Istanbul, Johannesburg, London, Montreal, Munich, Nairobi, New York, Nice, Nicosia, Paris, Rome, Teheran, Vienna, and Zurich. It

Table 95. International Air Trafic in 1950, 1960, 1969, and 1972[1]

	1950	1960	1969	1972
Aircraft landing	2,272	2,926	8,844	11,141
Passengers arrived (thousands)	82.8	111.6	566.7	871.3
Passengers departed (thousands)	33.8	111.8	548.2	841.9
Freight unloaded (tons)	1,410	1,486	12,452	15,225
Freight loaded (tons)	536	2,030	13,844	26,524
Mail arrived (tons)	167	321	989	1,436
Mail dispatched (tons)	74	202	783	1,078

[1] Including one-day visitors.

Table 96. Development of El Al's Productivity and Exploitation of Capacity

	1964/65	1966/67	1967/68	1968/69	1971/72
Flying hours	19,518	23,443	26,846	34,431	45,572
No. of passengers	231,793	314,404	364,360	464,915	678,920
Cargo (in tons)	6,459	8,863	13,000	14,758	20,515
Exploitation —%	55.6	60.5	65.1	64.6	68.2

holds 17th place amongst the 103 members of IATA in terms of the scope of its operations. At the end of 1971, the permanent staff in Israel and abroad numbered approximately 4,290. Since the Six-Day War, the company has been running at a profit. Table 96 shows its growth in recent years.

Air piracy and attacks on airliners and installations serving civil aviation have in recent years become a world problem, causing dislocation, expense, and danger. Between mid-1968 and the fall of 1972, passengers and aircraft of El Al and other companies operating flights to and from Israel were a target for the Arab terrorist organizations. El Al and the Israel government have taken measures to guarantee regular and normal air links with other countries.

Internal Aviation. The Arkia company (heir to Aviron, which started flying in 1936), began to operate internal airlines on the establishment of the state. It is jointly owned by El Al and Ḥevrat ha-Ovedim in equal shares; the share capital is IL664,000. The fleet consists of 5 twin-engined Heralds, which seat 50 passengers, and four-engined Vickers Viscounts, seating 80 passengers. The company's home airfield is Sedeh Dov outside Tel Aviv, but the Viscounts operate out of Lydda. There are regular services to Eilat, Jerusalem, Rosh Pinnah, Masada, Sharm el-Sheikh, and Nicosia. In 1958, it carried 70,000 passengers, in 1964—158,000, and in 1972 approximately 350,000. It employs a staff of about 310. Arkia has made an important

An El Al Boeing 707 at Lydda airport. Courtesy Government Press Office, Tel Aviv.

An Arkia airplane in Eilat. Photo I. Zukerman, Tel Aviv.

contribution to the development of tourism and industry in Eilat, which would have been impossible without regular air contact with the center and north of Israel. After the Six-Day War, when new tourist attractions and holy places came under Israel's jurisdiction, pilgrim and tourist traffic increased sharply. This gave rise to a considerable increase in private flying and in the number of small commercial, companies dealing in internal charter flights for tourists, publicity, flying lessons, etc. The leading companies of this type are Netivei-Kanaf, Arkia, Shaḥaf Ya'af, and Sheḥakim.

Agricultural Aviation. Agricultural aviation is highly developed and makes no small contribution to the war against pests infesting citrus, cotton, and other crops, leading to savings in manpower and helping to modernize Israel agriculture. The experience accumulated in this field is placed at the disposal of other developing countries. Agricultural aviation on a large scale commenced in Israel as early as 1950, when 2,500 dunams (about 600 acres) were sprayed by Piper aircraft: in 1972 the area sprayed was more than three million dunams (about 800,000 acres). In the same year Chimavir, the oldest company of this type, operated 25 aircraft, including 20 of the Pony type, 5 of Snow type: Merom had 16, all of them were large crop-spraying Snow aircraft, and Masok had five helicopters for spraying. Another company in this field was Executive.

Aircraft Industry. At the beginning of 1953, the Bedek ("Overhaul") Institute started operations at Lydda airport with a staff of about 70. In 1957 it began to produce the Fouga-Magister, a twin-jet trainer of French design, for the Israel Air Force and for export, and changed its name to Israel Aircraft Industries. I.A.I. developed rapidly and comprises a number of divisions and subsidiary companies dealing with aeronautical technology. In the early 1960s it carried out far-reaching modifications of the Boeing B-77, the Stratocruiser. In 1967, the company began to plan an original Israel aircraft, and early in 1970 the test flights of the Arava, a STOL (short takeoff and landing) aircraft which can operate on improvised runways, were made. It 279 weighs 12,500 lbs. and can carry 20 passengers or two tons of freight. The company acquired from the Rockwell Standard Corporation of the U.S. the manufacturing rights for the Jet Commander, a twin-jet executive aircraft, which was redesigned and named Commodore-Jet. In 1970, Israel Aircraft Industries employed more than 12,000 workers. In 1968/69, turnover was IL140 million; IL100 million had been invested in 150 plants.

Training Facilities. At the Faculty of Aeronautical Engineering at the Haifa Technion, aeronautical research and the training and education of aeronautical engineers have been expanded. There are also five vocational high schools which train aircraft technicians. A flying club, with branches throughout the country, teaches gliding, flying, and model aircraft building. Many of Israel's pilots and technicians started their training at the club.

Administration and Control. The government's Civil Aviation Authority is responsible for regulation, development, and assistance. It issues and enforces safety regulations and awards licenses to air and ground crews, grants licenses for the manufacture of new aircraft, and maintains contact with countries interested in purchasing them. At the beginning of 1970, Israel had aviation agreements with 18 countries; in 11 of these the rights were exploited. In addition, there were unofficial aviation links with companies in three countries. With the growth in aviation after the Six-Day War, the Authority made regulations for flights paths, air traffic control, and communications and navigation aids. Its planning activities are mainly concerned with investments in infrastructure, airfields, and other facilities required to keep pace with traffic forecasts and technological developments are taken into account.

TELECOMMUNICATIONS. Under Ottoman rule there was no telephone service in Erez Israel and only a few Morse telegraph circuits for public use. The British occupation forces in 1917–18, and the Palestine civil administration from 1920 started building an urban and interurban system. The first directory, published in 1919 by the British army,

Automatic telephone exchange at Nazareth. Courtesy Government Press Office, Tel Aviv.

recorded 138 subscribers in Jerusalem, Jaffa, and Haifa. By May 1948 the number in the area of independent Israel had grown to 10,400—13 per 1,000 of the population.

The development of telecommunications was particularly urgent for a dynamic country like Israel, and large funds were devoted to the purpose in the development budget. The system was managed first by the Ministry of Communications and from 1952 by the Ministry of Posts. The number of direct lines grew in 25 years to 477,000 and the number of telephones to 675,000 (in March 1972), while telephone density increased more than sixteenfold to 160 per

1,000, despite the quadrupling of the population during the period. While in 1948 the telephone system was largely automatic in the main cities, it was manual for trunk calls. By 1968 the system had become fully automatic, enabling any subscriber to dial directly to any other in the country.

Israel is divided into 11 dialing zones, each having a code number (e.g., 02 for Jerusalem and 03 for the Tel Aviv area) for use when dialing from another zone. The system consists of 80 switching centers (automatic exchanges) interconnected by a transmission network of underground cables and microwave radio links, on which carrier systems are superimposed, providing from 12 to 240 speech channels. The inland telegraph system consists of point-to-point teleprinter channels for the transmission of telegrams between post offices or messages between subscribers all over the country. The telex system was established in 1956 and had some 1,670 lines in 1972; planning anticipates a growth to 5,000 by the 1980s. Teleprinters are equipped for transmission of either Hebrew or Latin characters.

For over 20 years Israel's telecommunications with the outside world had to be conducted by radio. From a single telegraph channel and a single telephone channel with the United States in 1948, an extensive radio communications network was developed on the basis of direct high-frequency radio links with terminal and transit centers in Europe and the U.S. In November 1968, a submarine cable was inaugurated between Israel and France, providing 96–128 telephone channels, compared with 21 by radio, with much less interference and semi-automatic dialing, requiring only the intervention of the international telephone operator at the calling end. In 1973, a satellite communications station, with 400 international lines, was opened.

POSTAL SERVICES. *In the Ottoman Period.* The first regular services in the Land of Israel were established by the Great Powers by arrangement with the Sublime Porte in the mid-19th century under the Capitulation Treaties. In 1852 France, which had opened a shipping line to the Orient, established post offices in Jerusalem, Jaffa, and Haifa. At about the same time, Austria opened offices in Jerusalem and Jaffa, with Russia and Italy following suit. Austrian postal agencies were also set up in the Jewish villages of Rishon le-Zion and Petaḥ Tikvah, the latter with its own stamps. In 1865, the Turkish government began to establish its own network of post offices. The foreign post offices used the stamps of their own countries with the face value in Turkish currency superimposed. They competed with one another and often had their postmarks printed in Hebrew to attract business. Competition also helped to increase efficiency, and at the beginning of the century a letter would reach Vienna within five days—a reasonable speed at the time. All foreign countries closed their post offices on the outbreak of World War I, except for Germany and Austria, Turkey's allies, who continued to deal with army mail.

Under the British Mandate. When the British occupied Palestine (1917), the military authorities established a civilian postal service as part of the network of the Egyptian Expeditionary Force, and a countrywide civilian postal service was set up during the period of the British Mandate, with a monopoly confirmed by the Post Office Ordinance of 1930. The service was organized on the British pattern, and the senior officials were almost entirely British. Large modern offices were opened in the main towns, with agencies in smaller places. The pillar boxes were exact replicas of the British ones: bright red with the royal arms embossed on them. Stamps, postmarks, and public notices were printed in the three official languages, English, Arabic and Hebrew, but internal directives were exclusively in English. At the end of the Mandatory period in 1948, there were 97 post offices and agencies in the area that became independent Israel, but most of the villages had no satisfactory postal services.

In the State of Israel. Improvised postal services were organized in Jewish areas when the de facto partition of Palestine began even before the departure of the British, using Jewish National Fund stamps overprinted with the

Table 97. Posts and Communications[1] (1948/49—1969/70)

	Unit	1948/49
Postal Services		
Post offices and branches	Number	—
Postal agencies	"	—
Mobile post office	"	—
Localities served by mobile post offices	"	—
Rented post office boxes	1,000	—
Mail sent abroad[2]	1,000 kg.	—
By air mail	"	—
Number of parcels sent abroad	1,000	—
By air mail	"	—
Telephones		
Capacity of exchanges	1,000	—
Connected trunk lines	"	10.9
Standing applicaions	"	11.0
Telephones		18.4
Length of telephone lines	1,000 km.	1.1
Length of telephone wires	"	137
Telephone calls	"	
Local and interurban trunk calls	C. Pulses—10⁶	44.3
International[3]	1,000	0.9
Thereof: Incoming calls	"	—
Telegrams[3]	"	
Telegrams dispatched	1,000	616
Thereof: Sent abroad	"	347
Telegrams received from abroad	"	84
Telex calls		
International	1,000 min.	—
Local	C.P. 1,000	—

[1] Budget years; data on mail sent abroad, telephone calls, and telegrams refer to the yearly postal activity; the other data refers to March 31 of each year.

1950/51	1960/61	1967/68	1969/70	1971/72
64	114	173	178	184
77	218	285	321	356
6	29	32	35	39
—	550	559	582	596
—	15.9	31.8	38.7	44.5
—	—	1,324	1,545	1,739
—	169	352	489	563
17	131	217	232	235
—	41	119	128	134
—	80.2	331.1	417.0	477.0
17.1	67.9	244.5	332,9	418.0
12.0	19.5	35.3	44.9	83.8
	122.5	358.5	474.8	586.0
3.1	8.1	15.0	—	—
179	761	3,093	—	—
63.8	255.9	750.6	1,058.6	1,209.4
14.6	41.6	197.1	683.8	1,204.3
5.9	20.9	117.9	369.2	675.4
995	1,126	1,467	1,467	1,496
471	455	646	676	729
429	444	709	691	760
—	116	985	1,347	2,431
—	2,513	5,065	8,642	11,687

[2] Excludes parcels.　　[3] Includes calls to ships at sea.

word *do'ar* (post). At the same time, preparations were made for the establishment of the new state's postal system, which was run first as a department of the Ministry of Communications and, since 1952, by the Ministry of Posts (renamed in 1971 the Ministry of Communications). The service still operates under the Ordinance of 1930, given the force of law in 1948. The ministry runs a wide network of post offices, postal branches, and postal agencies of various types—a total of 580 at the end of 1972. An unusual feature is the mobile postal service, which came into operation in 1950. Post offices on wheels run according to a fixed timetable, staying for 10–15 minutes at each place on their route and providing all postal services, including those of the postal bank. At the end of 1972 there were 39 mobile postal routes, embracing 600 villages. Many services are operated gratis, including the delivery of letters from soldiers and material for the blind, and many others are run at a loss, such as the delivery of telegrams, parcels (particularly books), and newspapers, losses being offset by profits from other services. Israel has postal and telegraphic connections with every country in the world (with the exception of the Arab countries and Pakistan, who refuse to cooperate). She has been a member of the Universal Postal Union since 1949 and participated in its activities. The scope of the services provided by the ministry has been growing steadily since its inception, and the annual average growth of 11% is higher than in many other countries.

Philatelic Services. During the Mandatory period the stamps bore the name Palestine in the three official languages, English, Hebrew, and Arabic, with the letters א״י—the initials of "Ereẓ Israel"—in parentheses after the Hebrew name. They depicted characteristic views and

Series of four stamps showing postmen in Ereẓ Israel issued by the Israel Post Office on Stamp Day, December 14, 1966. Designed by   M. and G. Shamir. 1. Austrian postal service, 1854. 2. Ottoman period. 3. Mandatory period. 4. State of Israel. Jerusalem, B. M. Ansbacher Collection.

ISRAEL اسرائيل

0.12

ישראל

ISRAEL اسرائيل

0.15

ישראל

יום הבול
תשכ"ו
JOURNÉE
DU TIMBRE
1966

יום הבול
תשכ"ו
JOURNÉE
DU TIMBRE
1966

1

2

ISRAEL اسرائيل

0.40

ישראל

ISRAEL اسرائيل

1.00

ישראל

יום הבול
תשכ"ו
JOURNÉE
DU TIMBRE
1966

יום הבול
תשכ"ו
JOURNÉE
DU TIMBRE
1966

3

4

landmarks, such as the Dome of the Rock, the Citadel (Migdal David), and Rachel's Tomb.

Early in 1948, as the end of the Mandate approached, it became known that the British had given orders to destroy stamps and postal stationery on their departure, and the preparation of new stamps became imperative. As the name of the Jewish state-to-be was not yet decided, the words *Do'ar Ivri* (Hebrew Post) were given instead of the name of the country. The designs, by Otto Wallish, were based on ancient Jewish coins. The printing of the stamps in two weeks by inexperienced workers on unsuitable machinery under war conditions was no small achievement. Today a complete set of these stamps, consisting of nine denominations from 3 to 1,000 *perutot*, is a highly prized collector's item.

Better printing methods, such as photo-offset and photogravure, have gradually been introduced and the best Israeli artists have vied in the creation of attractive, colorful stamps, which have received worldwide recognition. Notable are the various "definitive" series showing emblems of the tribes, signs of the zodiac, and city coats-of-arms; the airmail series, showing birds and landscapes; and the stamps issued annually to mark Independence Day and Rosh Ha-Shanah. Other issues commemorate distinguished Jews, outstanding themes in the history and development of Israel, and various aspects of Jewish tradition.

Israel stamps have attracted collectors everywhere. There are stamp clubs, united in the Association of Israel Philatelic Societies, in every town in the country. Philatelic circles specializing in the study and collection of Israel stamps are to be found in the U.S., Great Britain, Germany, Holland, and elsewhere. Collectors of stamps connected with Judaism have their own separate organization. The government Philatelic Services have done much to popularize Israel stamps, and a sizable revenue is earned from collectors.

16 TOURISM

As a land sacred to three religions, Erez Israel has continuously attracted travelers from all over the world. But while in the past they went as pilgrims to the Holy Places, Israel today also offers many other attractions as a tourist center. It is a meeting place between East and West, between arid desert and flowering countryside; it contains not only holy places and historical sites, but also development areas and kibbutzim, seaside resorts and places of entertainment. The development of tourism was first the responsibility of various government departments; then, from 1955, of the Government Tourist Corporation under the aegis of the prime minister's office. A separate Ministry of Tourism, for publicity, organization, and development, was set up in 1964. It assists investors to establish tourist services and hotels, is an active partner in basic investments, organizes the training of hotel and other staff, and encourages the development of tourist attractions. The Tourist Corporation serves as a parent company for all government companies dealing with tourism.

Owing to differences in climate, lake and sea resorts are available all the year round: Tiberias, the Dead Sea region, and Eilat in winter, and Mediterranean coastal towns, such as Ashkelon, Herzliyyah, Netanyah, Caesarea, and Nahariyyah in the summer. Tourists are drawn by both Jewish and Christian holidays: Passover, Easter, and Independence Day in the spring, Feast of Weeks (Shavuot) in the summer, the Jewish New Year and Feast of Tabernacles (Sukkot) in the autumn, and Hanukkah and Christmas in the winter. Events have been arranged to encourage tourism, including the annual summer music and drama festival, sporting events, international congresses, summer camps for youth, and working holidays in the kibbutzim.

Tourist services are continually being expanded. All categories of accommodation are available, from youth hostels, Christian hospices, and camping sites to luxury hotels. Seventeen foreign airlines fly to Israel, in addition to El Al, while the ships of ten passenger lines call regularly at Haifa port. Lydda (Lod) is Israel's international airport, and the Atarot (Kalandia) airport near Jerusalem can also accommodate international traffic. Internal air transportation is provided by the Arkia and other airlines.

Despite the adverse influence, from time to time, of the security situation, the development of tourism has been rapid: from 43,000 tourists and a foreign currency income of $6,565,000 in 1956 to 727,000 with a foreign currency income of about $220,000,000 (apart from fares by sea and air) in 1972, when tourism was the country's second-largest source of foreign currency. The average length of stay was 15 days. Over 55% of the tourists were Jewish: 47% came from the Americas and 42% from Europe.

GLOSSARY

Agora, Israel coin, 1/100 of Israel pound.

Aliyah, immigration to Erez Israel.

Bank of Israel, Israel's central bank established in 1954 with the sole right to issue currency.

Betar, youth organization of the Zionist Revisionist party (now the Herut movement) founded in Latvia in 1923.

Comecon (initials of Council for Mutual Economic Assistance), economic organization including: East Germany, Bulgaria, Hungary, Poland, Mongolia, Rumania, Czechoslovakia and U.S.S.R.

Capitulations, treaties signed by the Ottoman sultans and the Christian states of Europe concerning the extraterritorial rights of their subjects.

Druze, a religio-political community inhabiting parts of Israel, Syria and Lebanon.

Egged, Israel public transport cooperative.

Fellah (Ar.), peasant.

Haavarah, a company, established in Tel Aviv in 1933, for the transfer of Jewish property from Nazi Germany to Palestine.

Haluz (pl. Haluzim), pioneer, esp. in agriculture, in Erez Israel.

Hebrew University, University in Jerusalem opened in 1925.

Hevrat ha-Ovedim, a roof organization for the ramified enterprises run by the Histadrut, founded in 1923.

Jewish Agency, international, nongovernment body, centered in Jerusalem, which is the executive and representative of the World Zionist Organization, established in August 1929.

Jewish Colonial Trust, the first Zionist bank incorporated in London in 1899.

Jewish Colonization Association (ICA), philanthropic association to assist Jews in depressed economic circumstances or countries of persecution to emigrate and settle elsewhere in productive employment, founded by Baron Maurice de Hirsch in 1891.

Jewish National Fund, the land purchase and development fund of the Zionist Organization, founded in 1901.

Jordan Project, an Israel project to channel part of the Jordan river water to the Negev (southern area of Israel). The project started in 1953 and was concluded in 1964 and is part of the National Water Carrier.

Kibbutz, larger-size commune constituting a settlement in Erez Israel, based mainly on agriculture but engaging also in industry.

Knesset, parliament of the State of Israel.

Ma'aser ("tithe"), due given to the priests and the poor.

Mekorot, water company established in 1937.

Mizrachi Women, the women's organization of the religious Zionist movement Mizrachi.

Moshav, smallholders' cooperative agricultural settlement in Israel.

Nahal (fighting pioneer youth), a regular unit of Israel Defense Forces that educates its members toward cooperative settlement in Erez Israel.

Palestine Office, central agency for Zionist settlement activities in Palestine, including land purchase and aiding immigration to Palestine, founded in 1908 by the World Zionist Organization and functioning in this capacity until the eve of World War I.

Perutah, Israel coin, 1/1000 of Israel pound; in circulation until 1962.

PICA (the Palestine Jewish Colonization Association), society for Jewish settlement in Palestine, founded in 1923 by Baron Edmond de Rothschild; active until 1957 when its property was transferred to the State of Israel.

Pioneer Women, worldwide labor Zionist women's organization founded in New York City in 1925.

Reparations Agreement, an agreement between West Germany and the State of Israel and Diaspora Jewry for reparations to the Jewish victims of the Nazi regime. The agreement came into effect on March 21, 1953.

Sinai Campaign, campaign (Oct. 29–Nov. 5, 1956), when Israel army reacted to Egyptian terrorist attacks and blockade by occupying the Sinai Peninsula.

Six-Day War, war (June 5–June 10, 1967), when Israel reacted to Arab threats and blockade by defeating the Egyptian, Jordanian and Syrian armies.

Tabu, name of the land registry in Palestine until 1948.

Tahal, a corporation established by the government of Israel in 1952 by merging the water resources department of the Ministry of Agriculture with the engineering division of Mekorot Water Company.

Technion, Israel Institute of Technology, Israel's only engineering university, founded in 1912 and situated in Haifa.

Templers, German sect which founded settlements in Erez Israel in the 19th and the first quarter of the 20th centuries.

Third Aliyah, pioneer immigration to Erez Israel in the years 1920–1923.

War of Independence, war that lasted from Nov. 30, 1947 to July 20, 1949, when the Jews of Israel fought Arab invading armies and ensured the establishment of the new State.

Weizmann Institute of Science, Israel scientific institution, founded in Reḥovot in 1949.

Werko (Ar.), name given to property tax in Palestine until 1948.

Wizo (Women's International Zionist Organization), women's Zionist movement founded in July, 1920.

Yishuv, the Jewish community in Erez Israel in the pre-State period.

BIBLIOGRAPHY

Economic Affairs: PALESTINE: 1880–1948. R. Nathan et al., *Palestine: Problem and Promise* (1946); UN Economic Survey Mission for the Middle East, *Report*, 1 and 2 (1949); Palestine Office of Statistics, *Statistical Abstract of Palestine* (1936–45); The Jewish Agency for Palestine, Economic Department, *Economic Facts and Figures* (1949) THE STATE OF ISRAEL: N. Halevi and Klinov-Malul, *The Economic Development of Israel* (1968); D. Horowitz, *The Economics of Israel* (1967); A. Rubner, *The Economy of Israel* (1960); Israel. Economic Planning Authority, *Israel Economic Development* (1968); Israel. Central Bureau of Statistics, *Statistical Abstract of Israel* (1950–); Bank of Israel, *Annual Report* (1955–); H. Ben-Shaḥar, *Interest Rates and the Cost of Capital in Israel, 1950–1962* (1965); M. Heth, *The Legal Framework for Economic Activity in Israel* (1967); M. Bruno, *Interdependence, Resource Use and Structural Change in Israel* (1962); A. L. Gaathon, *Capital Stock, Employment and Output in Israel 1950–1959* (1961); Israel Prime Minister's Office, Economic Planning Authority, *Israel's Economic Development* (1968); Israel Investment Authority, *Israel Investor's Manual* (1968[2]); P. Uri—(ed.), *Israel and the Common Market* (1972); M. Bruno, *Economic Development Problems in Israel* (1970); A. L. Gaaton, *Economic Productivity in Israel* (1971); D. Horowitz, *The Enigma of Economic Growth. The Case of Israel* (1972); E. Kanowsky, *The Economic Impact of the Six-Day War* (1970); H. Pack, *Structural Change and Economic Policy in Israel* (1971).

Taxation: A. Morag, *Mimmun ha-Memshalah be-Yisrael* (1967), incl. bibl.; A. Witkon and J. Neeman, *Dinei Missim* (1969[3]).

Foreign Exchange Rates: IMF, *International Financial Statistics* (1948–); Pick's Currency Yearbook (1955–).

Foreign Trade: N. Halevi and R. Klinov-Malul, *Economic Development of Israel* (1968); D. Patinkin, *Israel Economy: First Decade* (1958); Israel Bureau of Statistics, *Statistical Abstract of Israel* (1950–); Bank of Israel, *Annual Report* (1955–).

Water and Irrigation: Y. Prushansky, *Ha-Mayim be-Yisrael* (1961, 1963²); Israel, Ministry of Education and Culture, Information Office, *Ha-Mayim be-Yisrael* (1968); idem, *Ha-Mayim be-Yisrael* (periodical, 1955–); Israel, Water Authority, *Ha-Mayim be-Yisrael—Tizrokhet u-Tefukah 1962–1968* (1970); *The Mekorot Water Co. and its Role in Israel's Development* (1963); *Sheloshim Shanah li-Mekorot* (1967).

Agriculture: A. Bein, *Return to the Soil* (1952); D. Gazit, *Toledot ha-Hityashevut ha-Hakla'it be-Erez Yisrael* (1962); Israel Government, Central Bureau of Statistics, *Statistical Abstract of Israel* (1950–); Israel Government, Ministry of Agriculture, *Reports* (Heb., 1967, 1968); idem, *Pe'ulot Misrad ha-Hakla'ut bi-Yehuda u-ve-Shomron* (1968); S. Hurwitz, *Ha-Hakla'ut ba-Mizrah ha-Aravi* (1966); H. Halperin, *Temurot ba-Hakla'ut ha-Yisra'elit* (1956); R. Weitz and A. Rokach, *Agricultural Development: An Israeli Case Study* (1968); N. Michael, *Ha-Haklaut be-Israel 1949–1969* (1970); S. Pohoryles, *Haklaut be-Israel, Degam shel Tikhun Kalkali* (1973).

Afforestation: C. R. Conder, *Tent Work in Palestine* (1879); H. Prutz, *Kulturgeschichte der Kreuzzuege* (1883); J. Weitz, *Avodat ha-Yi'ur shel ha-KKL* (1940); M. Zohary, *Mavo le-Ge'obotanikah shel Erez Yisrael* (1944); J. Weitz, *Mediniyyut ha-Yi'ur be-Yisrael* (1950); Y. Gindel, *Ha-Ya'ar ve-Yi'ur ha-Arez* (1952); Gindel, in: *Ariel*, no. 19 (1967), 13–24.

Energy Sources: Water resources of Palestine, Preliminary Project, P. Rutenberg (Jerusalem, 1920); Electricity Concessions Ordinance 1927: *Official Gazette of the Government of Palestine* (March 7, 1927), 154–86; Israel Electric Corporation, *Annual Reports* (1923–); *Israel Government Year Book* (1953/54–).

Oil and Gas: B. Wade, in: *Oil News*, 9 (1921), 594–7; F. J. Fohs, in: *Bulletin of the American Association of Petroleum . . .* 11 (1927), 12; B. K. N. Wyllie, in: *Geology Magazine*, 68 (1931), 806; M. and D. Ball, in: *Israel Economic Forum* (1955).

Mineral Resources: M. J. Attia, in: International Geological Congress. 20th, Mexico, 1956, *Manganese Symposium* II: Africa: 143–71; Y. Bartura, *Type Sections of Paleozoic Formations in the Timna' Area* (1966); Y. K. Bentor, in: International Geological Congress. 19th, Algiers, 1952 (19th session) sect. 11, 93–101; idem, *Clays of Israel* (1966); N. Glueck, in: *Ha-Mishar, ha-Ta'asiyah ve-ha-Melakhah be-Erez-Yisrael bi-Ymei Kedem* (1937), 51–60; J. Kenat, in: *Symposium on Salt, 2nd., Cleveland. 1965, Second Symposium on Salt (Papers)* (1966); L. Lartet, in: *Annales des sciences géologiques,*

296

1 (1869), 5–116; 3 (1871), 149–329; D. Neev and K. O. Emery, *Dead Sea Depositional Processes* . . . (1967; = *Geological Survey of Israel Bulletin,* 41, 1967); Y. Shaḥar and U. Wuerzburger, in: *World Petroleum Congress, 7th,* 1967. *Proceedings* (1967), 719–28; R. F. Tylecote et al., in: *Journal of the Institute of Metal,* 95 (1967).

Banking and Commerce: Bank of Israel, *Annual Reports* (1956–); M. Heth, *Banking Institutions in Israel* (1966); W. Schick, *Das Bankwesen Israels* (1964); Bank Leumi le-Israel, *Annual Reports* (1951–); idem, *Sefer ha-Yovel* (1954); *Prospectus of Israel Discount Bank* (1964); Workers' Bank, *Annual Reports* (1924–), particularly 1961 "40 Years"; I. A. Abaddy (ed.), *Jerusalem Economy* (1950); J. Gross, *Ha-Bursah le-Neyarot Erekh* (1972).

Insurance: Breuer, in: *Ḥod ha-Ḥez,* 6–7 (1965), 11–20; Israel Central Bureau of Statistics, *Statistical Abstract of Israel* (1949–), chapters on Insurance Companies.

Communications: Israel, Misrad ha-Taḥburah, *Meshek ha-Taḥburah be-Yisrael* (1967); B. Katinke, *Me-Az ve-Ad Hennah* (1961); *Israel Government Yearbook; Statistical Abstract of Israel* (annual); Bank of Israel, *Annual Reports* (1955–).

Postal Services: I. Livni, *Livni's Encyclopaedia of Israel Stamps* (1968); H. U. Ribalow, *The History of Israel's Postage Stamps* (1956); F. W. Pollack, *Turkish Post in the Holy Land* (1962); A. Popik, *Toledot ha-Do'ar be-Erez-Yisrael* (1966).

Tourism: *Israel Government Year-Book* (1968/69); Israel Ministry of Tourism, Annual Report (1967); Israel Economic Planning Authority, *Israel Economic Development* (1968), 513–25.

INDEX

300